PLAIN TEXT

PLAIN TEXT

THE POETICS OF COMPUTATION

> DENNIS TENEN

STANFORD UNIVERSITY PRESS
STANFORD, CALIFORNIA

Stanford University Press
Stanford, California

Printed in the United States of America on acid-free, archival-quality paper

Library of Congress Cataloging-in-Publication Data

Names: Tenen, Dennis, author.
Title: Plain text : the poetics of computation / Dennis Tenen.
Description: Stanford, California : Stanford University Press, 2017. |
    Includes bibliographical references and index.
Identifiers: LCCN 2016052467 (print) | LCCN 2016054558 (ebook) |
    ISBN 9781503601802 (cloth : alk. paper) | ISBN 9781503602281 (pbk. : alk. paper) |
    ISBN 9781503602342 (electronic)
Subjects: LCSH: Literature and technology. | Digital media--Philosophy. |
    Electronic publications. | Electronic publishing.
Classification: LCC PN56.T37 T47 2017 (print) | LCC PN56.T37 (ebook) |
    DDC 809/.93356--dc23
LC record available at https://lccn.loc.gov/2016052467

Designed by Bruce Lundquist
Typeset at Stanford University Press in 8.5/14 Euphemia

To Bill Todd and Elaine Scarry,
whose influence on my thought grows with time

CONTENTS

ACKNOWLEDGMENTS

The book's faults, to quote Will Durant, are all mine. Its strengths, however, derive from the support of a community.

This project would not have been possible without the generous support of Harvard University's Comparative Literature Department. Publication was subsidized in part by Harvard Studies in Comparative Literature. Initial sketches of the book appeared in conversation with Aleksey Berg, Jacob Emory, Anders Engberg-Pedersen, Elena Fratto, Natalia and Ilya Kun, Guy Smoot, Simos Zeniou, and many others who made Dana-Palmer House their home away from home. Readers will recognize the influence of Svetlana Boym, Peter Gallison, Richard Moran, Elaine Scarry, William Todd, and Roberto Mangabeira Unger. Their thought was formative in the manuscript's early stages.

A fellowship from the Berkman Center for Internet and Society gave me the time and means to develop a deep research archive. I would like to thank Yochai Benkler, Urs Gasser, John Palfrey, Rebecca Tabasky, Jonathan Zittrain, and especially Jeffery Schnapp for their support. Members of the Cooperation Group in particular had a profound, if not an obvious, intellectual impact on my work. Echoes of discussions with Mayo Fuster, Jerome Hergueux, Benjamin Mako Hill, Andrés Monroy-Hernández, and Aaron Shaw can be found on the pages of every chapter.

The book came to fruition at Columbia University. Junior colleagues Ratik Asokan, Emily Fuhrman, Jessica Hallock, Tobias Pester, Phil Polefrone, and Zachary Roberts helped with line edits and gave insightful feedback. Senior colleagues Sarah Cole, Nick Dames, Michael Golston, Stathis Gourgouris, Marianne

Hirsch, Jean Howard, Matt Jones, Sharon Marcus, Edward Mendelson, Frances Negrón-Muntaner, Bruce Robbins, and Gayatri Chakravorty Spivak had a hand in individual chapters. The book became stronger with their guidance. Kaiama Glover, Bernard Harcourt, Matt Hart, Marguerite Holloway, Lydia Liu, Anupama Rao, Jesús R. Velasco, and Bill Worthen offered valuable advice. Columbia University's seminar on comparative media provided an important forum for several of the book's chapters, involving Stefan Andriopoulos, Noam Elcott, Brian Larkin, Reinhold Martin, Rosalind C. Morris, and Felicity Scott, among others. The Columbia University Summer Grant Program in the Humanities and a Lenfest Junior Faculty Development Grant supported the concluding stages of manuscript preparation. Weekly meetings with members of the Experimental Methods Group—Alex Gil, Susanna Allés Torrent, Grant Wythoff, and others— grounded my thought in practice, among many inspiring projects.

Manan Ahmed and Durba Mitra, both members of our co-presence writing group, deserve a special mention and my heartfelt gratitude. We shared the same space daily for almost two years as we worked on our respective projects. Ahmed's *Book of Conquest: The Chachnama and Muslim Origins in South Asia* (Harvard University Press, 2016) and Mitra's "Indian Sex Life: Women and the New Science of Society" were at various stages of development at the same time. Their warmth, humor, and intelligence brightened every page.

Both Matt Gold of the City University of New York (CUNY) and Jentery Sayers of the University of Victoria assigned early drafts of individual chapters to their students. The experience was immensely helpful in imagining my audience. Siddhartha Lokanandi and Ann Kay line-edited extensively. Barbara Herrnstein Smith and Johanna Drucker advised on individual chapters. Raja Adal, Janet Vertesi, and Susan Zieger were some of the most insightful public respondents to the text on the conference circuit. I am particularly thankful to Wendy Hui Kyong Chun for the opportunity to meet and discuss this manuscript in person.

Emily-Jane Cohen and her team at Stanford University Press expertly guided the book to publication. I received careful consideration and comments from Matthew Fuller, Ray Siemens, and two other anonymous reviewers. I would like to thank Micah Siegel, Anubhuti Maurya, Marthine Desiree Satris, Mimi Braverman, Derek Gottlieb, and Gigi Mark for their patience, hard work, and attention to detail.

Finally, a book extracts its heaviest toll from those closest to the author. My family and my partner Yoora gave it the needed time, space, and love.

PLAIN TEXT

> COMPUTATIONAL POETICS

An Introduction

As I write these introductory remarks, a ceiling-mounted smoke detector in my kitchen emits a loud noise every three minutes or so. A pleasant female voice also announces, "Low battery." This is, I learn, a precaution stipulated by the U.S. National Fire Alarm Code (NFPA 72), §11.6.6 (2013). The clause requiring a "distinctive audible trouble signal before the battery is incapable of operating" is encoded into the device. The smoke detector literally embodies that piece of legislation in its circuitry. We thus obtain a condition where two meanings of code—as governance and as machine instruction—coincide. Code equals code.

I am at home, but I also receive an alarm notification on my mobile phone. Along with monitoring apps that help make my home "smarter," the phone contains most of my library. I often pick it up to read a book. The phrase "reading a book," however, obscures a number of metaphors for a series of odd actions. The "book" is a small, thin black rectangle: three inches wide, five inches tall, and barely a few millimeters thick. A slab of polished glass covers the front of the device, where the tiny eyes of a camera and a light sensor also protrude. On the back, made of smooth soft plastic, we find another, larger camera. At the foot of the device, a grid of small perforations indicates breathing room for a speaker and several microphones. To "open" a book, I touch the glass. The machine recognizes my fingerprint. I then tap and poke at the surface until I find a small image that represents both my library and my bookstore, where I can "buy" and "borrow" books. However, buying or borrowing books does not involve the possession of physical objects. Rather, I agree to a license that grants limited access to data, which the software then assembles into something resembling a book on-screen. I tap again to begin reading. The screen dims to match room ambiance as it fills up with words. A passage on the first page appears underlined: other readers in my social circle must have found it notable. I swipe across the glass surface to turn a "page." The device emits a muffled rustle to reinforce the pretense of manipulating paper. The image curls ever so slightly as another "page" slides into view. My tiny library metaphor contains hundreds of such page metaphors.

Despite appearances, this electronic metaphor-making device in my hand has more in common with smoke detectors than it does with the several paper volumes scattered on my desk. The electronic book and smoke alarm contain printed circuit boards, capacitors, and resistors. Both draw electric current. Both require firmware updates, and both are governed by codes, political and computational. Smoke alarms and mobile phones connect to the Internet. They communicate with distant data centers and with each other. Yet I continue to "read" these devices as though they are familiar, immutable, and passive objects: just books. I think of them as intimate artifacts, friends even, wholly known to me, comforting, and warm. The electronic book is none of those things. Besides prose, it keeps my memories, pictures, words, sounds, and thoughts. It records my reading, sleeping, and consumption habits. It tries to sell me things, showing me advertisements for cars, jewelry, and pills. It comes with a manual and terms of service. It is my confidant, my dealer, my spy.

Plain Text concerns the nature of digital inscription, the material trace that gives rise to textual phenomena and, more broadly, to all cultural artifacts in which computers mediate. We—readers, writers, interpreters—find ourselves today in an unprecedented, since the Middle Ages, position of selective *asemiosis*: the loss of signification.[1] Many contemporary texts, such as poems inscribed into bacteria and encrypted software, exist simply beyond the reach of human senses.[2] Other forms of writing are illegible by design, in ways that prevent access or comprehension. Increasingly, we write not in the sense of making marks on paper but in simulation. Key presses leave lasting traces in computer memory, which then appear on-screen redoubled and ephemeral. On disk, marks endure in a form legible only to those who possess the specialized tools and training necessary to decipher them.

I appeal to the idea of plain text in the title of this book to signal an affinity with a particular mode of computational meaning making. Plain text identifies a file format and a frame of mind. As a file format, it contains nothing but a "pure sequence of character codes." Plain text stands in opposition to "fancy text," that is, "text representation consisting of plain text plus added information."[3] In the tradition of American textual criticism, plain text alludes to an editorial method of text transcription that is both "faithful to the text of its source" and is "easier to read than the original document."[4] Combining these two traditions, I mean to build a case for a kind of a systematic minimalism when it comes to our use of computers, a minimalism that privileges access to source materials, ensuring legibility and comprehension. I do so in contrast to other available modes of human–computer interaction, which instead maximize system-centric ideals such as efficiency, speed, performance, or security.

The title of this book further identifies an interpretive stance that one can assume in relation to the making and unmaking of literary artifacts. Besides visible content, all contemporary documents carry with them a layer of hidden information. Originally used for typesetting, this layer affects more than innocuous document attributes such as font size or line spacing. Increasingly, devices that mediate literary activity also embody governing structures. For example, the Digital Millennium Copyright Act, passed in the United States in 1996, goes beyond written injunction to require in some cases the management of digital rights at the level of hardware. An electronic book governed by digital rights may subsequently prevent readers from copying or sharing stored content, even for the purposes of academic study.[5] In other contexts a device may monitor and report on reader activity.

Machine instruction thus embodies new forms of technological control. To speak truth to power—to retain a civic potential for critique—we must therefore perceive the mechanisms of its codification. Critical theory cannot otherwise endure apart from material contexts of textual production, which today emanate from the fields of computer science and software engineering. Conversely, a tighter coupling with the critical tradition can reveal technology's often occluded political implications. For example, creating a novel algorithm that predicts crime by analyzing one's reading habits also invites the dystopian possibility of thought policing, unless, that is, such algorithms remain legible, in public view, and under continual counterscrutiny. A vibrant discursive practice of textual exegesis is crucial for the preservation of whatever ideals that demand a literate populace.

THESIS AND ARCHIVE

Plain Text is a response to a particular situation of a literary scholar encountering the field of software engineering. For a long stretch of my professional life, these two areas of activity remained separate. I worked at one and studied the other. At the time, I simply did not think that code had much to do with poetry. Initially, my two selves—the scholar and the engineer—spoke different languages. Reconciling them was and continues to be a disconcerting process by which things dear and familiar to me in both worlds grew strange and unfamiliar, showing themselves to be sometimes less than and sometimes more than I comfortably expected. Nothing could be assumed from the start. Field-specific language, down to its foundations, had to be examined for hidden assumptions that prevented dialogue. With time, I saw that code and poetry have much to do with one another. Writing this book has taught me to embrace the remaining incongruence.

The idea for *Plain Text* came in a moment of realization after I was asked one of those seemingly naïve but fundamental questions that can set research in motion down a long and winding path.

A childhood friend who shares a love for reading asked why he could not lend me a digital copy of the novel that he recently purchased from a major online retailer.[6] In my struggle to answer, I realized that some of my deepest intuitions about literature relied on assumptions firmly attached to print media. Despite my professional experience as a programmer and my academic training in literary studies, I could not readily explain the mechanisms by which electromagnetic charges transformed into pixels and pixels into words. Where to begin? To recount the passage of digital text one has to know something about chip architecture, operating systems, file permissions, networking, and encryption. I could describe parts of that system, but my knowledge was also riddled with unexamined gaps. It did not amount to a coherent story.

Worse yet, it quickly became apparent that these technical details affect all higher-level interpretive activity. To read together—to form a shared understanding of a text—we have to convene on the same page, which was made difficult in my friend's case by imposed geographic restrictions. The text changed as it passed hands. I had to draw on philology and sociology of literature to reflect on textual variants, recensions, and authorship attribution. Digital text is more obviously entwined with its reception history: reader reviews and algorithmic recommendation engines. Despite the new purchase, my friend's electronic copy of the text was already marked and highlighted. It was synchronized with other media: audiobooks and related television promotions. The work was preprocessed, in both the technical and the social senses of the word, to privilege certain meanings and modes of comprehension.

The task of coming to terms with these emergent contingencies entails an expansive research program, which can be commenced here only in part. The digital literary ecosystem is evolving rapidly. A historical approach to its development extrapolates its trajectory into the future. Crucially, digital knowledge ecologies are only just coming into being; they are still pliable, still in their formative state. Their cultural importance necessitates active commentary and experimentation. Without it, we risk the dominion of what Langdon Winner has called autonomous technology, a condition by which complex systems begin to irrevocably determine our politics. "Modern people have filled the world with the most remarkable array of contrivances," Winner wrote. We are then surprised to find them resistant to change. "The human kind faces a woefully permanent bondage to the power of its own inventions," he concluded. And I hope, along with him, that it is still possible to "reconsider and reconstruct" those outcrops that in retrospect impoverish culture, to "learn and start again," and to retain the "prospect of liberation."[7]

To these ends, *Plain Text* tells a story of a major morphological shift affecting cultural production, particularly as it relates to the mechanics of reading and writing. Were I to interrupt a digital typist to ask, "Where do these words reside?" I would likely receive several conflicting answers in response. In some sense, the words are on-screen, where they can be viewed. In another sense, they are somewhere within the machine, on remote and hermeneutically sealed surfaces: silicon chips, hard drives, flash memory cards. In yet another sense, visible signs are still further removed from the contexts of their production. The word is in the wires. It spreads across servers, routers, and data centers. What was once apparent takes on a more complex structure, stretched across planes and temporalities. The book—this book, any book—gains a new shape. Digital texts form a live lattice, a multidimensional grid, that connects a letter's tactile response at one's fingertips to its optic and electromagnetic traces. In aggregate, these *textual laminates* incorporate the scaffolding of synthetic inscription. I cannot consequently pass a digital note to another person in the same sense that one passes notes in class, on paper. It is impossible to give the entire structure over. Text is irrevocably intertwined with its stratified material contexts. It means—

it becomes—something else when recreated under conditions that are not fully congruent to my own.

Much contemporary anxiety about the intrusion of computational culture into the everyday can be traced to such fundamental reshaping of the sign. Its fracture leads to its multivalence. The lattice expands into spaces between signs, where forces of capital and control intervene to monitor and monetize.[8] Reading and writing are no longer solitary activities. Who shares the page? What entities contest newly found space bearing digital inscription? The answers lie in our ability to perceive latent topographies.

Reflecting on the development of Morse code in 1949 in the *Proceedings of the American Philosophical Society*, Frank Halstead mentioned the difficulty of finding a home in either the arts or sciences for what he called code development: "It is a matter somewhat related to the general art of cryptology, yet it is not wholly divorced from electrical engineering nor from general philology."[9] As Halstead anticipated, research into codification would lead to a rich multidisciplinary archive of materials on the history of literary theory, semiotics, telegraphy, and electrical engineering from the mid-nineteenth century to the end of the twentieth century. That archive includes patents and technical manuals, formalist manifestos, studies of animal communication, human–computer interaction textbooks, and foundational texts in aesthetics and literary theory.

I deploy the archive to argue that extant theories of interpretation evolved under conditions tied to static print media. By contrast, digital texts change dynamically to suit their readers, political contexts, and geographies. Consequently, I advocate for the development of *computational poetics*: a strategy of interpretation capable of reaching past surface content to reveal platforms and infrastructures that stage the construction of meaning. Where "distant reading" and cultural analytics perceive patterns across large-scale corpora, computational poetics breaks textuality down into its minute constituent components. It is a strategy of microanalysis rather than macroanalysis.[10]

In *Plain Text* I also argue that some of the ideological afflictions of the contemporary public sphere (e.g., the acquiescence to routine surveillance and censorship) relate to our failure as readers and writers to come to terms with the changing material conditions of digital text. A society that cares about the long-term preservation of complex discursive formations, such as free speech, privacy, or online deliberation, would do well to heed the textual building blocks at their base. The structure of discursive formations (documents and narratives) has long been at the center of both computer science and literary theory. By using primary sources from both disciplines, in *Plain Text* I uncover the shared history of literary machines, bringing computation closer to its humanistic roots and the humanities closer to their computational realities.

I make a historical case for the recovery of textual thought that is latent in the machinery of contemporary computing. Just as literary scholarship cannot survive without awareness of its computational present, the design of computational platforms cannot advance without greater awareness of its cultural contexts. The political struggle for meaning making, the very opportunity to engage in the act of interpretation, thus begins and ends with the material affordances of the epistemic artifact.[11]

The future of reading and writing is inexorably intertwined with the development of computer science and software engineering. Even if you are not reading these words on a screen, my message has reached you through a long chain of machine-mediated transformations: from the mechanical action of the keyboard on which I typed my manuscript, to the arrangement of electrons on magnetic storage media, the modulation of fiber-optic signal, the shimmer of the flowing liquid crystal display rendering the text, and on to the typesetter's shop and the printing press. Computation occupies the space between keyboard and screen, which in turn gives rise to higher-order cultural institutions: from social media platforms to massive shared archives. Cultural techniques that guide our use of such technologies are formative of the society as a whole.[12] Daily choices such as choosing a text editor, a filing system, or a social networking platform cannot therefore be addressed in shallow instrumental, system-centric ideals. Complex computational systems do not give rise to ideals any more than financial markets do. From the many available visions of human–computer interaction, I argue for choosing ones that align with a humanist ethos, whatever the reader's politics.

THEORY
Displacement
Plain Text is ultimately an exploration of textual space.[13] I am thus inherently concerned with the dynamics of settlement and displacement, which frame my historical argument and form its theoretical underpinnings.

I mean "settlement" in the way one lives among and within one's own notebooks, bookshelves, and archives. Smart toasters and electronic heart valves differ from their dumb mechanical counterparts in that they similarly give grounds to inscription. Computers perform reading and writing operations at scale. To support that activity, engineers necessarily create vast, in terms of information capacity, expanses. Commercial, private, and public interests rush in to colonize newly opened territories. Boundaries are drawn. Areas of exclusion are created, even in our most intimate spaces: bedsides, living rooms, kitchens, the body and the mind. A diabetic is not able to modify her insulin pump software; the smart television contains proprietary firmware that is controlled at a distance and without explicit consent. The struggle is not one for virtual but for concrete grounds for inscription.

These intimate territories are remote, however, in that they unfold at quantum scale. Individuals who are not privy to the mechanics of micromolecular writing are hence in peril of unprecedented dispossession. I am concerned here with our basic ability to shape discourse—to read and write—along surfaces that are not available for immediate scrutiny. Poetics—the affordance of literary space—physically limits the possibility of interpretation. An illegible sign is one that never enters the hermeneutic circuit.

In making the case for a computational poetics, I am helped by recent scholarship in the historically and philosophically inflected studies of media and technology.[14] My notion of poetics also builds on the long history of literary theory, in the genealogy of formalist and structuralist schools. My approach is not limited, however, to the canonical, straight-ahead structuralisms of Roman Jakobson or Jonathan Culler. Rather, I am borrowing from a more peripheral tradition represented best by such third-culture thinkers as Viktor Shklovsky and Vilém Flusser, consummate immigrants both, who extracted a methodology out of the fabric of their displacement.

Flusser in particular considered the condition of unease that comes with migration, both physical and mental, to be a kind of information processing. His thought was influential in making sense of my own displacements, first as a refugee fleeing the dissolution of the former Soviet Union, next as a transplant into Silicon Valley from a strict literary education, and now as a lapsed engineer among humanists. These vantage points offer a singular view onto the material conditions of contemporary intellectual life.

Both Shklovsky and Flusser wrote lucidly about the dynamics of settlement. Their work sheds light on an irresistible compromise at the core of all technology by which we trade critical understanding for comfort. Habit covers the various homes we make for ourselves in the world "like a fluffy blanket," Flusser wrote. "It smoothes the sharp edges of all phenomena that it covers, so that I no longer bump against them, but I am able to make use of them blindly."[15] When we sit at our desks, for example, we fail to see "papers and books that are lying all about."[16] We are used to them being there as they are. We do not, therefore, parse them as information. Like water that surrounds fish, habituated things pass into the background of experience. Mediums become media. They cease producing meaning, become stages for meaning making, and like a stage disappear from view.

Losing sight of the material contexts of knowledge production is politically perilous, because those who own the contexts set the terms of engagement. Estrangement arrests material concealment. Exile allows the displaced to once again transform habituated media into meaningful information. In exile, "everything is unusual," Flusser wrote.[17] Migrants experience the world as ex-perience (er-fahrung, literally "a driving out"). Discovery, Flusser concluded, "begins as soon as the blanket is pulled away," where familiar objects can pass into view again.[18]

To take a simple example, one could write "a field of study" without much thought about figurative space. Shklovsky would have readers pause to consider the implications.[19] In what sense do ideas resemble (or not) a field? A poet could take things further and elaborate: "to scythe a verdant field of literary study." The verb (to scythe) and the adjective (verdant) create an unexpected transference of new qualities not present in the original image (intellectual field). These qualities overdetermine or saturate the metaphor, exposing its conceit. One can do to fields of grass what one cannot to ideas. Subsequently, we realize that the two domains, intellectual and horticultural, do not map onto each other perfectly; they leave a semantic remainder, the chaff. Readers discover intellectual "fields" for what they are: habituated metaphors, neither natural nor self-apparent. Metaphors are made strange again through purposeful defamiliarization. To take the technique to its logical conclusion, a writer could depict several fictional characters in the act of scything a field of grass while discussing the relative merits of structuralism: a discussion about the field on a field. Such literary artifice would make actual the implied connections between fields of grass and ideas. The writer shows what was merely told before. The technique of defamiliarization renews the figure: discarding hardened clichés while suggesting novel linkages between constituent concepts—ideational chaff, leaves of mental grass, combines of thought.

I would like to effect a similar sense of estrangement when it comes to our use of technology. The formalists understood habituated metaphors to lessen the vitality of experience. Shklovsky quotes from the diaries of Lev Tolstoy, who, while dusting his room, could not remember if he had already dusted his sofa. Tolstoy wrote, "Because actions like these are habituated and unconscious, I could not remember . . . whether I dusted and forgot or just did so without thinking—it was as if the action never happened. . . . Thus when life passes without conscious reflection, it passes as if one has not lived at all."[20] Shklovsky added that life so habituated disappears into nothingness when the automatization of experience "consumes things, clothing, furniture, your spouse, and the fear of war."[21]

The formalists rarely quoted Marx directly. Yet Marx resonates throughout. For Marx, dead metaphors marked alienation from humanity.[22] The point at which material artifacts disappear from consciousness is also one where they appear within the social sphere as fetishes.

Shklovsky changed Marx's German *Entfremdung* (alienation), which for Marx always denied life, into the Russian *ostranenie* (estrangement), literally an "othering," of the kind that affirms it. The difference is one of agency. In the first case, subjects are treated like objects by others. In the second, subjects recognize and reject the objectified other within. Formalist estrangement, which is sometimes also translated as defamiliarization, arrests the momentum of tacitly received habit. Once estranged and extracted like a splinter, ossified experience can be revitalized.

Our challenge today is to uproot ourselves from the comforts that rapidly descend on the dwellings of our intellectual life. By dulling the senses, seemingly inconspicuous conduits of agency—electronic books and smart desks—acquire a sense of intelligence of their own. Devices that "watch," "hear," "see," and "think" give rise to object-oriented ontology and the Internet of Things. A new generation of objects clamors for participatory intelligence. They claim space in the home, near heart and hearth. Smart phones, smart lightbulbs, smart thermostats, smart homes, and smart watches enter the networked public sphere in the role of independent agents.[23] A conversation begins about their personhood: their levels of trust, friendships, rights, and accountability.[24] Marx's table that "evolves out of its wooden brain grotesque ideas" becomes Microsoft Surface and PixelSense, that is, actual smart tables, intellect itself, commodified.[25]

If we hope to understand digital culture and especially literature "under conditions of high technology," as Friedrich Kittler would write, we can do so only from the position of humanism. One cannot otherwise lament the systematic erasure of the human from the literary process and, at the same time, advocate for a post- or antihumanism. Unlike Kittler, who wrote that under conditions of high technology "literature has nothing more to say," I believe that literature and literary analysis continue to have a voice in contemporary life.[26] Technology does not—cannot be allowed to—determine literary silence. Rather, as the material grounds for all reflective textual activity recede from view, readers face the prospect of selective illiteracy.[27] The command of technologies such as networking and encryption separates those able to read and write under conditions of high technology from those who no longer are, which is another dispossession.

When we mistake things for animate actors, we further diminish our ca-pacity for critical analysis or collective action. Objects that surround us log our reading habits, social interactions, and intimate conversations. Agents that benefit from trade in such personal data are neither cyborgs nor posthuman assemblages. The bargain that trades critical understanding for comfort benefits specific individual interests. To address objects as though they could respond in kind shifts our attention from seats of power to things powerless, inarticulate, and indifferent to our protestations. One can no more extract justice from a smart desk than hold a bureaucracy accountable. Notions of justice and accountability presuppose a robust model of agency, which is absent in the assemblage.

The internal exile that we must undergo for smart books and smart desks to come into view cannot compare in difficulty to the experience of physical displacement that follows natural disaster, war, poverty, or political instability. Yet our systematic reluctance to take on even those small intellectual discomforts that could lead to acts of localized dissent and disobedience—to write using free software, build open archives, or share memories in private—cannot be said to exist outside complex systems that perpetuate inequity and violence globally. The emotional affirmation that accompanies exuberant technesis (e.g., the ecstasy of constant communication) brings with it governing structures invoked in the name of law enforcement and national security. Comfort and security constitute the same ill-conceived bargain that leads to critical disempowerment. But where it is difficult to imagine or to enact strategies of digital disobedience on a universal scale, we can begin to address them through numerous minute local transactions that in aggregate brace everyday literary exchange. This we can do here and now. Computational poetics begins with machines in our immediate proximity, closest to thought and touch.

Picking up an electronic book and taking it apart may be against the law in some jurisdictions.[28] Given the extent to which emergent thought things— epistemic artifacts such as electronic books and smart phones—participate actively in the production of meaning, we can no longer use strategies of interpretation at the level of ideology or representation alone.[29] The praxis of close reading must reach down to the silicon bedrock: material entities and physical structures that bear the weight of interpretation. Literary theory, a discipline fundamentally engaged in the exegesis of figurative trope, is therefore crucial to the understanding of new computational environments, which have enveloped intellectual life through metaphoric substitution. To read the machine is to learn how it is made, but it is also to unpack the rich metaphors that guide our tactical engagement with the word: the boot in rebooting, the wares in software, the bug and the joystick, the interpreter and the shell.

Settlement

Estrangement cannot be practiced effectively in monologue. To produce meaning, Flusser reminds us, it needs to become a dialogical, dialectical practice. Perpetual exile is otherwise uninhabitable.[30] Without the shelter of one's home, everything turns to noise. Information cannot exist without dwelling, "and without information, in a chaotic world, one can neither feel nor think nor act," Flusser wrote.[31] Estrangement thrusts the displaced into the chaos of unsettled existence. With time, they make a new home, from which they can once again "receive noise as information" and produce meaning: "I am embedded in the familiar so that I can reach out toward the unfamiliar and create things yet unknown."[32] A dialectics of exile leads to "informed renewal" of shared space, through what Flusser called a creative dialogue between the settled and the displaced.[33]

In *Plain Text* I thus model the reciprocal movement to "making strange" on the diverse practices of reverse engineering. Similar in method to what Matthew Kirschenbaum called forensic argumentation, reverse engineering recalls the formalist strategy of structural decomposition.[34] The function of case studies in an engineer's education, as Henry Petroski explained in his *Invention by Design*, is to understand the ways by which one gets "from thought to thing."[35] From thought to thing would be an apt definition of poetics and an alternative subtitle to this book. Along with literary and historical exposition, each of my chapters contains at least one literary thought thing. Each enacts a deconstruction—a literal taking apart—of that device. A reification of the ideal, the epistemic object is meant to augment and refine theory.

The reverse engineering of literary devices reveals that not all texts are created equal. In print, traditional distinctions between form and content lie flat. A printing press embeds ink into paper, leaving no space between type and page. Materially minded critics such as Johanna Drucker, Katherine Hayles, and Jerome McGann have urged literary scholars to reevaluate textuality in its media-specific contexts.[36] Their work reminds us that the flatness of digital text is an illusion. Low-level operational intuitions that govern textuality—ideas about form, content, style, letter, and word—change profoundly as texts shift their confines from paper to pixel.

A substantial gap separates visible text from its storage medium. The two sites of inscription, screen and electromagnetic storage, are physically incongruent. One must be translated, transformed into the other. Control codes govern the process of transfiguration, which brings with it physical control at the level of platform and architecture. This is a layer where, for example, we can find spyware and censorship filters, digital rights management, and advertisement delivery.

I propose to begin, then, with this obvious sense of difference between paper and pixel: Where print is governed by law from without (think, for example, of England's Obscene Publication Acts), digital text is governed by code from within.[37] I go further than others to maintain that digital text *is* code, in the sense that it is always parsed and potentially executable.[38] Control binds to content inextricably to become an organ in the same unified corpus.

Changing material conditions of textual transmission alter the theoretical vocabulary of literary criticism. The ease with which some digital texts can be reproduced, for example, has the unexpected effect of destabilizing the material bases for authorship attribution. Text that is easy to copy is easy to cite or plagiarize. The physically diminished notion of authorship makes certain ways of talking about such constructs as authorial intent and fidelity to the original difficult to sustain. Practices of collaborative and machine-assisted writing (e.g., Wikipedia, automatic news summarization) further erode notions of authorship based on individual genius.

The author is not dead, however; authors continue to live and collect royalties.[39] Autopoiesis (literature writing or discourse speaking itself) does not displace the social institution of authorship.[40] Codification merely makes the flows of poiesis less apparent. Although it is difficult to find specific parties responsible for massive spam campaigns or to credit individual Wikipedia writers, spammers do routinely find themselves in court just as notable Wikipedia contributors receive "barn stars" in recognition of their efforts.

Extant models of literary transmission assume movement through passive and immutable media. Paper constitutes the document of record, which, once archived, does not change its contents. Philological techniques like genetic criticism and forensic reading make it possible to reconstruct if not authorial intent, then at least a trace of an author's hand. In some cases— think manuscripts and folios—we may even ascribe properties such as fidelity to original works of art. When media are immutable, one imagines a causal chain of custody between works and their creators, who at some point must have occupied the same contiguous time and space: The closer a parchment to Shakespeare, the higher its evidentiary (and market) value.

The transition between the Gutenberg press and Project Gutenberg, an online library containing thousands of texts, complicates the linkage. Unlike pen and paper, which come in direct contact with each other during writing, the bridge between keyboard and screen passes through multiple mediating filters. Writing itself becomes a programmed experience. We do not write onscreen in the conventional sense of etching marks into a static host. The act is a simulation displaced in time and space. We neither immediately touch nor see the textual conduit. The visible does not correspond to the actual. An erased word on paper, for example, implies the physical destruction of ink. By contrast, a simulated digital erasure, of the kind that happens when a writer presses the backspace key, does not necessarily correspond to the erasure of content on disk. The "erased" word could persist and even multiply across other storage drives and devices. Erasure in that sense no longer nullifies; it bears witness. It can be used to train algorithms or indicate the intent to conceal. The changing materialities of digital inscription thus ultimately entail wide-ranging political consequences.

The illusory affordances of the fractured sign, as described, require a poetics capable of reconstructing a sequence of willful delegation: from thought—someone's thought—to thing. A discipline of close attention to the minute particulars of encoding, transmission, storage, and the decoding of texts reclaims a measure of intent and thereby authorial responsibility. In many cases we may not care to speak of it. One would hardly find Tolstoy at fault for his *War and Peace*. In other contexts, as when unsolicited advertisements clutter bandwidth to the exclusion of other forms of speech, we must.

This may seem strange at first: to recover the subject in the physical minutiae of the encounter between text and machine. The point of contact between human, text, and device is significant because it is in the liminal zone of semiotic exchange where subjects disappear into machines and where machines step forth as animated and seemingly intelligent actors. Our ability to apprehend the politics of smart objects depends on the formulation of their poetics: how they are made.

METHOD

> We cannot separate the two things: head and hand. . . . The science of life . . . is a superb and dazzlingly lighted hall which may be reached only by passing through a long and ghastly kitchen. . . . We shall reach really fruitful and luminous generalizations about vital phenomena only in so far as we ourselves experiment and, in hospitals, amphitheaters, or laboratories, stir the fetid or throbbing ground of life.[41]

My approach to writing *Plain Text* stems from the desire to enact theory capable of addressing the grim picture Friedrich Kittler painted at the end of his influential monograph *Gramophone, Film, Typewriter*.[42] By all accounts, Kittler was neither a technological romantic nor a Luddite. I hence understand his *Gramophone, Film, Typewriter* as a call to action. When Kittler wrote that "media determine our situation," he challenged his readers to choose between complicity and defiance.[43] It was not a statement of fact but the articulation of a question: What can one do to counteract technological determinism? In what follows, I outline several intellectual lineages—materialist, pragmatist, and experimental—that frame my answer.

Critical theory at its best aims to see "the human bottom of nonhuman things."[44] As such, it is one of our most powerful tools for analysis and resistance against technological determinism. Max Horkheimer wrote that the issue "is not simply the theory of emancipation; it is the practice of it as well."[45] My thought and practice is inspired by scholars of media and technology (Bernard Stiegler, Christina Dunbar-Hester, Tiziana Terranova, and Lilly Irani among others) who have turned the tools of critical theory toward the instrumental contexts of knowledge production.[46] I join them to argue that in treating the instruments of intellectual production uncritically, all of us, readers and writers, accumulate a debt that accrues both technical and ethical interest. It is one thing, for instance, to theorize about the free movement of literary tropes across cultures and continents and quite another to have that theory appear in print behind paywalls inaccessible to most global reading publics.[47] Similarly, a theoretical distinction between form and content, when instantiated in specific file formats such as Microsoft Word (docx) or Adobe Reader (pdf), establishes divisions of labor between editors, booksellers, and offshore typesetting firms.[48] One group trades content in an economy of prestige, another controls distribution for corporate profit in a market economy, and yet another labors invisibly on formatting in an economy of survival. Distinctions of labor persevere so long as theory persists in the abstract. A materialist critique cannot achieve its stated aims without purchase on the material world. Contemporary knowledge workers stare into rectangular black boxes for a considerable part of their days, suspecting, in the absence of other feedback, that their gaze is met in bad faith. Bad faith points to a misalignment between thought and action.[49]

Connecting theories of meaning making to their practice offers a way out of the conundrum. The solution to connect meaning with operational meaning thus belongs equally to a species of pragmatism, as it does to critical theory. William James articulated the approach concisely when he wrote that "reality is seen to be grounded in a perfect jungle of concrete expediencies."[50] For James and other pragmatists, truth could not be found outside that jungle, in the abstract. It always entailed real consequences, causes, and effects.[51] In his essay "Pragmatism's Conception of Truth," James asked, "How will the truth be realized? . . . What concrete difference will its being true make in anyone's actual life? . . . What experiences will be different from those which would obtain if the belief were false?"[52] Frank Ramsey, the young British philosopher close to Ludwig Wittgenstein, would later write in a similar vein about meaning "defined by reference to the actions."[53]

For a pragmatist, truth-carrying propositions of the shape "X is Y" (as in "the author is dead" or "art is transcendent") raise the questions of where, when, for whom, and what is at stake in maintaining that? Following the pragmatic insight of James and Ramsey, I proceed with the conviction that abstract categories such as literature, computation, and text cannot possibly be reduced to a number of essential structural features. Rather, to borrow from Wittgenstein's *Philosophic Investigations*, categories denote a set of related practices that share some familial characteristics.[54] In our case, imagine a tree diagram in which the branches of computation and textuality intersect and diverge in ways that we have yet to untangle.

In an approach to *doing* theory, *Plain Text* joins the experimental turn steering the academy toward critical practice, especially in fields long dominated by purely speculative thought. The experimental turn represents a generation's dissatisfaction with armchair philosophizing. Recall the burning armchair, the symbol of the experimental philosophy movement. Joshua Knobe and Shaun Nichols, some of the early proponents of the movement, explain that "many of the deepest questions of philosophy can only be properly addressed by immersing oneself in the messy, contingent, highly variable truths about how human beings really are."[55] The emergence of spaces where research in the humanities is done exemplifies the same trend. In naming the locations of their practice "laboratories," "studios," and "workshops," humanists reach for new metaphors of labor. These metaphors aim to reorganize the relationship between body, space, artifact, knowledge, and inscription. In my lab and elsewhere, researchers have taken to calling this approach the experimental humanities.

As an example of what I have been calling here the experimental turn in the field of early modern history, consider the preface to the recent volume *Ways of Making and Knowing*, edited by Pamela Smith, Amy Meyers, and Harold Cook. They write that the "history of science is not a history of concepts, or at least not that alone, but a history of the making and using of objects to understand the world."[56] Smith translates that insight in her laboratory, where, together with students, she bakes bread and smelts iron to recreate long-lost artisanal techniques. For those who experiment, book knowledge and artifactual knowledge connect in practice.

Artifactual knowledge—from typesetting software to e-book readers and word processors—shapes our everyday encounter with literature. Such technologies should not be understood as value-neutral conduits of information. I follow Lewis Mumford and Langdon Winner to argue that technology affects the exercise of textual politics in subtle and profound ways.[57] Artifacts cannot hold beliefs about politics. Rather, political power is exercised through them. For example, stairs do not discriminate against the mobility impaired; the human failure to enforce accessibility through specific legal and architectural choices does. Typesetting software, e-book readers, and word processors similarly embody implicit communication models: ideas about deliberation,

In conversation w/ ooo → agency of things — but is it agency of ppl through things?

ethics of labor, discursive values, and views about "natural" human aptitude for interpretation. The maker of the electronic book encodes how the book is sold and where, minimum and maximum font size, the visibility of marginal notation, the possibility of sharing, the availability of critical apparatus. Content in that sense is meant for further processing, in a way that maximizes its extracted value. Contemporary documents are capable of structuring the literary encounter to these ends according to a reader's economic status, gender, race, age, location, or physical ability.

To what extent does the book in front of you sanction access? Whatever the answer, a function of understanding the text includes an explication of its physical affordances. The experimental approach to reading enables critics to lay bare the device. A literary scholar's version of baking bread and smelting iron is to make literal the archaeology of media at the level of the mechanism. In *Plain Text* we will unearth and excavate textual machines. In practicing archaeology, I contend that cardinal literary-theoretical concepts, such as word, text, narrative, discourse, author, story, book, and archive, are thoroughly enmeshed in the underlying physical substratum of paper and pixel. It follows that any attempt to articulate the idea cannot attain its full expressive potential without a thick description of its base particulates.

Luckily for us, reading and writing are not esoteric activities. They are readily available for introspection. I therefore occasionally encourage readers to encounter the immediate contexts of their reading anew: to put down the book or to lean away from a screen and to look at these textual artifacts with strange eyes. In this movement of the body, I want to disrupt the mind's habituated intuitions, pitting them against knowledge at hand and fingertip knowledge, as when ruffling through the pages or typing at a keyboard. How ephemeral is an electronic text, for example? The pragmatic answer lies not in reductive universal propositions—very or not at all—but in contingent technological affordances attached to specific reading devices. What can a reader do with this text, here and now? Where is it stored? Are readers given dispensation to copy and paste? Do they have legal permission to quote at length, to perform publicly, or to otherwise transmediate? Will this text disappear when its reader closes the book's cover?

PLAN OF THE PRESENT WORK

The pathways of inscription winding their way through the device exist in relation to distinct communities of computational practice. A researcher cannot for this reason expect to discover a single theoretical framework that captures the complexity of digital text in motion. An engineer's use of the words *code* and *poetry* differs from that of a poet's. The changing contexts evoke a corresponding shift in operational definitions. This book is thus neither a total history of modern computing nor a survey of literary theory. Rather, the argument herein progresses from the action of the alphanumerical keyboard switch, through copper and silicon, to liquid crystal and the floating gate, and on toward the reader and the community. It is but one of many possible passes through a cavernous black box.

The first chapter begins with a question: What does it mean to turn a page when neither pages nor the action of turning them corresponds to the implied analogy? A close reading of the metaphor leads to an intellectual history of human–computer interaction. It progresses from the conversational programming school of design to the direct manipulation school, the latter shaped by theories from cognitive linguistics and immersive theater. The logic of directness culminates in the rapidly developing field of brain–computer interfaces. The chapter concludes with a moment of speculative formalism, in which I consider the possibility of affective literature that eschews language and representation.

At the core of the book's second chapter lies the notion of a modernist literary device, understood both as literary technique and thought experiment about intelligent machines, directly connected to the birth of modern computing. A section on literary technique in the work of Percy Lubbock, Walter Benjamin, and Mikhail Bakhtin opens the discussion. Materialist poetics rise concomitantly alongside a mechanistic, rule-based view of language. In this chapter I reconstruct a series of thought experiments first in the writing of Ludwig Wittgenstein and then in Alan Turing's seminal paper on an imaginary computer capable of reading and writing. The verbs *to read* and *to write* imply a type of cognitive processing. What does it mean to read and to write for a machine? What about broken mechanisms of comprehension? At once device and algorithm, the Turing machine blurs the boundaries between software and hardware, code and content, intelligence and its imitation.

In the third chapter the intellectual history of literary formalism collides with format theory found in both textual criticism and computer science. The concept of format, as I describe it, mediates between a text's intrinsic rules for construction and its extrinsic shape, transforming one type of structure (a series of bits arranged into tracks and sectors) into another (letters arranged into sentences and paragraphs). A history of document formats illustrates the theoretical discussion. Formatting comes into being with several control characters, which are limited in function to actions such as carriage return and stop transmission. With time, formats encompass all manner of machine instruction, including technical means of enforcing digital rights management, copy protection, and other legal instruments. A manufacturer's ability to censor or to surveil digital text is thereby contained in the formatting layer: from electronic books that modify themselves to suit the reader's geographic location to smart contracts that contain the rules of their own execution.

The fourth chapter begins with an apparent paradox. A camp of media theorists and textual scholars in the 1990s conceived of electronic texts as a near immaterial phenomenon. Text shimmered and glared; it was discussed in terms of ephemera, hypertext, light writing, and electricity. A generation of theorists that came after insisted on the weighty materiality of electronic media. Reading began to engage the morphology of rare metals, media archaeology, hard-drive forensics. Both accounts, I argue, capture an aspect of the same underlying condition. The perceived image of an archived inscription splits from its source. The sign plausibly resides both on the screen and on the hard drive. It fractures in some real sense, diverging at the site of its projection from the site of the archive. Using materials from the history of telegraphy in the late nineteenth and early twentieth centuries, I chart the gradual fissure and ultimate illegibility of the newly composite sign. Marks made on punch cards and ticker tape protruded through the medium. Although difficult to read, these forms of machine writing were readily visible and therefore amenable to analysis. The advent of magnetic storage forced the composite inscription into an opaque conduit. Unable to perceive magnetic polarities without the aid of a machine, readers often manipulated text blindly. In this way a typist would type several sentences without seeing the printed output. The chapter identifies a milestone in the history of human textuality: the moment at which the inscription passed from view, giving rise to the sometimes conflicting but nevertheless consistent accounts of digital textuality.

The fifth and final chapter charts the emergence of screen reading. Screens restore a measure of visibility lost to electromagnetic inscription, with one major side effect: Fidelity between visible and archived inscription cannot be guaranteed. Screen reading further happens on screens that refresh themselves at a rate of about 60 cycles per second (Hertz). The digital word is technically an animation; it moves even as it appears to stand still. This property attunes the reader to a particular mode of apprehension, affecting not just the physics but also the aesthetics of digital media. Works by philosophers Henri Bergson, John Haugeland, and Nelson Goodman construe a phenomenology of screen-based digital perception. The digital emerges not as a medium's intrinsic property but as a structure imposed from without. In the extreme, that means that a censored *electronic* text can appear in practice as a perfectly *analog* artifact, despite being digital in all other senses of the word. Conversely, texts in print are already born digital, in the sense that all literary works are already to some extent amenable to "reliable processes of copying and preservation."[58] Properties that make media digital or analog reveal themselves to be neither universal nor essential to the medium. The medium is not the message. As I argue in the conclusion of the chapter, reliability and preservation of textual copies may mean one thing to a literary scholar, another to a software engineer or a legal professional, and something entirely different to a librarian. It matters not what the text is but what we can do with it.

In a short conclusion I gesture toward the contemporary political consequences of the material covered, discussing also the possibility of machine phenomenology in relationship to humanism. Computational poetics, I maintain, encourages users to become active thinkers, tinkerers, and makers of technology. I further encourage those who may have considered themselves mere users of computation to apply the same critical acuity they employ in the close reading of prose and poetry to the understanding of code and machine. For text to render on-screen properly, it must be encoded or translated from machine-transmittable code into human-readable shape. Encoding constitutes a primitive field of textual activity—a system of semiotic exchange—visible at the crossroads of computer science and literary theory. Encoding finally matters because how texts are encoded, transmitted, and stored decides who gets to decode, receive, and revise.

CHAPTER 1

> METAPHOR MACHINES

Jean Baudrillard's sometimes enigmatic comments on the genesis of simulacra in the late 1980s are beginning to come into focus for me only now, when code has already conquered culture. Today, computers interject ubiquitously. We drink our morning coffee from brewing machines that use fuzzy logic. At night we go to bed surrounded by smart alarm clocks and sleep activity monitors. Baudrillard wrote, "At the limit of an always increasing elimination of references and finalities . . . we find 'the programmatic sign,' whose 'value' is purely *tactical*."[1] Like good theater, we experience the machine in immersion, suspending disbelief. This leads to what Baudrillard called the "ever-increasing loss of resemblances and designations."[2] The programmatic sign circumvents critical reflection in favor of affect. Its value is tactical in the sense that it appeals to practical reason alone, by invoking purely instrumental terms, such as efficiency, performance, disruption, and innovation.

Code, as we encounter it here, elicits pleasure and catharsis. In this, the programmer and the user occupy distinct and unequal positions in the epistemological hierarchy. Code is not usually meant to be decoded by those it acts upon. Recipients of codified control are spared the friction of signification, remaining instead in the state of *asemiosis* and therefore nescience. In return, code compels exacting obedience. Baudrillard understands the essence of the programmatic sign to lie in the "micromolecular structure of command and control."[3] The appeal to structure at the molecular level draws readers' attention to the perils of selective illiteracy. As inscription, code settles within remote materialities, at strata not immediately perceptible to human senses. Users are thereby confronted with the choice to persist in the simulation pleasurably or face the difficulty of microscopic reading, which requires special tools and training. Value is further derived from the resulting imbalance of critical acumen.

The programmatic sign so conceived splits its energies between screen and hard drive. On the screen, at the site of projection, the programmatic sign simulates familiar materialities: buttons, bins, files, folders, drawers, desktops, windows, tiles, wood grain, drop shadows, chrome. At the site of storage, from which the sign emanates, the language changes to the vocabulary of control: central processing units, compilation, commitment, extraction, command, condition, initiation, handling, function, persistence, and execution. In the rift between the sites of storage (what is) and projection (what appears to be), the programmatic sign undergoes a series of structural transformations. What originates from (1) the keyboard as the mechanical action of a switch becomes (2) an electric signal that (3) leaves electromagnetic marks in computer memory, which (4) morph into phases of liquid crystal on-screen, leaving behind (5) letters that emanate outward as light. Programming languages bridge the passage between bodies, archives, and screens, breaking thought up into differentiated units for transfer. Simulation emerges in the reassembly of fractured media into a seemingly continuous integrated whole, whereby texts dissolve into letters and pixels, which then congeal back into holistic literary works.

Roman Jakobson called such construction and deconstruction of meaning the "profuse exchange of ritualized formulas" or the phatic function of language.[4] Code, like the phatic utterance, facilitates the exchange of information through convention. The words "Hello world" on paper or in plain text format take up 11 bytes. In the Portable Document Format (PDF) they make up more than 24,000 bytes. The added information is directed not toward the receiver of the message but toward the channel itself. Code describes the rules of engagement between author and reader. It makes concrete and constrains the physical capabilities of the medium. The codified phatic function is more profuse than it is in speech, where it is limited to occasional metacommentary: Can you hear me now? It is also less apparent in that it contains other (machine) languages and registers that are physically inaccessible to the recipient.

Programming at its essence is a phatic activity. Code shapes and commands. At the same time, it conjures fantastical metaphors to occlude the structure of shaping and commanding. The simulacrum created by code obscures the incongruence between visible signs and a medium's underlying material affordances. What you see is not always what you get. We are instead confronted with a composite image, which under examination reveals a complex process of transfiguration between the visible sign and the sign at the site of its inscription.

The simulation is without a referent. It bears little resemblance to material substrata of electronic reading. We believe we are handling books; our ideas about reading and interpretation subsequently rely on that initial physical point of contact with paper. But when reading electronically, we are handling something other than print material. The semblance to paper guides our intuitions about the medium and its associated affordances: to scroll, bookmark, or turn pages. We have far fewer intuitions about the affordances of inscription at the micromolecular level. As we "turn" simulated pages, electric charges embedded into a solid-state medium cross the impenetrable oxide barrier, reaching their destination, the floating gate, through quantum tunneling. Electromagnetic inscription exploits the wave-particle duality of matter and its corollary, the Heisenberg uncertainty principle.[5] A digital text thus comprises numerous improbable events at quantum scale.

What can be said about practices of reading and interpretation grounded in such remote physicalities? For now, only that they continue to unfold figuratively, removed from the material conditions of knowledge production. Metaphor sustains our lives in digital worlds artificially by analogy to habituated media. We already know what to do with paper; electronic books therefore replicate paper. Replicators dull the discomfort of contact between human and machine. They hinder efforts to master poetics at quantum scale: the ability to inject electrons, draw lattices, manipulate arrays, affect solid states of being. It is tempting to view media ecosystems that host our digital lives as a kind of a natural element like water or air. But we should not forget that computational ecologies are always constructed environments. They are not governed by laws of physics in the same sense that clouds or oceans are. They form part of a massive tactical effort to bring private spaces of inhabitance—think the Home folder on your computer, your family photo album, your digital bookmarks—under the purview of computational control. Simulations encode political structures that should not be naturalized, lest we succumb to the complacency of technological determinism.

My goal in this chapter is therefore to interrupt the frictionless advance of the computational metaphor, to separate resemblances from their designations, the apparent shape from a command in the imperative. What does it mean to turn a page in a medium that sustains neither turning nor pages? I rely on the language of cognitive metaphor theory to tell a story of metaphor's influence on computation at a formative moment in the history of human–computer interaction. I approach this tradition from within, taking on its language and assumptions in the first few sections of the chapter. In the later sections I narrate the historical transition from literal computing, by which users gave explicit commands to their machines, to the so-called direct manipulation model, in which they began to occupy virtual, figurative environments. The chapter draws on archives from graphic design, literary theory, and computer science, fields that came into direct contact in the 1970s, 1980s, and 1990s. The trajectory from the conversational to the direct model of human–computer interaction points to a speculative possibility by which human and machine couple in seemingly unmediated, affective ways. I acknowledge and finally reject the idea outright in my conclusion.

VERISIMILITUDE

Metaphors structure human habitation within simulated environments. "People do not think like computers," a group of engineers from Interval Research Group wrote in a patent application describing "methods and systems for providing human/computer interfaces." According to their description, metaphors "permit more efficient and medium independent communications between people and computers."[6] Metaphor mediates in the symbolic transference between human and machine, in the liminal space where two disparate systems of representation meet to exchange information. "Certain encoded information is translated into certain decoded information," the engineers concluded.[7]

Interfaces translate machine states (the configuration of open and closed circuits) into pictures, numbers, and letters, which are all species of human cognitive states. In essence, a computer is a system for such metaphoric transference of properties. "A user interface is represented on the display screen in the form of metaphoric objects, called icons," wrote another group of engineers employed by the Xerox Corporation. An icon, they continued, "may be a representation of a virtual object, such as a virtual floppy disk." Crucially, a virtual object can be accessible either in what the authors referred to as a "host system world" or an "emulating processor world," even when "virtual floppy disk[s] may have a filing system alien to the host system world."[8] An arrangement of information on-screen—the poetics of emulated space—are incompatible with arrangements of electromagnetic charge on disk—the poetics of inscription.

To reflect on metaphoric function in everyday computation, consider the following passage from a patent filed by Xerox in 1991. It describes an "electronic library metaphor," which includes

> a shared books with data base metaphor, a reference books metaphor, and a card catalog metaphor in one system that allows large object ori- ented data bases to be organized and accessed in an exclusive environment and in addition allows access to screen icons, creates a visual hierarchy of related and shared objects, and allows mutually exclusive access to the metaphors within the library.[9]

The invention ultimately enables the "organizing, accessing, and query- ing of information unique to physical libraries in an electronic workstation environment."[10]

A related invention describes "methods, systems, and computer program products for the display and operation of virtual three-dimensional books." Its purpose, according to the authors, "is to mitigate the limitations of the small screen space," that is, to transform the constrained physical dimensions of screen space into an unconstrained virtual space. To achieve this effect, the system contains "two basic types of information: content information and display/manipulation information." The authors explain that content "refers to the text and image data for the underlying document," where display and manipulation protocols refer to the "data defining how the text and image data is to be presented to the user." The separation of physical and virtual spaces allows users to "touch," virtual "books and bookcases," which "fly" from one "space" into another (see Figures 1.1 and 1.2).[11]

Set aside for the moment the peculiarity of being able to patent a meta- phor. Note instead the ambiguity of technical language introduced by the split between "two types of information," one describing the virtual space and the other the physical space. How does one "access" a metaphor, for

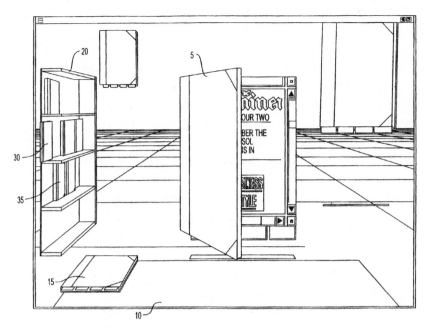

FIGURE 1.1. Visual metaphors extend the affordances of the represented object into virtual space, as illustrated by this drawing from the Card et al. patent showing a sample interface for viewing a three-dimensional book. Source: Stuart Kent Card et al., "Methods, Systems, and Computer Program Products for the Display and Operation of Virtual Three-Dimensional Books," Patent US7015910 B2, filed December 21, 2000, issued March 21, 2006, sheet 3.

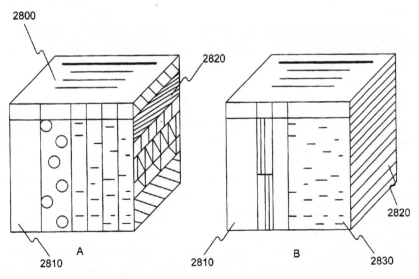

FIGURE 1.2. Card et al. imagine "alternate display techniques for information about a big book." The virtual object offers new possibilities for interaction. Source: Stuart Kent Card et al., "Methods, Systems, and Computer Program Products for the Display and Operation of Virtual Three-Dimensional Books," Patent US7015910 B2, filed December 21, 2000, issued March 21, 2006, sheet 4.

example? If someone were to "check out" a book from the electronic library, would she behold a book or its metaphor alone? What is lost or gained in the translation of library space into electronic workstations? What mechanisms would ensure the integrity between the metaphor and its underlying data structure? Metaphor theory strains to answer such questions.

Traditional metaphor theorists see metaphor as a linguistic phenomenon. To say "The day stands tiptoe on the misty mountain tops" is to use the verb *stand* in a novel linguistic context. Days have no literal legs to stand on. In the 1980s scholars such as John Searle, George Lakoff, and Mark Turner argued that metaphors were broadly cognitive phenomena that mapped distinct ontological categories across conceptual domains.[12] In the modified view, even such basic semantic concepts as "quantity, state, change, action, cause, purpose, means, modality" were metaphoric in nature.[13] Lakoff and others further argued that beyond figurative, lyrical language, metaphors also structure everyday experience.[14] Thus the analysis of such common phrases as "Things are looking up" and "I can't get that tune out of my mind" reveals the underlying figurations "Good things are up" and "The mind is a container." The idea that "good things are up" generates a number of further metaphors, such as "Profits are going up" and "We're moving on up."[15] "The mind is a container" produces "open your mind" and "close-minded."

In the cognitive view, metaphors perform a number of "conventional mappings from one domain to another."[16] Lakoff mentions, for example, the common trope of "a state is a person" implicit in the ideas of "friendly" and "hostile" states.[17] These tropes imply that ideas—about agency, emotion, and mental life—that are usually attached to people can also extend to state actors. Similarly, to say that someone is "boiling mad" instantiates the common trope of "anger is a hot liquid in a container." In this case, familiar properties associated with physics transfer to emotion. Lakoff explains that such domain mappings tend to follow rules: "Mappings are not arbitrary, but grounded in the body and in everyday experience and knowledge."[18] Finally, domain mappings obey what Lakoff calls the invariance principle, by which "the image schema structure of the source domain is projected onto the target domain in a way that is consistent with inherent target domain structure."[19] Keep these rules in mind, as they will become important later on in our conversation.

The kind of resemblances that we have been discussing so far (e.g., those between documents and their icons) are further referred to as *structural metaphors*. Structural metaphors do more than orient concepts, as Lakoff and Johnson wrote in the 1980s. Grounded in "systematic correlations within our experience," structural metaphors transfer organizing principles from one domain to another.[20] Thus, to say "The world is our oyster" is to suggest that something in our approach to interacting with oysters resembles our approach to life. The ease of eating one, for example, transfers to the ease of living in the other. The transferred property implies more than a semantic similarity, one of meaning; it also implies a structural similarity, one of interface. The metaphor suggests an arrangement that, like an oyster, can be shucked, or that it might contain a tasty hidden morsel. Structural metaphors organize one thing in the shape of another. They are tools for extending insight from known domains to lesser known ones. They hold great explanatory and exploratory power by which simple things, like oysters, shed light on complex things, like worlds.

In their capacity to aid explanation and exploration, metaphor machines present us with a special case of conceptual domain blending. They enact rather than merely suggest a transference of structuring principles from one system to another, from physical libraries to electronic workstation environments in the earlier example. Metaphors that can be touched and handled in some way exist neither wholly in language nor wholly in mind. Rather, they are at hand, in action. John Carroll, one of the pioneers in the field of human–computer interaction, summarized the role of metaphors in the design of computing systems as follows:

> Professional programmers might learn a new system X by metaphorizing at least initially from what they already know about system Y. More casual or naive end-users might rely on metaphors drawn from more distant knowledge domains, e.g. on what they have already learned about electric typewriters. . . . The implications of this proposal are simple and direct. If people employ metaphors in learning about computing systems, the designers of those systems should anticipate and support likely metaphoric constructions to increase the ease of learning and using the system.[21]

In essence, Carroll imagines the kind of human–computer interfaces that incorporate Lakoff and Johnson's conceptual blending in practice. The simulacrum of a familiar gesture of discarding a crumpled piece of paper can thus guide the deletion of electronic documents.

Apple's influential *Human Interface Guidelines*, at the core of its desktop interfaces in the 1980s and today, echoes Carroll's proscriptions.

> You can take advantage of people's knowledge of the world around them by using metaphors to convey concepts and features of your application. Use metaphors involving concrete, familiar ideas and make the metaphors plain, so that users have a set of expectations to apply to computer environments. For example, people often use file folders to store paper documents in their offices. Therefore, it makes sense to people to store computer documents in computer-generated folders that look like file folders. People can organize their hard disks in a way that's analogous to the way they organize their file cabinets.[22]

Apple's designers understood that the mapping of concepts between the physical world and the computer-generated world is imperfect. Actual file folders, for example, can hold a limited number of documents. Their storage capacity is constrained by the physical properties of paper, cut into a particular shape. A computer folder, by contrast, holds a nearly unlimited number of files. To be more precise, the electronic folder metaphor is subject to different constraints from those that limit the use of paper files. How does one explain the incongruence between these physicalities to a lay computer user? The Apple manual advises designers to borrow some of the logic from the source domain (paper) while retaining new possibilities made possible in the target, digital domain. Designers are to "strike a balance between the metaphor's suggested use and the ability of the computer to support and extend the metaphor."[23] In theory, users handling virtual folders can thereby recognize the medium's novel capabilities beyond those suggested by iconography. A perceptive user realizes that some attributes of the paper domain map onto the virtual, whereas others do not, and that virtual objects further contain possibilities not conveyed by analogy.

A number of patents from IBM, Xerox, and Microsoft invoke the logics of structural metaphor and domain blending. Consider U.S. Patent 5,907,845 by Paula J. Cox and colleagues of International Business Machines. The invention describes "a library metaphor that allows a user to organize the online books in a manner that has meaning and utility." Its authors continue to explain that although "the actual books may be stored in many separate and distinct locations . . . the bookcase provides a familiar classification system." The creation of bookcase metaphors must also involve "the creation of appropriate links to the actual online book/bookshelf/bookcase." Book metaphors ultimately provide "an easy to understand and intuitive model for a user who might not be familiar with on-line viewing tools."[24]

Another metaphor machine can be found in the collaboration between the influential product design firm IDEO and Xerox in the 1990s. The two companies collaborated to produce an early "file manager shell" called PC Catalog, later renamed TabWorks. In describing the design process, IDEO developers wrote about defining "key elements of the metaphor" contained in the image of "tabs" and "catalogs": "The book *cover* opened to display three *rings* binding a set of divider *tabs*, each containing one or more *pages*." Pages, in turn contained "items" or "icons representing documents or applications."[25] In a similar binder-based software application, IBM engineers describe "contents of the notebook metaphor," which are "displayed as a stack of sheets." Thus "the interface . . . permits a user to directly manipulate the sheets in the notebook metaphor."[26]

Note again the awkward conceptual slide between objects and their representations. Users cannot in fact "manipulate metaphors directly." Metaphors mediate. They are precisely a method for indirect contact, through transference of properties. Direct manipulation suggests an object's immediate availability to hand. Users do not handle objects immediately, however. They take hold of images. Actual data objects are occluded in favor of their mimetic representation. Paper and page metaphors substitute for the reality of floating gates and electromagnetic charges.

The analysis of such fundamental incongruence between physical domains is crucial to our contemporary political predicament, in which structures of digital control often advance by metaphoric substitution: The camera light is off, but the camera continues to record. The light, in this case, occludes a persistent mechanism of surveillance. Metaphor machines contain the promise of productive domain mapping. However, we lack the means to verify the success of appropriate property transference. In the following sections I examine the dynamics of this subtle sleight of hand—more closely and on its own terms. Because metaphor theory influenced interface design historically, it can also help diagnose modes of metaphoric failure. How do metaphors break and what happens to zombie-like dead metaphors, empty of sense yet functional in ways that no longer honor the initial contract between incongruent logics and physicalities?

DEATH AND INCONGRUENCE

Metaphors are said to be motivated when a number of concepts from one domain extend into another domain to produce insight.[27] Lakoff explains that to say "to spin one's wheels" when referring to someone who is thinking is to apply a reader's knowledge of automobiles to the mental realm. Wheels that spin without moving the vehicle forward waste energy. The metaphor suggests that something similar happens mentally as well.[28]

In his influential essay on metaphor the English literary critic I. A. Richards wrote that "when we use metaphor we have two thoughts of different things active together and supported by a single word, or phrase, whose meaning is a resultant of their interaction."[29] Richards's radical contribution to metaphor theory lies in the observation that metaphors operate in language, thought, and action ubiquitously. They do not, as previously thought, exist merely in the realm of poetic language. Richards believed that thought itself is metaphoric in that the mind continually searches for patterns and comparisons.[30] Motivated metaphors produce insight: We use them to explore and make sense of the world.

Some metaphors, however, are more productive than others. The poetic use of metaphor does not merely carry meaning across known domains; it produces new and unexpected connections between them. To this effect, Richards cited Percy Shelley, who wrote the following in defense of poetry:

> [Poetic] language is vitally metaphorical; that is, it marks the before unapprehended relations of things and perpetuates their apprehension, until the words which represent them, become, through time, signs for portions or classes of thoughts instead of pictures of integral thoughts; and then if no new poets should arise to create afresh the associations which have been thus disorganized, language will be dead to all the nobler purposes of human intercourse.[31]

In highlighting the continually regenerative power of poetic metaphor, Shelley anticipated what the cognitive school of metaphor theory was to confirm by empirical means more than a century later.[32] Metaphors do not "die" as such. They continue to live but also become naturalized, that is, understood literally. They create connections, which with time become habituated and invisible. Taken for literal truth, metaphors lose their quality of mediation or literally "ferrying across,"[33] as when the idea of dead metaphors itself no longer evokes death.[34] Metaphors wither; once a connotation is lost, it becomes a denotative statement lacking any exploratory or explanatory potential. In Shelley's view, all metaphors are destined to become habituated in this way, only to be reborn in poetry.

At the height of their generative powers, metaphors produce new meaning. At their nadir, they block judgment and perception. Creative juxtaposition between two previously unrelated conceptual domains brings novel aspects of experience to light. With time, however, metaphors fail to perpetuate understanding; they become commonplace instrumental shortcuts. In the words of Viktor Shklovsky, we "cease to experience" the trope.[35] Vilém Flusser similarly wrote that habituated idiom proceeds "smoothly," giving us no pause, without "bumps or interruptions."[36]

Lakoff famously took exception to the idea of dead metaphors, arguing that even those metaphors that are thoroughly habituated can play a vital part in structuring everyday experience. He gave an example with the following sentence: *He still can't quite grasp the basic ideas of quantum mechanics.* "Grasping," in this case, is used as a synonym for "understanding." It indicates a transference of properties between physical (grasping) and mental (understanding) realms. Lakoff argued that, despite being commonplace, the metaphor is alive, because it continues to perform a function: naming a mental activity that we would otherwise find difficult to explain with precision. Such metaphors are less dead than other, perhaps more novel, one-off poetic tropes that fail to circulate widely.[37] A metaphor dies in the sense of being overused, but it dies also in another sense for not being used at all.

For Lakoff, truly dead metaphors are ones where the original source image no longer makes sense. He gives the example of the English word *pedigree*, which originally referred to the French *pied de grue*, "crane's foot." The foot was historically used in a typographical flourish to decorate familial tree diagrams.

In the previous example of metaphoric mental "grasping," both sides of the domain transference were readily available to us. We understood something about grasping things and extended it to the mind's capacity to take hold of ideas. By contrast, most English speakers no longer perceive the *pied de grue* contained within *pedigree*. In the case of a commonplace, the metaphor is merely tired from frequent use, whereas in the crane's foot example it is completely dead. All habituated metaphors such as "grasping ideas" and "pedigree" lose a measure of their symbolic connotation with time. Unlike "pedigree," however, the metaphoric nature of "grasping ideas" is at least available for casual interpretation. It therefore retains its generative powers. According to Lakoff, the underlying metaphor "The mind is like a hand" produces other meaningful phrases, such as "You have to *let go* of this idea." The crane's foot in the English "pedigree" by contrast has stopped generating novel connections. The conventional notion of dead metaphors, Lakoff objects, does not appropriately differentiate between the two cases of metaphor dysfunction.[38] Metaphors sometimes die but continue to produce new linkages, as is the case with grasping ideas. At other times, they die in the sense of one domain becoming no longer accessible to its user, as is the case with pedigree.

Furthermore, note that wholly unmotivated metaphors do not live at all. Thus the Mad Hatter poses his famous nonsensical riddle in Lewis Carroll's *Alice in Wonderland*: How is a raven like a writing desk? The complete dissimilarity between the domains, that of animals and that of furniture, prevents any productive congruence.[39] Little domain mapping happens between ravens and writing desks. Not having been born, the metaphor dies in yet another sense.

With these comments on broken and dead metaphors in mind, I return to computer screens and ask, How do interface metaphors live or die by these definitions?

When we discard a document into a trash can, to return to our recurring example, we intuitively expect the computer to erase it. This would fulfill Lakoff's invariance principle, which, if you recall, describes transference from a source domain "in a way that is consistent with the inherent structure of the target domain."[40] But the computer does not do this. We empty the trash but have no means to verify the realization of the implied transference. Our ability to actually erase data stands in an arbitrary relationship to the depicted figure. Indeed, the act of emptying trash cans often ceases to be metaphoric at all. When data are not erased, the icon no longer stands for the action it depicts. The transferred property of erasure is not simply missing in transit; it is manifestly misrepresented.

DISSIMULATION

Readers know how paragraphs, pages, files, and folders relate to paper and would like for their digital images to behave in a similar way. The principles of metaphor-driven design contain an implicit model of human–computer interaction, which suggests that humans prefer to manipulate digital information stored on computational media by the means of familiar mediating structures (paragraphs, pages, files, and folders) associated figuratively with the affordances of print media.

One affordance of paper is that it can be folded. It therefore becomes possible to earmark a page by folding a corner. Patently, digital media cannot (as yet) fold the way paper does. Readers seeking a mechanism for digital recollection may not be familiar with the affordances of the newly inhabited medium. Consequently, the affordances of digital media are presented through metaphor. In this way, a virtual "earmark" on a "page" represents a numerical pointer to a specific address in computer memory. A "page" stands for a range of related addresses that correspond roughly to the information visible on an analogous page in print. Similarly, one "drops a folder into a trash can" or "drags and drops a file" or "bookmarks a page" on a screen. Such metaphors rely on habituated insight where properties of one medium extend into another. We do not literally drag or drop bits, but we use metaphors of paper and trash cans to help us manipulate bits and bytes as though they were common household objects. The metaphor opens figurative possibilities. It also obscures actual physical contingencies of interacting with bits and bytes, logic gates and electromagnetic traces.

Metaphoric substitution encourages readers to extend their facility with one sort of media (paper and ink) to another (screen and pixels). But what readers gain in facility, they lose in critical faculty. Alienated from the material conditions of information storage and retrieval, readers gain access to metaphor alone. Thus we go through the motion of "turning pages" but in actuality modulate points of light on-screen. We "highlight a passage," which constitutes an action that may also send information about the highlighted passage to a data aggregation service. We "share a book," which really means assigning a temporary license to another user. "Where is my text?" I ask when downloading a paper from an online journal.[41] It is in your Home folder, my colleague answers. But unless one of us is familiar with the material contingencies of file storage, neither has a mental map of any physical location corresponding to the Home folder, the default location of personal files on many systems. When confronted with the actual affordances of digital text, users grasp for neutered metaphors. We "reside" in such "homes," "own," "share," and "create" only in the simulacrum.

Interface metaphors conceal structures of algorithmic governance and control over the transmission of symbolic goods. Print offers a relatively static and stable medium by comparison. Ink and paper do not change much in transit. By contrast, the vessels of computation are capable of altering their contents dynamically. For example, imagine my asking you to read Shakespeare's *Hamlet* by sharing a print copy of the text. I am fairly certain that the text will remain unaltered as I pass it into your hands. By contrast, the computed sign adjusts itself to new contexts. An electronic version of *Hamlet* could change based on the new reader's geographic location, mood, or consumption habits. In fact, most texts we consume today come to us in such a computationally constructed way. The front page of the *New York Times* viewed in Beijing will differ from that viewed in New York. The two "pages" or "sites" are in some sense two completely different textual variants. In another sense, the "front page" identifies the same location of the same text in two diverging and dynamically composed versions. Whatever is meant by "today's edition of the *New York Times*" in that sense denotes differing surface phenomena that emanate from the same source.

The key to understanding the loss of resemblances that accompanies ubiquitous simulation lies in the inner dynamics of the metaphor machinery. A functioning metaphor, according to Lakoff's definitions, is one that transfers structural properties of one domain into another. Thus to say "Life is a stage" is to transpose something about theater onto life. In literary terms, *theater* is the "tenor" and *life* the "vehicle" of the composite figure.[42] Simulations work differently. Where the tenor of a literary metaphor *transfers* properties across domains, the computational tenor *substitutes* them, confusing "signs of the real for the real."[43] It is a subtle difference that engenders not-so-subtle effects. For example, it would be one thing to say "You are the apple of my eye" and quite another to actually confuse apples for eye pupils. Baudrillard gives us the example of a map that no longer corresponds to any territory. He calls such a condition of pure simulation without a referent "hyperreality."

Hyperreality emanates from the momentum of an expected correspondence between representation and the thing being represented. One expects a weather simulation to model actual observed meteorological conditions.

Would it still be a weather simulation if the model was broken in some way or, in the extreme, if it had no correspondence to the physics of clouds, wind, and water whatsoever? The hyperreal model breaks further still by usurping rather than imitating or merely obscuring the underlying reality. It begins to simulate itself, according to its own rules, entering a state of dissimulation. Such dissimulation no longer corresponds to any conditions on the ground. Severed from their referent, signs attain the status of things represented: a map of a map, a symbol that folds onto itself, weather simulation confused for weather.

We know that physical affordances of liquid crystal displays (LCDs) and electromagnetic storage differ drastically from those of paper, goat skins, or parchment. For example, an English-language character occupies eight basic units of information (bits) on a disk, whereas a print character occupies one basic unit (letter). A disk can tolerate millions of rewrites, whereas the paper medium wears out after only a few. Paper inscriptions are visible to the naked eye, whereas digital inscriptions are not. Still, simulations maintain an illusion of similarity. We encounter what is called *skeuomorphic* design, by which screen reading retains the ornaments of print. In this way, electronic book readers mimic the bent corner of a well-thumbed book. Skeuomorphic metaphors extend visual cues from one medium to another. A reader already knows how to turn book pages. Book devices therefore simulate page turning to ease the cognitive burden of transitioning from paper to pixel. Instead of issuing arcane commands meant for the machine, readers perform the more habituated motion of swiping across the screen. The gliding motion enacts a kinetic analogy (a type of a metaphor) as though transposing properties of paper to glass.

Our grasp on the medium weakens the more convincing its simulacrum. By definition, simulation "assumes a form resembling that of something else," whereby one referent is exchanged for another.[44] To drag and drop a document into a trash can on the screen should in theory correspond to an analogous set of data manipulations on disk. Yet discarding a file in this manner does not necessarily include deletion of data from the storage medium, as expected. The document icon disappears visually, but its electromagnetic trace endures. Such loss of resemblances could in theory remain insignificant. Does one care whether a file is actually erased or not when performing deletion? Perhaps not. But in some cases, when it really matters (e.g., under the threat of censorship or persecution), the incongruence exposes the frailty of our alienation from the material contexts of digital labor. Under duress, one may demand that the thing stay deeply deleted. The problem of metaphoric immediacy reappears in the unfulfilled promise of mimesis. In many contexts the metaphoric vehicle claims to bridge domains and to ferry content across faithfully, without meddling or damaging its contents. But if metaphors do meddle—if they mediate while dissembling and dissimulating—by what process can one ensure the efficacy of transference? What entity makes good on the promise of verisimilitude?

Readers ultimately bear the burden of confirming the appropriate transference of properties between domains. In pretending to turn virtual pages uncritically, we otherwise lose sight of the metaphor. If we hope to practice anything like interpretation or close reading of digital content, we must begin at the physical site of its inscription. A truly materialist poetics would analyze embedded representation in the context of the surrounding medium. More than superficial embellishment, skeuomorphic metaphors enacted at the digital surface affect all higher-order meaning-carrying units, from individual letters to words, paragraphs, chapters, pages, and books.

Why do readers tolerate misleading media metaphors then? Why not simply make use of novel interfaces afforded by new technology? The literature in human–computer interaction suggests a formalist answer: habituation.[45] The initial effort it takes to inhabit a new cognitive environment discourages curiosity. Smart designers therefore rely on acculturated practice, the turning of pages in our case, to minimize adaptive friction. Digital poems, novels, physician's scripts, and legal contracts resemble their paper counterparts in order to enable familiar actions. And as they perform that mimesis, by imitating paper pages, reading appliances also monitor, adjust, warn, and control. The new affordances pass under the guise of the old.

Dissimulation conceals structuring principles large and small. Some occluded details remain inconsequential, such as the limit on how many keys can be pressed at once without overwhelming keyboard circuitry when typing. Other concealed details are of paramount importance. Digital rights management chips and censorship filters interfere directly and in ways that are often purposefully hidden from the reader. For example, the U.S. Digital Millennium Copyright Act prohibits physical circumvention of copyright protections.[46] An electronic book encrypted to prevent copyright infringement could also prevent readers from examining codes and codices embedded into the device, rules governing accessibility, preservation, or freedom of speech. Material

affordances of inscription at that deep, bottom-most meaning-bearing medium influence all higher-level practices of interpretation.[47]

Traditional theories of textual interpretation rely on properties and assumptions attached to print media. For example, Hans-Georg Gadamer famously imagined the artistic transformation of abstract "free play" into
concrete material structure (*Gebilde*) that is both "repeatable" and "permanent."[48] Similarly, in his *Interpretation Theory*, Paul Ricoeur wrote about the
"range of social and political changes" related to the invention of writing.
Ricoeur attributes the "birth of political rule exercised by a distant state"
and "the birth of market relationships" to the stability of communication in
print. The constitution of archives enables history; the fixity of law, justice.
"Such an immense range of effects suggests that human discourse is not
merely preserved from destruction," Ricoeur wrote. It is also "deeply affected
in its communicative function."[49] Digital text offers no such permanence.
What is meant by "fixed" "durable," and "repeatable" changes with the device. Such properties come to us under the guise of surface representation.
Nothing is guaranteed in the passage of digital text from one pair of hands
to another. Formatting expands its purview beyond typographical convention. It includes the capability to substitute words, summarize automatically,
generate discourse by algorithmic means, or erase wholesale. What does
it mean, then, to read and interpret texts that change depending on their
contexts? How can literary analysis—close reading, philology, hermeneutics—
persist without the fixity of print?

Dissimulation is perhaps necessary, because the reading and writing
of digital data can involve processes far outside everyday experience. For
example, in reading data from solid-state (flash) memory, a circuit imparts
electric charge through quantum tunneling onto a connected series of floating gate transistors (Figure 1.3).[50]

Whatever the complexities of solid-state storage architecture, the difference
in the structure of information on pages and floating gates is apparent. The
arrangement of one has only an arbitrary connection to the other. Consequently, changes in the structure of the symbolic domain, which manifest in
the erasure of words on-screen, do not necessitate corresponding changes
in the physical domain, which manifest in the discharge of the floating gate.
Information endures despite intended erasure.

Dwellers of virtual realms believe in verisimilitude as a matter of faith.
We hope that the analogy of turning pages or erasing words on-screen will

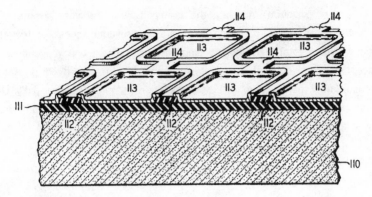

FIGURE 1.3. Remote materialities at the site of the inscription: nonvolatile solid-state memory. A drawing from Boyle and Smith's patent shows the quantum tunneling mechanism where an "avalanche" of particles tunnel through a classically insurmountable barrier to charge a floating gate, representing a single bit of information. Source: W. Boyle and G. Smith, "Information Storage Devices," Patent US3858232 A, filed November 9, 1971, issued December 31, 1974, sheet 7.

entail similar actions on disk. But we waver when asked to authenticate the particulars of the simulation. At times, "erased" data is simply hidden from view. At other times, instead of disappearing, it proliferates across deep surfaces, shared without consent with agents not privy to the original contexts of inscription. As was the case with Baudrillard's map, metaphors of reading and writing digitally break in that they no longer resemble any familiar terrain. Dissimulation mimics known materialities absent their actual physics. It suggests a structuring of one kind while enacting another.

Micromolecular writing, of the kind perceived already by Kittler and Baudrillard in the 1990s, today demands the corresponding practice of microscopic reading.[51] I imagine here the inverse of Kittler's literature without humans: cryptic, illegible, and under the conditions of high technology. The methodology of computational poetics insists on recovering the full shape of the inscription, across surfaces and domains. It makes the extent of the dissimulating figure available for interpretation.

What happens in the metaphoric transfer between cognitive structures (contracts, poems, novels) and device-things that simulate them (screens, drives, readers)? Estrangement, the exegesis of metaphor, reveals the rules that govern transference from one medium to another. A materialist poetics can subsequently allow one to consent to or, conversely, to resist elements of imposed structure. That is not to say that meaning-making structures can ever become fully transparent or produce plain, unambiguous meaning.

A true cipher precludes not just the ambiguity but the very possibility of interpretation or misinterpretation. It physically prevents access. In the continuum between total legibility and illegibility, digital text today occupies the space somewhere right of center. It is illegible in part and by dispensation. Archivists know this problem well: the simulation of print decays rapidly. Digital documents—computer games and proprietary text formats—become inaccessible as the platforms used to decode them themselves pass into oblivion.

MIMESIS

"An interface is by nature a form of artistic imitation: a *mimesis*," Brenda Laurel wrote in her important 1984 essay "Interface as Mimesis." She went on to argue that "if designing interfaces feels like painting on cave walls by flickering torchlight, it is only because we, the designers, have not availed ourselves of better illumination: the science of the mimetic arts, poetics."[52] Laurel, who started her academic career in theater studies, went on to work for Apple, Activision, Atari, and Sun Microsystems among other companies. Her work, widely cited in technical literature, reminds us of the close connection between poetics and human–computer interaction.

The nexus of these fields is all the more important today, because immersive computational environments structure experience beyond the merely instrumental. Computers increasingly mediate the interface between the public and the private, art and politics, mind and body. The simulacrum requires that we advance a reflective "science of the mimetic arts" lest we lose a sense of what I call, channeling Michael Taussig, mimetic alterity.[53] The suspension of disbelief must remain, as it was in Samuel Coleridge's original formulation, a willful act, containing further a "semblance of truth" required to animate the shadows of imagination.[54] An involuntary or, worse, forced suspension of disbelief can lead only to a state of total critical disempowerment.

The history of human–computer interaction passes through several distinct stages, each defined by their relationship to semiosis. I periodize the development as follows:

1. Early computers were programmed by physically manipulating a complex arrangement of wires and relays. With time, that configuration could be abstracted into symbolic states, signified by visible marks on paper and later invisible electromagnetic marks on tape.
2. In the next stage of development, physical arrangements of gates and

relays were further codified into an artificial language. Programmers oper-ated with a constrained vocabulary, sending and receiving messages to the machine in a dialogue, dubbed "conversational programming," that resembled human communication.[55]

3. As computer use spread, the paradigm of so-called "direct interaction" or "direct manipulation" shifted emphasis from verbal cues to visual cues and from symbol to icon. Communication was and continues to be direct in the sense of felt immediacy and immersion. Compared to a verbal symbol, an icon appears to have a more direct relationship to the remote materialities of computational media, less arbitrary than the symbol.[56]

4. Finally, one imagines an indexical connection between human and ma-chine by which brain states and machine states could correspond through a physical rather than a merely visual linkage. The so-called "direct brain interfaces" bypass inscription (word and picture) altogether, making use of neuroprosthetics (implants and surface electrodes) to connect human and machine.[57]

It would be a mistake, however, to conflate claims to directness, at any stage of interface development, with the absence of mediation. A morpho-logical grammar always intercedes. The passage between disparate media, brains and machines, requires a rule book that specifies the dynamics of transformation. The grammar sets the terms of engagement.

Before the 1980s the dominant paradigm of interacting with machines was the dialogue.[58] Already in 1950, Alan Turing imagined a conversation between an artificially intelligent poet and its critic.

> *Interrogator*: In the first line of your sonnet which reads "Shall I compare thee to a summer's day," would not "a spring day" do as well or better?
> *Witness*: It wouldn't scan.
> *Interrogator*: How about "a winter's day"? That would scan all right.
> *Witness*: Yes, but nobody wants to be compared to a winter's day.
> *Interrogator*: Would you say Mr. Pickwick reminded you of Christmas?
> *Witness*: In a way.
> *Interrogator*: Yet Christmas is a winter's day, and I do not think Mr. Pickwick would mind the comparison.
> *Witness*: I don't think you're serious. By a winter's day one means a typical winter's day, rather than a special one like Christmas.[59]

The goal of conversational programming was to provide a similarly natural-ized dialogue between operators and machines. Although machine under-standing of informal human speech did not develop in earnest until the twenty-first century, interactive computing environments such as DIALOG and JOSS were designed to lessen the cognitive burden of speaking machine languages by translating them into dialogue systems that understood a lim-ited number of English words.

JOSS, an experimental online computing system created by the Rand Cor-poration in 1963, consisted of a typewriter connected to the JOHNNIAC com-puter. Before JOSS, programmers would interact with the JOHNNIAC machine by means of keyboard and punch card, initially using octal number notation and then binary assembly language.[60] These methods of programming were time-consuming and prone to error. "An octal desk calculator was nice to have," a historian of the system would later quip.[61]

The JOSS experiment introduced the idea of an interpreter that sat be-tween the human operator and the machine, facilitating communication in a friendly, conversational manner. Think of JOSS as a "user's computing aide and a single contact with the computer," wrote the system's designers.[62] Instead of feeding punch cards into a mechanism, as was done before, op-erators would use a typewriter. Instead of flipping switches, they typed words. JOSS thus referred both to a simple language for machine instruction and the new remote console way of interacting with computers. JOSS and the user would take turns controlling the typewriter. The interpreter understood simple commands such as Do, Go, and Type, which it would then translate into machine instructions. When encountering an unspecified command, the interpreter mimicked human confusion, responding simply, "Eh?"[63]

This new mode of conversational interaction could also be seen in one of the earliest text adventure games, the *Colossal Cave Adventure*, designed by Will Crowther in 1975.[64] The following dialogue illustrates the call-and-response game play typical of the genre:

```
You are standing at the end of a road before a small brick
building. Around you is a forest. A small stream flows out of
the building and down a gully.
> enter
You are inside a building, a well house for a large spring.
There are some keys on the ground here. There is a shiny
```

```
brass lamp nearby. There is food here. There is a bottle of
water here.
> get keys
OK
> get lamp
OK
> exit
You're at end of road again.
```

Although more accessible and interactive than communication in octal or binary machine code, the conversational model posed several significant challenges. It was meant to resemble human communication in all its richness and variety, but in fact the machine "spoke" and "understood" only a limited number of words. Researchers from the U.S. Air Force academy wrote:

> The lower cost of computer access and the proliferation of on-line systems produced a new breed of users, people whose expertise was in some area other than computer technology. As their initial fascination with conversational computing wore off, users reported experiencing feelings of intense frustration and of being "manipulated" by a seemingly unyielding, rigid, intolerant dialogue partner.[65]

The conversational intermediary of *Colossal Cave Adventure* understood 295 commands and knew about 1,600 words in response, arranged into several hundred canned phrases.[66] Faced with an unfamiliar word, it could only repeat, "That's not a verb I recognize."

By the 1980s a new breed of metaphoric interfaces gained widespread prominence. If *Colossal Cave Adventure* epitomized the conversational model of computing, games like *Pong*, *Space Invaders*, and *Donkey Kong* heralded the paradigm of direct manipulation. Direct manipulation, according to Ben Shneiderman, the researcher who coined the term in 1982, involved three key principles:

1. Continuous representation of the object of interest.
2. Physical actions or labelled button presses instead of complex syntax.
3. Rapid incremental reversible operations whose impact on the object of interest is immediately visible.[67]

The primary goal of direct manipulation therefore was to achieve accord between visual representation and the object of interest. Shneiderman mentions the calculus of Leibniz as a direct influence. Leibniz developed a system of symbolic notation, at the root of his calculus, to express, in his words, "the exact nature of a thing briefly and, as it were, picture it."[68] For Leibniz, the symbol, an accurate and portable picture of an idea, could subsequently reduce the mental effort required for abstract thought, leading to a "great advantage for discovery."[69]

Symbolic notation made it possible for mathematicians to represent infinitely small and infinitely large numbers in print, ideas that would not otherwise fit on the page or in the mind.[70] For Shneiderman and others, computer games like *Pong* similarly enabled the direct manipulation of complex abstractions, for example making it possible for a player to control a virtual table tennis paddle by rotating a physical knob on a gaming console. The knob's movement corresponded "directly" to the movement of the paddle— clockwise for up and counterclockwise for down—thus achieving an analogy between the "operation" and its "impact on the object of interest."[71] Without such direct linkage the physics of game simulation would be too complex for players to handle effectively by writing code or by controlling the paddle through dialogue, in conversation.

Direct manipulators argued that the arbitrary nature of the sign to its signifier hindered the conversational model of human–computer interaction. For example, when using EMACS, a text editor commonly found on Unix systems of the time, one would enter the command k in combination with other keys to delete or "kill" a file, whereas on other systems, Shneiderman complained, k stood for "keep a file," the opposite of killing it.[72] In the conversational model the command stood in a contingent relationship to the intended effect, whereas in the direct manipulation model the dial and paddle were related mimetically.

In the language of Peircean semiotics, the direct manipulation paradigm favors the iconic relationship between representation and object of interest, by which the two relate through shared elements of structure and composition.[73] Consider the *Pong* game controller. The dial's rotation mimics the movement of the paddle it represents. Like an onomatopoeic word, the one resembles and imitates the other. Direct manipulation interfaces like *Pong* involve mimetic visual metaphors meant to overcome the deficiencies of purely symbolic conversational commands. Although there are numerous verbal ways to instruct a machine to return a serve, dials constrain a player's instrumental vocabulary in one dimension: clockwise or counterclockwise. These movements are less arbitrary than words, because they contain a direct topological mapping of properties.

In their field-defining work on human–computer interaction, Edwin Hutchins, Donald Norman, and James Hollan wrote," "There is an economy here [referring to direct manipulation] in that the user's knowledge of the structure of the surface acoustical form has a non-arbitrary relationship to meaning. . . . The same sort of thing can be done in the design of interface languages."[74] Influenced by insights from cognitive metaphor theory about structural domain mapping, direct manipulators thought that the mimetic icon required less explanation than arbitrary symbol. The transference of iconic qualities was intuited; the icon contained its own explanation.[75] Instead of querying a "dictionary" of arbitrary commands, the user could rely on habituated affordances of real-world objects, such as table tennis paddles and paper trash cans. The evolution from conversational to direct models of human–computer interaction could thus be viewed as a shift from a symbolic system of representation, in which signs stood in an arbitrary relationship to their referents, to an iconic one, in which they related mimetically.[76]

Crucially, direct manipulation designers aimed to suspend disbelief. The feeling of directness came through a complete immersion in the mimetic context of virtual worlds.[77] The mimetic icon usurped its object of interest through use. Screen icons themselves became objects of interest, at the expense of the underlying physics. Direct manipulation theory imagined the handling of representations, not objects, as evidenced by the somewhat strained language of metaphor machines in which metaphors can be "accessed," "organized," "handled," and "manipulated."[78] These interactions are direct in the sense of concealing the mediated nature of virtual experience. The goal is to manufacture what Laurel and others called an "interactive mimesis" and "first personness"—the experience of "directly living and acting within the world established by the computer."[79]

Hutchins, Hollan, and Norman wrote, "When an interface presents world of action rather than a language of description, manipulating a representation can have the same effects and the same feel as manipulating the thing being represented."[80] Actual instruments of manipulation—keyboards, screens, and machine instructions—were meant to disappear, lest they puncture the illusion. "The user of a well-designed *model world* interface can willfully

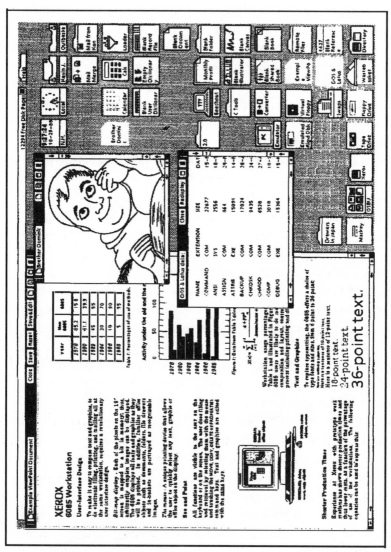

FIGURE 1.4. Metaphor-driven user interface design. The on-screen menus for the Xerox 6085 Daybreak workstation include "icons," "folders," "windows," "drawers," "buttons," and "wastepaper basket." An image of "Brother Dominick" is in reference to a Xerox advertisement that featured a medieval scribe who is asked to copy hundreds of pages by hand. Source: J. Johnson et al., "The Xerox Star: A Retrospective," Computer 22, no. 9 (September 1989): 13. © 1989 IEEE. Reprinted with permission.

suspend disbelief that the objects depicted are artifacts of some program and can thereby directly engage the world of the objects," Hutchins and colleagues wrote.[81] The dialogic model of tool use encouraged by *Colossal Cave Adventure*—"get keys," "get lamp"—was seen to stand in the way. Instead of working with "objects of interest"—instead of being part of a story—the protagonist was "using the computer."[82] "End users are not interested in *making* representations," Laurel wrote. "They want to move around *inside* one," favoring the mimetic context over their actual, physical surroundings.[83] By contrast, fully immersive environments could support the "sensation of directness," in which direct (i.e., iconic) expressions "behave in such a way that a user can assume that they, in some sense, *are* the things they refer to."[84]

Principles of direct interaction stood against what Laurel called the mediator's ill-formed presence. Conversational computing prevented the unmediated "pleasure" and "catharsis" of direct engagement.[85] Intermediaries of *Oregon Train* and *Colossal Cave Adventure* took the place of players: They swung swords for them, took a beating, and reported on the second-hand experience. Laurel wrote:

> In the file management example, the intermediary takes the form of command menus that are invoked in order to activate processes in the program that will create the desired results. The user does not have the experience of pushing files around, stowing them and grabbing them, or blowing them away. Instead, the user has the experience of communicating with the file management intermediary.[86]

In combination, the ideas behind cognitive domain blending and direct manipulation gave rise to the now ubiquitous WYSIWYG (what you see is what you get) interfaces put into mass production by Apple, Xerox, and other companies in the early- to mid-1980s. The Xerox 8010 Star workstation, introduced in 1981, and the Xerox 6085 Daybreak workstation, introduced in 1985, heralded the era of accessible, metaphor-driven personal computing, characterized by the use of virtual graphical objects like windows, icons, desktops, folders, and buttons (Figure 1.4). The Star and Daybreak workstations were some of the earliest machines to put the principles of metaphoric domain blending and direct manipulation into action. The interface was meant to reveal the structure of simulated objects intuitively, without training or lengthy written explanation. Laurel wrote that mimetic interfaces used "logic and aesthetics to create representations that *engage* humans in pleasurable ways."[87] The mimetic context is simply "the experience we desire," Laurel concluded. Immersion finally enabled actors to experience "the full pleasure of the mimetic form."[88]

Designers advocating direct manipulation understood the compromise that came with an emphasis on such immersive and pleasurable experiences.[89] Effective mimesis assumes user familiarity with a source domain. For example, we understand what to do with virtual folders because we know how paper folders behave in real life. However, direct mimetic manipulation does not tell us anything new about the capabilities of such virtual folders. Immersion precludes critical reflection beyond the predefined confines of a modeled world. Users gain access only to what the simulation warrants. Like a theme park ride, it is a scripted experience, which leads to predetermined modes of engagement.

Problematically, the ideas behind mimetic immersion contain a logical fallacy. The literature on direct manipulation often alludes to car steering. Steering wheels are a paradigmatic example of interfaces by which inputs and outputs correlate directly. Thus instead of issuing complicated commands, the driver turns a wheel. A movement to the right compels a corresponding rightward motion of the vehicle. A direct, causal link exists between a car's steering wheel and its axle. Similarly, when interacting with a game such as *Space Invaders* by using a joystick, players experience the immediate correspondence between movements of the controlling mechanism and the spaceship on-screen. The car and the spaceship are the player's direct objects of interest.

However, to return to our simple and recurring example, authors attempting to delete sensitive information are not interested in the virtual representation of their documents. The direct object is not mimetic. They want to erase documents, not their icons. In cases such as these, inhabitants of a virtual world are concerned with objects outside it. Direct manipulation instead veils the direct object from view, suspending the rules of physical interaction in favor of the virtual. Far from being direct, the document's interface (an iconic image) usurps the physical object (the file itself). By such circuitous logic, direct manipulation occludes the mechanisms of mimesis.

The occlusion is a loss of resemblances and designations of the kind described by Baudrillard. At its logical extreme, the simulacrum supplants the thing being simulated. It appears as hyperreality, the experience of unmediated interaction without awareness or sense of the underlying referent. All objects of interest in such a model world are fabricated objects. They are thus limited to the external, artificial constraints imposed by their makers. Manufactured metaphors present us, the users, with compelling, possibly cathartic, experiences. The metaphor eventually subsumes all spheres of social activity mediated by computers.

The history of human–computer interaction began with the manipulation of physical switches, first by hand and then by proxy, through removable storage media such as paper tape and punch card. The next phase was dialogic and conversational. Conversational computing introduced the idea of a mediating agent, an interpreter, which could translate a limited number of natural human language commands into a specialized vocabulary of signals that changed machine configuration states. The direct manipulation school dispensed with visible machine states, leading us closer to immersive mimesis in which virtual environments resemble real-world objects and their properties by analogy. Viewing that history in light of metaphor theory, I find myself ill at ease with the possibility of a totalizing mimesis: More compelling the simulation, more it is removed from its material contexts and more concealed the logistics of its production.

SPECULATIVE FORMALISM

To what extent do we, as a society, need to perceive the mechanisms that animate such machine metaphors? One does not need to understand the physics of internal combustion to drive, the argument goes. Why insist on physics when it comes to computers? Computers, I would like to reflect in conclusion, are dissimilar to cars in that they are epistemic, not just purely instrumental, artifacts. They do not just get us from point A to point B; they augment thought itself, therefore transforming what it means to be human. They have the potential to affect all symbol-bearing fields of human activity. Contemporary automobiles are increasingly computers to the extent that they host inscription. They contain texts that can be interpreted, not in a fanciful way by which all culture is a text, but literally, by involving a succession of printed marks within a conduit. Self-driving "smart" cars differ from their mechanical "dumb" counterparts in that they contain symbolic content. A law governing pedestrian traffic embodies also a model of reading and comprehension; it is meant to be understood by its subjects. Codes governing self-driving vehicles do not answer to the same political ideals. They are not always legible or open to interpretation. We must insist on reading them for the same reason we read books and codices. They augment not just the foot but our collective sense of shared intelligence. The structure of symbolic representation—its storage and codification—constitutes our cognitive and ultimately cultural scaffolding.

In his paper "The Genesis and Speed of Telegraph Codes," published in the *Proceedings of the American Philosophical Society* in 1949, Frank G. Halstead noted that "the practical upper limits of [telegraph transmission] speed will also be limited by the ability of some human beings to operate a keyboard, until such time as electrical connection [can] be made direct with the receiver's central nervous system."[90] Halstead's prognoses are well in the realm of contemporary technical possibility. Direct brain to computer interfaces are common enough today to be turned into a toy.[91] Society stands at the threshold of a new symbolism.

Early brain–computer interfaces relied on either imprecise "noisy" electroencephalographic (EEG) scalp sensors or electrode implants that required invasive surgery. In 2004, a team of scientists developed a way to control "a one-dimensional computer cursor rapidly and accurately" using electrocorticographic (ECoG) activity recorded from the surface of the brain.[92] And in 2015 a quadriplegic woman piloted an F-35 joint strike fighter using her brain in a simulation developed by the University of Pittsburgh's Human Engineering Research Laboratories in collaboration with the Defense Advanced Research Projects Agency (DARPA).[93]

On the surface, the advance of brain–computer interfaces seems to bring us closer to the trajectory of growing immediacy: Witness the "no interface" movement in graphic design and its continuing promise of ever more direct interaction. Golden Krishna's *The Best Interface Is No Interface*, Steve Krug's *Don't Make Me Think*, and Nir Eyal's *Hooked: How to Build Habit-Forming Products* are some of the best-selling titles advancing this argument. Military applications aside, we must prepare for a future in affective, mystical arts, the ultimate loss of references and resemblances, where semiotic systems are to be experienced emotively past the senses: literature without language or representation, painting beyond media, asemiosis—messages lacking a sign.

However futuristic such possibilities may seem to us today, we should not lose sight of the constructed nature of human–computer interaction in all its forms: paper, ink, code, silicon. Media mediate. But they also grow opaque through habituation. As technological dreams become reality, they grow mundane. We neglect to marvel at the altitude of artificial flight or the speed of telecommunication. Habit dulls the instrument. The tool recedes from view. We forget its dangers. It becomes a seemingly harmless extension of the mind and body.

I do not mean to dismiss the mastery of those engaged in creating the illusion of directness. Pleasure and catharsis are important in some contexts. In other contexts we must privilege critical thought, analysis, and interruption. A "momentary breach"—a measure of discomfort in the fit between bodies, keyboards, and screens—ensures our ability to shape the encounter on our own, tactical terms: to opt in when useful and to opt out when necessary.[94] I am not concerned here with the metaphysical entailments of a possible posthuman future. The illusion of directness belies the very human mechanisms of command and control. Simulations ultimately embody specific power structures in an economy of exchange between physical and mental resources. There are those who extract rents from virtual, mimetic inhabitance and those whose dwelling becomes a commodity.

Recall in this regard the Heideggerian insight into the mediated nature of tool use. In *Being and Time* Heidegger wrote about the particular *handiness* of a tool, for example, a hammer: "The less we stare at the thing . . . the more actively we use it, the more original our relation to it becomes and the more undisguisedly it is encountered as what it is, a useful thing."[95] For Heidegger, tools had to be understood through use. They were otherwise inaccessible to reason or theory alone. A hammer comes into focus through what he called circumspection (*Umsicht*), the peripheral awareness of the object ready-to-hand (*zuhanden*).[96] One relates to the tool in the process of manipulating it while concentrating on the task at hand: The seamster is not interested in the needle, only in the work of sewing.[97] Later, Heidegger would connect his account of tool use with philosophy itself, as a mode of truth seeking or unconcealment.[98] When used properly, tools reveal some truth about the world, about the people using them, and about tool use itself. In this sense the Greek *techne* is for Heidegger related to *poiesis*, or bringing forth.

Contrary to the kind of technology that reveals and brings forth, Heidegger also describes instrument use of the kind that conceals and blocks poiesis. Such technologies determine rather than reveal. They are a "destined" kind of revealing that unfolds along a predetermined narrative, in which the answer is already given. A forester who walks the wood simply to cut it down can discover its nature only as a commodity, in what Heidegger calls a standing reserve. The forester who measures felled timber becomes subordinate to the organization of cellulose. The wood is "challenged forth" by the need for paper, the paper by the press. The press consequently organizes the public, set on "swallowing what is printed, so that a set configuration of opinion becomes available on demand." In following a determined path, technology turns humans into human resources. Modern technology is "no more a human doing," Heidegger concludes.[99] Proscribed tool use strips users of their powers of self-determination. They learn nothing new about themselves nor the world.

In closing, I would like to imagine the possibility of indexical interfaces, the kind of signs that connect to their objects of interest through palpable causal linkages: smoke and fire, tissue damage and pain. In other words, is it possible to inhabit virtual worlds in the mimetic alterity? The question is of vital political importance, because whether we have answers or not, implements of symbolic manipulation—books and pens that once lay safely at an arm's length—move inevitably closer to the mind's eye. For now, screens and hard drives, mechanisms of memory storage and image projection, remain extrinsic to the body. They are at this moment still amenable to limited circumspection. The political consequences of technology become more difficult to imagine in proportion to their habituation. Today, people who forgo the use of electronic tablets, smart phones, laptops, and notebooks could seem merely whimsical or quaint. What if tomorrow they are judged mentally deficient or barred from participating fully in public life?

Heidegger wrote that the human is endangered not by technology but by its determination.[100] The ability to read and write has always been politically fraught because of its potential to alter human experience. It is no accident that the struggle for universal literacy often accompanied political revolutions. Poets are important to the revolution not because they create beautiful aesthetic objects but because they retain the noninstrumental emancipatory potential of reading and writing. What can be said in parallel about digital literacy, the poetry of embodied and embedded devices? What if we fail to develop a sense of computational poetics in the face of frenzied instrumental development? How would one empty the hand, the mind, in breach of technesis?

CHAPTER 2

> LAYING BARE THE DEVICE

The Modernist Roots of Computation

"The weakest point in our present day universe is the incapacity of man to meet the machine, the cultural conserve, or the robot, other than through submission, actual destruction, and social revolution."[1] So wrote the Austrian American psychiatrist Jacob L. Moreno in his idiosyncratic, sprawling, and now seldom read volume *Who Shall Survive?*[2]

Humanity, according to Moreno, faced two major threats: human aggression and the aggression of robots—"cultural conserves" and "zootechnical animals." When Moreno referred to robots, he meant all devices, social structures, and products of the mind that persevere autonomously to compete for attention. Moreno thought that conserves diminish the human capacity for cultural production. Robots create the illusion of "finished, perfected product[s]," which substitute for creativity.[3] In this way, musical records obviate musicians, just as books do authors.

An "avalanche of ghosts" from the past enters into an evolutionary contest for cultural survival.[4] Unlike speech, which is extinguished as soon as conversations end, written words persist and proliferate. They survive and continue to shape the social and mental worlds to come. Moreno wrote:

> The author is immaterial; the book goes to all places and to all people, it does not care where it is read and by whom. Many robots have further in common the attribute of comparative immortality. A book, a film, an atomic bomb, they do not perish in the human sense, the same capacity is always

there, they can be reproduced *ad infinitum*. . . . Our human world is increasingly filled with robots and there seems to be no end to new forms and new developments.[5]

The musician and the author struggle to survive in competition with historical records. The conserve reduces humans to "machine-addict[s]" who reside in a "jungle of robots" that suffocates spontaneous activity.[6]

Similar to King Thamus from Plato's *Phaedrus*, Moreno thus distrusted rote mechanization of thought. Moreno believed that, in the name of comfort, safety, and prolonged life, technocracy disempowers the very subjects whose lives it claims to preserve. The zootechnical animal exchanges the human capacity of self-determination for the promised certainty of a better future. The eugenic dreamer and the technological dreamer have this one idea in common:

> to substitute and hasten the slow process of nature. Once the creative process is encapsulated in a book it is *given*; it can be recapitulated eternally by everybody without the effort of creating anew. Once a machine for a certain pattern of performance is invented a certain produce can be turned out in infinite numbers practically without the effort of man. . . . Once that miraculous eugenic formula will be found a human society will be given perfect and smooth at birth, like a book off a press.[7]

Knowledge, in Plato's terms, is thereby replaced with the simulation or imitation (*homoiōmata*) of knowledge.[8] It is given and received passively, bypassing the critical faculties. Robots appear to us in their perfected state, whereas the labor and struggle for their production is elided.

Instrumental and institutional mechanisms alike fell under Moreno's suspicion: plow, pen, book, gun; central planning, corporate governance, legal codex.[9] All robots in that sense constituted a species of autonomous agency, a problem long in the background of Western liberal thought.[10] For Moreno, books and bombs resembled one another because they both embodied volition detached from its human sources. Once in motion, both books and bombs seem to act in the world autonomously. The projectile acts at a distance; once launched, it completes its grim mandate even if the command to act is withdrawn. Technologies of the word similarly decouple readers from writers. Books persist to mean in the absence of their authors. Once

decoupled, seemingly autonomous paper agents—folders, novels, contracts—
clutter the social sphere, continuing to structure human experience in the
absence of the originating accord. Agency so detached operates without
consensus or comprehension. Books are "robot[s] par excellence," Moreno
wrote.[11] They elongate the causal chain of agency to effect change in mental
states across time and space. Yet books and bombs are not social actors in
a true sense. One cannot assign blame to them. They do not figure independently in our models of justice or responsibility.

Moreno's claims and his language might seem archaic today, but they
were not unusual in the larger context of early-twentieth-century post-Kantian
humanism. In Moreno's work one discerns the influence of Marx's critique of
the fetishism of commodities, a dynamic by which "definite social relation
between men" assumes "the fantastic form of a relation between things."[12]
Moreno arrived at a similar conclusion by way of another logic. In creating
some of the earliest examples of social network graphs, he found (and objected to) the presence of things in the position of social actors. His objection to the automatization of human experience also echoes that of his near
contemporaries, such as Viktor Shklovsky, Martin Heidegger, Walter Benjamin,
and Hannah Arendt.

Moreno helps us see the book in a new light. If, as he suggested, the
book is always a robot for enacting action at a distance, it is all the more
robotic as a device that draws electricity, an electronic book. In the 1930s
one could view Moreno's rhetoric about books and bombs as fanciful, tech-
nophobic even; a century later his concerns appear prescient. The unintended
consequences of automated and disembodied agency, from artificially intelligent personal assistants to market trading algorithms, worry contemporary
scientists, legislators, and philosophers.

Today, a machine that looks like a book can also function as a gun or a
trigger. Electronic books read on mobile phones, tablets, and personal computers make up a part of the same digital framework that powers drones and
aircraft carriers. Computers in the service of the world's largest purveyors of
literature are also used by air traffic controllers and by covert intelligence
agencies.[13] Cellular phones, once devices for voice telecommunication, are
now used both to read books and to detonate remote explosives.

These conditions compel us—historians, philologists, etc.—to reconsider the
cozy relationship we have had with books since Gutenberg. My task in this
chapter is to illuminate the blueprint of computation implicit in all electronic

reading and writing devices and thereby make them strange again. In a recip-rocal movement, I also aim to place modern computers within the long history of the book, to view them as technique for literary and not just mathematical symbolism. To do this, I construct a history of the literary device, based on materials drawn from the first half of the twentieth century. I am interested here broadly in the concepts of device and technique that emerged in the thought of Russian, German, and English philologists, whose work I cover in the first section of this chapter. Subsequent sections trace the concomitant emergence of literary device in another sense, as a thought experiment staged by Ludwig Wittgenstein and completed by Alan Turing in the 1920s and 1930s. These experiments lead us to consider a number of fantasti-cal broken reading and writing machines that define the limits of symbolic thought. They culminate in the schematics for a specific mechanism, which lies at the modernist roots of contemporary computational culture.

TECHNIQUE

What kind of a *thing* is a literary *device*? The formalist concept of a device is in part an artifact of an unfortunate translation from the Russian *priem*. The word would be better translated as "technique," in the sense of "method," "approach," or "procedure." "Device" contains these meanings as well, but in modern usage it often carries a more concrete connotation, as an "object, machine, or piece of equipment that has been made for some special pur-pose."[14] The ambiguity is instructive. A spirit of latent materialism—thingness—haunts literary theory from Viktor Shklovsky to Percy Lubbock and Frederic Jameson. The critic wants to approach the work of art as a thing, akin to a statue, and to understand the technique of its coming into being, as a mode of production. But the thing recedes from view because to encounter matter as an object unto itself is to strip it of figurative, symbolic potential. Tech-nique in that brute sense of the word is a matter of transformation, trans-figuration even, of matter into idea: the way in which a novel, for example, is borne out of an arrangement of purely physical properties like paper and ink. The critic becomes a physicist of sorts. A thick description of material particulates lies at the basis of interpretation. Books, sensors, computers, and other smart objects are distinct from other forms of inorganic matter in that they are *epistemic things*.[15] Unlike silicon or dead wood, they give space to inscription; that is, they compound with symbolic goods to become cognitive artifacts: objects assembled both at hand and to mind.

I am getting ahead of myself, however. "Laying bare the device," according to Shklovsky, who coined the phrase, means making explicit the implied mechanisms of a literary trope, particularly in cases where such tropes turn "stale," "automatic," and "naturalized," that is, bereft of their evocative power.[16]

Vladimir Nabokov, a writer conspicuously aware of his literary-theoretical heritage, used the formal technique of laying bare the device often and with relentless clinical precision. In the short story "A Guide to Berlin," to which D. Barton Johnson attributes our first glimpse of Nabokov's "mature virtuoso style," Nabokov wrote:

> In front of the house where I live, a gigantic black pipe lies along the outer edge of the sidewalk. A couple of feet away, in the same file, lies another, then a third and a fourth—the street's iron entrails, still idle, not yet lowered into the ground, deep under the asphalt. For the first few days after they were unloaded, with a hollow clanging, from trucks, little boys would run on them, up and down, and crawl on all fours through those round tunnels, but a week later nobody was playing anymore and thick snow was falling instead; and now when, cautiously probing the treacherous glaze of the sidewalk with my thick rubber-heeled stick, I go out in the flat gray light of early morning, an even stripe of fresh snow stretches along the upper side of each black pipe. . . . Today someone wrote "Otto" with his finger on the strip of virgin snow, and I thought how beautifully that name, with its two soft o's flanking the pair of gentle consonants, suited the silent layer of snow upon that pipe with its two orifices and its tacit tunnel.[17]

This tightly wound vignette dramatizes a distinctly formalist concern. The pipes embody the literary device. Usually found beneath the street, they now sit idle and visible on the surface. Even when exposed, the structure fails to captivate for long. Disused, it once again passes out of sight, covered in snow. Concerned with surfaces, the narrator "probes the glaze" of the street and finds a palindrome written in snow. The inscription "OTTO" not only resembles the pipes visually but is in itself a surface-revealing inscription that makes the pipes visible again. The mimetic surface inscription draws attention to the word's visual shape and acoustics. It invites readers to perform the symmetry of its consonance as they pronounce the word. The round vowels and the interrupting obstruents of "OTTO" contort the body in accordance with the sound image: reverse mimesis, the body as sound pipe.

The moment of corporeal reenactment transcends the representational and paper-bound confines of the medium. The pipes reach beyond page. The performance makes the "making of the literary technique obvious," obvious. The metaphor implicit in the idea of laying bare the device is thereby revealed. In this lies the prevalent characteristic of Nabokov's mature work, which often seeks to transcend the diegetic, fictional world through sheer recursion of literary technique, where each successive turn of abstraction pushes the buried symbol closer to the reader.

Despite such emphasis on devices, formalist poetics (both in art and in scholarship) fell short of producing an explicit theory of technique. In this section I reconstruct the notion of technique in the thought of three major literary theorists of the interwar period: Viktor Shklovsky, Percy Lubbock, and Mikhail Bakhtin. I do not mean to suggest that the group amounts to a coherent school of thought. Rather, I am interested in observing the development of technique as a concept in parallel traditions at a formative time in the history of literary technology. I am consequently going to do something unusual in this chapter: juxtapose relevant patches of literary theory and material culture, which converge on a mechanistic view of reading, writing, and interpretation. These observations evidence fragments of a larger history. The reader should not mistake them for a complete canvas. I arrange them in this way to provoke a response and to find curious early intersections between disparate intellectual traditions—literary theory, philosophy, and electrical engineering—that entwine to form the fabric of contemporary computational culture.

Viewed in the context of technological development, the emergence of technique as a critical category illustrates the broader concerns of the machine age. The notion of technology itself does not fully find its place in the critical literature until the 1950s–1970s, judging by the rash of titles like Martin Heidegger's *Die Frage nach der Technik* (1954), Jacques Ellul's *La technique ou l'enjeu du siècle* (1954), Lynn White's *Medieval Technology and Social Change* (1966), and Viktor Fekiss's *The Technological Man* (1969). Calling for the institution of a new field in 1959, editors of the inaugural issue of *Technology and Culture* wrote about the "neglect of the study of technology" amid a body of extant work that has "scarcely constituted" a systematic scholarly discipline.[18] "*Technology* is a word whose time has come," Langdon Winner would write in 1978 in his influential *Autonomous Technology*.[19]

Seen in this light, the pre–World War II concern with literary technique anticipates the postwar turn toward technology as a field of cultural analysis. Before technology, there was technique.[20] The formalist period in literary theory signaled a turn away from history and philosophy of literature toward the mechanics of literary production. The technical turn entailed a mechanistic understanding of language, in which linguistic phenomena were viewed as a system of moving parts, whose relationship to one another was determined by discoverable laws. The turn to technique also meant that the mechanisms of meaning production, on the sides of both authorship and apprehension, were made accessible to a mass audience. Russian formalists in particular understood their task as one of radical democratization of the literary sphere.[21] High literature, once the purview of a select few, could belong to the proletariat at large.[22] This also meant that literature was *composable*: It could be distilled into discrete and reproducible rules—technique over art—to be learned and shared widely.

The turn to technique gains significance in its instrumental context. The rise of formalist and consequently structuralist thought (along with philosophy's linguistic turn, which saw language as a system of rule-based games) parallels the rise of rule-based programmable media: punch cards, magnetic drums, and ticker tape. This is not to imply that thought and technology stand in a reductive causal relationship to one another. Rather, they form a feedback loop, in which instruments, practices, and explanatory models evolve through mutual reciprocation. Locating the literary-theoretical construct of the device within its technological context allows us to witness the contemporaneous evolution and mutual interdependence among art, engineering, and philosophy. The origins of computer science and literary formalism can be traced back to shared theoretical assumptions and technological contingencies coming to the fore of telecommunications in the first few decades of the twentieth century.

It is at this time that the formalist concept of technique began to abstract the idea of literary production from its irreproducible contexts. The emphasis on craft over art implied primarily a change in the artist's relationship to labor. Walter Benjamin had this view in mind when he wrote, decades later, about works of art that could no longer be thought of as "rigid, isolated object[s]." Rather, they had to be "inserted into the context of living social relations," determined by their relation to literary production.[23] For Benjamin, technique made literary works "accessible" to materialist analysis.[24] Whereas artistic genius was unique, craft carried with it a model of inheritance. Whereas genius was born, technique was shared. Whereas artists labored alone, craftsmen learned their trade in workshops, as part of a collective.

In a more general sense, the turn to technique could be seen as a rejection of Romanticism: for example, Schopenhauer's aesthetics emphasized individual creative genius that reached "beyond the objects which actually present themselves" toward the transcendent ideal.[25] Formalism dispelled the myth of lone genius creators, orienting artists instead toward discovery through handicraft. In his "Art as Device," Shklovsky wrote, "The work of poetic schools amounts to the aggregation and the discovery of new devices/ techniques [priem] for the arrangement and the processing of linguistic material, and, in particular, more so with the rearrangement of figure [obraz] rather than with its creation."[26]

Influenced by Herbert Spencer, the formalists imagined language to make up a natural, physics-based system, which tended toward the conservation of energy.[27] In his influential 1852 essay *The Philosophy of Style*, Spencer wrote about the limited reserves of the "recipient's mental energy":[28] "A reader or listener has at each moment but a limited amount of mental power available. . . . Hence, the more time and attention it takes to receive and understand each sentence, the less time and attention can be given to the contained idea."[29] The ideal writer thus strove to minimize mental exertion, following the law of what Spencer called the economy of composition: to say as much as possible in the most concise and direct way possible. Poetry for Spencer was exemplary in that regard; it habituated those "symbols of thought" and "methods of using them" that had proved themselves to be the most effective through continuous use.[30] Spencer's ideal of literature was of the most thrifty, economical kind. His emphasis on efficiency in language prefigured principles of industrial management, the goal of which was general competency, not genius. Rather than searching for some "unusual or extraordinary man," Frederick Taylor would later write, optimal production outcomes should rely on "clearly defined laws, rules, and principles as foundation," in other words, technique.[31]

Shklovsky agreed with Taylor and Spencer about the dynamics of everyday language, but not poetry. Poetry does not facilitate communication, he argued; it disrupts it. Poets arrange and process habituated material with the view of resurrecting the vitality of the word lost to everyday habituation. For Shklovsky, the deprogramming of received trope constituted the primary technique of specifically aesthetic language. Poetic estrangement counterbalanced prosaic habituation, by which complex things and ideas were replaced by shorthand. Thus, whereas everyday language (and industrial management) followed the laws of energy conservation, poetic language, according to Shklovsky, expended energy. It literally belabored (*zatrudnenie*) and made language difficult again. It prolonged rather than shortened apprehension (*vospriiatie*).[32] If, for Spencer, language was a labor-saving device and poetry its most economical expression, Shklovsky's idea of poetry was labor-intensive and extravagant.

Any literary innovation was, in the formalist view, bound to follow a cycle of habituation and renewal. With time, images once able to capture the imagination lost their vitality. Consequently, the evolution of aesthetic periods followed a course of arbitrary differentiation, in what Jean Moréas (a symbolist poet and art critic important in the history of formalism) called a cyclical evolution (*évolution cyclique*), by which dominant tropes in one period become clichés in the next. Art depletes itself, Moréas wrote, "from copy to copy, from imitation to imitation." What seems fresh today "dries up and shrivels" tomorrow.[33] Technique, in that sense, was seen by the formalists as a kind of information processing at the metalinguistic social level. The mechanics of the arrangement and the rearrangement of figure produced new meaning in habituated contexts. Such give and take powered the engine of literary development.

Reflecting critically on Shklovsky's materialist aesthetics, Mikhail Bakhtin would write in the 1920s that such an overly formal model of aesthetic genre formation was capable only of establishing a "chronological table of variance in the evolution of technical devices," because "in isolation technique cannot have a history."[34] The formalist model of literary development seemed meandering and meaningless to the more teleologically oriented critic. Bakhtin was also less inclined toward materialism. For example, he was careful not to reduce technique to questions of material arrangement alone, independent of the "aesthetic idea": "I am quite ready to join in the sentiment that 'in art technique is everything,' provided we understand that the aesthetic object cannot exist independent of the artistic work."[35] For Bakhtin, the work existed neither in the mind nor in the configuration of matter alone. Any immanent text—for example, an edition of Shakespeare's *Hamlet*—could not, for Bakhtin, exhaust the possibility of *Hamlet* as a transcendent work of art. Neither could works be reduced to pure ideas. Any notion of *Hamlet* the play must rest on firm material foundations—the textual witness—be it an original folio or a critical edition. "In art, technique is not mechanistic," Bakhtin wrote; rather, "technique animates and motivates the aesthetic object at every point."[36] Bakhtin thus rejected the dualism between ideational content and physical form. Idea and objects enter into a continual dialectic.

For Bakhtin, technique was that force which at any point of a text was capable of translating ideas into things and things into ideas; the mental conception of the word materialized into a specific arrangement of ink and paper. Within the ontological indeterminacy of art, which exists simultaneously as an object and idea, Bakhtin approximated the following formula: "Audiences are equivalent to creators, minus technique." Alternatively, authors "equal the audience plus technique."[37] Audiences experience art's coming into being, though they lack in craft. Technique in that sense is a "method of processing content through material."[38] We return to the notion of labor or procedure, which transforms raw material—things—into art, no longer mere objects limited by their physical manifestations. The goal of poetics becomes, in Bakhtin's words, the analysis of the "technical apparatus of aesthetic creation": the movement between works and objects of art and back from things to ideas.[39] Hence he arrives at the notion of aesthetics as a kind of dialectics between immanent and transcendent realms.

Even as formalism flirted with the idea of a materialist poetics, the "matter" of formal analysis was limited to the abstract notion of language, which, as is the case with any abstraction, can exist only in a categorical sense, for example, in a way that all whales are mammals. Mammals are not a thing in that sense. The category of language similarly comprises a theoretical aggregate of specific vernaculars. In giving names to literary phenomena (e.g., genres and periods), literary critics similarly move from material specifics to categorical abstractions. In this light, it becomes possible to view Nabokov's recursive metapoetics as a response counter to the critical method of induction. His prose works deductively, in that it attempts to convert ideas back into things. Nabokov reifies. His pipes and surface inscriptions protrude through the diegetic limits of a fictional world.

On the way to becoming things, words necessarily encounter their medium. Whatever the diegetic limits of fictional worlds, language is firmly constrained by paper. Nabokov's prose often reveals that outermost conceit of any novel, the book, where a literary device in its ideational sense meets the literary device in its proper, physical sense. Fictional worlds bump against the real at the bounds of a page. Recall, for example, the conclusion of Nabokov's 1936 *Invitation to a Beheading*, which ends with one such imagined dissolution of diegetic boundaries, at which point the novel's characters glimpse the material reality on the other side of the page. Nabokov wrote:

> Everything was falling. A spinning wind was picking up and whirling: dust, rags, chips of painted wood, bits of gilded plaster, pasteboard bricks, posters; an arid gloom fleeted; and amidst the dust, and the falling things, and the flapping scenery, Cincinnatus made his way in that direction where, to judge by the voices, stood beings akin to him.[40]

The passage gestures toward the real, arresting mimesis. In this way Nabokov exposes the incapacity of literature to actualize and to assume physical form. His characters are often dimly aware of their fictional predicament and struggle hopelessly to escape.

On the other side of the page, the material contexts of literary production similarly escape a reader's grasp. Critics endeavor to articulate the transition from thought to object. But the linkage between pen and paper, technique itself, disappears in reception. Echoing his Soviet colleagues in the influential *Craft of Fiction*, the English critic Percy Lubbock, who I do not think would mind being called a formalist, wrote, "To grasp the shadowy and fantasmal form of a book, to hold it fast, to turn it over and survey it at leisure—that is the effort of a critic of books, and it is perpetually defeated. . . . Nothing, no power, will keep a book steady and motionless before us, so that we may have time to examine its shape and design."[41] Note that the author's use of object-oriented vocabulary does not quite refer to objects. Lubbock's "grasping," "holding," and "keeping the book motionless" are still metaphors. The reader holds and keeps the thing before the mind's eye. Books escape the reader's mental, not physical, grasp. Nor do Lubbock's "books," "forms," "shapes," and "designs" refer to the outward material aspects of the literary artifact. These are again mental constructs, not material ones. When Lubbock mentions a book, he usually means the novel. His materialism is latent rather than explicit.

This confusion is not to Lubbock's detriment—it further underscores his thesis. Readers' unfamiliarity with what Lubbock calls the novel's "technical aspects" hampers their ability to understand how the novel comes to present itself to the mind in its entirety.[42] Critics grasp other more plastic art forms, such as sculpture or painting, whole and at once.[43] These exist synchronically in space limited to their physical dimensions. By contrast, narratives unfold in time, diachronically. To perceive a book, to read a novel, readers must therefore abstract from the physical object and extend it in working memory, past immediate perception. Meaning making of this sort involves the mental assemblage of linguistic minutiae, which eventually constitute a literary whole.

Critical reading in Lubbock's sense entails an account of the transformation from things to ideas: from words and sentences to stories, novels, and verse. Echoing Boris Eichenbaum in "How *The Overcoat* Is Made," Lubbock was interested in the mechanics of literary craft—how the thing is made. He promised to view "a few familiar novels . . . with some particularity" but without judgment or critique. "How they are made is the only question I shall ask," he wrote.[44] The book's author is ultimately a craftsman. It is therefore the critic's role to "overtake him [the author] at his work and see how the book was made."[45] The mechanics of intellectual production are here again central to the project of literary criticism. Books, however, "vanish" when we "lay our hands" on them, Lubbock wrote.[46] Critics must therefore choose to see either trees or forest. As the totality of the work comes into view, the technical details of craft—books as objects—disappear. Conversely, when viewed up close, technical particulates obscure sight of the work as a whole.

"The real heart and substance of the book," Lubbock wrote, "stands out more clearly for the obscurity into which the less essential parts of it subside."[47] To read in this mode is to deny books their materiality. When reading for pleasure, lay readers lose themselves in the elements of narrative immediately available for observation. For Lubbock, to read novels for pleasure is to "forget, if we can, that the book is an object of art."[48] By "object of art" Lubbock means the transcendent idea of the novel as opposed to the immanent work itself. To "objectify" elements of the novel that "strike us more keenly," as Lubbock phrases it, therefore means quite the opposite of what is usually meant by objectification. The complete mental idea of the novel congeals only at the conclusion of reading, that is, at the limits of the book as a thing: "Far from losing ourselves in the world of the novel, we must hold it away from us, see it all in detachment, and use the whole of it to make the image we seek, the book itself."[49] But to hold books away in this sense means also to internalize them completely. And by "books" Lubbock means the idea of a novel, not at all the thing itself. Thus to read critically is, paradoxically, also to arrest the coming-into-being of the work.

The difficulty of materialist poetics is reflected in its language, which continually conflates mental and physical constructs.

The Craft of Fiction ends on an ambivalent note. Lubbock sensed the inadequacy of his materialism: "If only there were one single tangible and measurable fact about a book." If only it could be "weighed like a statue" or "measured like a picture—it would be a support in a world of shadows."[50]

I want to end the section here, with a momentary failure of materialist poetics, to pick up another concomitant thread, one that will take us through some of the same concerns about the nature of symbolic representation and its relationship to the physical world. My aim is to disconnect the history of modern computing from its expected contexts of calculating machinery and to join it with literary theory, where, as we will see, it also finds a measure of congruity. I do so in the absence of direct evidence for an explicit intellectual connection.[51] My goal is not to prove that such a linkage exists, but rather to irreparably entwine the nominally discordant intellectual and material genealogies in a way that sheds light on our modern predicament, where books and bombs indeed share the same semiotic infrastructures. Along with such critics of contemporary computational culture as Bernard Harcourt and Frank Pasquale I would like to ask, How did we get here?[52] The thought of Ludwig Wittgenstein and Alan Turing leads to a number of broken reading and writing machines, which in aggregate suggest a possible answer to the quandary of materialist poetics, posed in the liminal space between thought and thing.

THOUGHT EXPERIMENT I

Modern computers, and by extension the electronic book, harken back to a cluster of related thought experiments prevalent in the philosophy of Ludwig Wittgenstein and subsequently Alan Turing, his longtime student and colleague. The story of Turing machines has been told before in many contexts but never with an eye to literary machines. The history of literary interpretation nevertheless occupies a central place in the early development of modern computing. To confront computers as literary devices, one must first understand their peculiar relationship to universal Turing machines. I would like to frame that discussion by drawing two further as yet unexplored historical genealogies that culminate in Turing's seminal essay on computable numbers: the first is intellectual and stems from Turing's tutelage under Wittgenstein, and the second is material and highlights the physical similarities between Turing's design and a number of attendant developments in printing and communication.

To read Shklovsky, Bakhtin, Lubbock, Turing, and Wittgenstein together is to recover a legacy of humanities computing that often gets overlooked in the history of computer science and software engineering. The literary perspective is important because it allows us to see the computer in a new light: more than a by-product of quantification, a metaphor machine. Turing machines should interest literary scholars because they embody a minimally viable model for generalized symbolic manipulation: reading and writing. Poetics should interest electrical and software engineers because it grounds computation in the long history of the written word. Turing's thought experiments were meant to solve a mathematical problem, but their pedigree lies also in the study of textual meaning making and interpretation. Wittgenstein and Turing posed a problem similar to that of the formalists and arrived at a similar conclusion: a generalized algorithm for language manipulation.

In his seminal 1936 paper on computable numbers, Alan Turing proposed a peculiar (for a mathematical treatise) thought experiment that addressed a problem in the field of elementary number theory.[53] His solution involved more than a formula. Instead, he imagined a machine that would substitute for calculation. Ultimately, Turing described a device that was meant to embody the symbol: It transformed external abstractions into physical states internal to the device. In doing so, his imagined device breached the boundary between idea and matter. It was exactly an instrument for transforming thoughts into shapes, of the kind approached by formalist poetics. In that sense, Turing's hypothetical machine was an advancement in the development of a long-standing thought experiment concerning the nature of human understanding and the beginning of a new, machine-assisted philological practice.

The question of an automated hermeneutics echoes through the canon of Western philosophic tradition. What does it mean to read and to understand something? Is it enough to repeat another's words, as Phaedrus did in response to Socrates? Could students be said to possess reason when they merely parrot thoughts, without actively thinking on their own? What of animal or machine intelligence? The question had been posed by Descartes, who wrote that it would not be sufficient for the "rational soul" to be "lodged in the human body like a pilot in his ship, except perhaps for the moving of its members" but that intelligence must be "joined and united more closely with the body in order to have sensations and appetites similar to our own."[54] Magpies and parrots can appear to speak, Descartes wrote, but can they show us that they understand? And what would that showing entail?

Recall also the experiments with combinatorial poetics of the seventeenth-century German Jesuit scholar Athanasius Kircher, the inventor of *Arca Musurgicae*, a music composition device, by which a composer not versed in music could combine predetermined musical phrases written on wooden planks to compose a score. In correspondence with Kircher, the German Baroque poet Quirinus Kuhlman argued that using a similar instrument to compose poetry would amount to *sed versus, non poema* (mere versification, not poetry). Would we call a naïve child using such a contraption a composer or a poet? No, he answered:

Sed lusus est ingeniosus, Ingeniose Kirchere, non methodus, prima fronte aliquid promittens, in recessu nihil solvens. Sine cista enim puer nihil potest respondere, & in cista nihil praeter verba intelligit; tot profert, quot audit, sine intellectu.

But [the poetry box] is just an ingenious game, ingenious Kircher, not a method, promising something on the surface, but solving nothing deep down. For without the box the boy can answer nothing, and with the box he understands nothing but words. He produces whatever he hears, without understanding, like a parrot.[55]

The child cannot create without mechanical assistance. Like the parrots of Plato, Kuhlman, and Descartes, it mimics creation on the surface. Nothing "deep down" in an automaton's mind corresponds to the outward appearance of thought. The child composes poetry without thinking—that is, without the appropriate deep structure that should accompany proper poiesis. If technique alone is to guide the creation of poetry in a way that was suggested by the formalists, would we recognize purely formal creation as art, or thought, or language? Or would it be for us mere versification? In other words, does technique matter? Do we care how the thing is produced—by machines or aliens—or do we care only about its effects?

The philosopher John Searle would later pose a similar question in his famous Chinese room thought experiment.[56] Can a contraption be said to "speak" a language if inside it contains only a dictionary for looking up the correct answers to any given query? A man inside the room sorts the answers blindly. He does not understand the language (Chinese, in the original thought experiment), yet the contraption appears to respond appropriately. But is it again enough to *appear* to understand, or should we say that understanding must always involve an analogous movement inward?

Searle argued that his room, a kind of robot for automated responses in a foreign language, does not properly speak a language in the way a fluent speaker does. For Searle and other so-called internalists, the external signs of whatever is meant by "speaking" and "understanding" must correspond to some appropriate internal mental states.[57] Plato, Descartes, Kuhlman, and Searle all pose a variation on the same thought experiment, which, in opposition to mere functionalism, aims to identify deep structure that characterizes cognitive phenomena, apart from their surface manifestation. Reading and writing should leave something behind, these thinkers intuit. Functional outward appearances are not sufficient. A text is assimilated. It leaves a trace. It is joined and united with the body, to paraphrase Descartes. Moreover, the trace must correspond in some way to the originating inscription. The two—text and body—achieve a measure of structural accordance.

Recall the famous *pharmakon* passage from Plato's *Phaedrus*, which explores the relationship between writing and its impression on the mind. At the conclusion of the dialogue, King Thamus objects to the technology (*ta tekhnēs*) of the written word, because he believes it will foster forgetfulness in the people who use it. Plato writes, "Their faith in extrinsic writing [*graphō ex then*], by means of foreign impressions [*allotrion tupōn*], will diminish their intrinsic [*endothen autous*] capacity to remember."[58] Plato thus contrasts the exterior figure of the inscription with memory, an intrinsic cognitive ability. The Greek *tupōn*, related to the English "type," literally means an impression. It is, in this case, also "foreign" or "othered" (*allotrion*). It comes from without. Like Moreno after him, Thamus finds thought externalized through typography problematic. For him, true memory and thought come from within. They are once again properly internalized.

For this reason, in the beginning of the dialogue Socrates asks his young collocutor to stop reciting a speech that the latter has learned by heart. Recitation is worth little for him. He wants Phaedrus to think for himself and not merely regurgitate another's ideas. The student must not perform as a mere parrot or an automaton would. To truly comprehend something and to make a show of it, readers assimilate, absorb, and make their own. Much can go wrong in that process. We expect that reading will ultimately leave an appropriate impression (*tupōn*) on the reader's mind. These typographic imprints presumably correspond to the stamp. For understanding to take place, writing must produce "true," in Descartes's words, feelings and appetites. But what is true, appropriate, or proper? What shapes does type (*tupōn*) impress onto the soul? It cannot be a letter's literal form. How, then, does one convert external images (*graphō exōthen*) into internal impressions? How can we incorporate foreign (*allotrion*) to us states of mind? How does one ingest inscription in a way that leaves an appropriate trace? Even the most mundane acts of reading contain such profound mysteries of comprehension.

THOUGHT EXPERIMENT II

Turing machines, which will come into view shortly, embody a stark solution to the problem of "appropriate comprehension." Complementary and somewhat contrary to well-settled narratives of early computing, which place Alan Turing's work in conversation with other computer pioneers such as Charles Babbage, Ada Lovelace, Konrade Zuse, and John von Neumann,[59] I propose considering the Turing machine, first, within the broad tradition of formalist poetics and, second, more narrowly, in response to a series of thought experiments proposed by Wittgenstein in the 1930s.[60] What follows is a reconstruction of a remarkably persistent idea that regularly resurfaced in Wittgenstein's writings for the duration of his career.

Wittgenstein broached the problem of reading machines and comprehension initially in his *Blue Book*, *Brown Book* and *Philosophical Grammar* (all compiled in the early 1930s), then in his lectures and remarks on the foundations of psychology and mathematics from the late 1930s, and finally in *Philosophical Investigations*, written between 1945 and 1949.

The earliest of these documents, *The Blue Book*, opens with a question of semantics: "What is the meaning of a word?" Wittgenstein cautions his students against choosing the easy answer, which holds that meaning resides in the head.

> It is misleading then to talk of thinking as of a 'mental activity.' We may say that thinking is essentially the activity of operating with signs. This activity is performed by the hand, when we think by writing; by the mouth and larynx,

when we think by speaking; and if we think by imagining signs or pictures, I can give you no agent that thinks. If then you say that in such cases the mind thinks, I would only draw your attention to the fact that you are using a metaphor, that here the mind is an agent in a different sense from that in which the hand can be said to be the agent in writing.[61]

Wittgenstein explains that when we see a sentence on paper, we assume that some structure analogous to that sentence exists in the mind. Perhaps, he speculates, we could even observe the brain directly in the process of writing, to check whether mental states correspond to the inscription. Both mental and written thought structures embody thought. Yet neither exists in isolation. Rather, we are witnessing the workings of a metaphor: the transference of properties between two distinct physicalities, one in the head and one on paper. Neither physical nor mental descriptions alone are sufficient for Wittgenstein to locate cognition. The subject escapes depending on our point of view. When the hand writes, it is the brain that thinks. But when the hand thinks, it is the brain that writes. Meaning thus lies in the transition from hand to head and from mind to paper. We might say that thinking takes place "on paper, in our head, in the mind," Wittgenstein writes, but, crucially, "none of these statements of locality gives *the* locality of thinking."[62] Thought is distributed throughout the body and among its extensions. We think by the sign, head, hand, and pen.

"Could a machine think?" Wittgenstein asks later in the first notebook.[63] The challenge, as he explains it, is not one of finding a machine that can do the job of manipulating signs. It lies in its ability to enact both sides of the metaphoric equation. "Doing the job" (manipulating external signs) must correspond to something else. Severed from its analogical structure, the chance manipulation of signs is a meaningless activity. Meaning, Wittgenstein suggests, resides in the metaphoric transference between something (symbol) and something else (machine state). Therefore a better question is, Can a machine hold private mental states? Can it feel pain in the sense of pain being the state of internal affairs not accessible to others?[64] If we believe machines to be capable of holding intrinsic states, then we can imagine something akin to machine intelligence, by which a spoken word or letter finds the appropriate inward representation. Understanding, in that sense, lies simply in the structural accord between something internal and something external.

Wittgenstein engages the question of automated semantics again in his *Brown Book*. He first defines reading mechanically as an activity devoid of meaning that involves "translating script into sounds," "writing according to dictation," or "copying in writing a page of print." What happens when a naïve child reads a newspaper? Wittgenstein asks, echoing Kuhlman and Descartes. The child's eyes, he answers, "glide along the printed words, he pronounces them aloud or to himself," but "other words he pronounces after having seen their first few letters only, others again he reads out letter by letter." Children act as "reading machines" when they pay no attention to what they read. A child reads "faultlessly like a reliable machine," Wittgenstein repeats, emphasizing the mechanical property of colloquially "mechanistic" reading.[65] Another hypothetical child merely pretends to read. The child guesses at the words and on occasion repeats things by heart without actually seeing them on the page.[66] Would any of these hypothetical scenarios rise to our conventional understanding of reading?

Wittgenstein continues to complicate such edge cases. He considers, for example, the case of a hallucinating patient who "reads" what to others looks like gibberish. Another fakes reading Cyrillic by memorizing the lines phonetically. Wittgenstein further imagines reading machines, which produce random sounds that occasionally, by accident, correspond to some existing texts. In each case, Wittgenstein writes, we envision two mechanisms: one visible and external and one hidden and internal. The reader eventually does more than mimic the mechanical motions of reading. Outward signs are insufficient to indicate comprehension. A body's motions—of gliding one's eyes across the page and saying the words out loud—must connect in some way to appropriate internal, mental representations.

We are tempted, then, to privilege the inward-facing signs of comprehension as the "real criterion for a person's reading or not reading."[67] However, no such internal mechanisms can be known to us or communicated to others properly. One can only intuit another's intimate experience of reading. Absent the ability to convey private mental states directly, reading pupils must verbally convince their teachers that a scanned sign had the intended effect. How can Phaedrus convince Socrates? How can he explain his comprehension? He could write an essay, perhaps. Texts beget texts. But what if his explanations are memorized as well? What can be done to convince others definitively of our having understood a text properly? This requires even more words, which are themselves subject to the same suspicions. The hermeneutic circuit is thus perpetually frustrated.

The *Blue* and *Brown* books conclude without a clear resolution. Wittgenstein describes something akin to affective hermeneutics, an "indirect way of transmitting [a] feeling." Communication, we would say today, is always mediated. Wittgenstein finally imagines the possibility of "direct" communication, capable of transmitting feelings immediately from one person to another in a way that "obviate[s] the external medium."[68] Barring that possibility, we are ultimately limited by our private sensations of knowledge. "Something which we can never know happens at the end," Wittgenstein writes.[69] Any sense of affirmation, the phatic utterance—Can you hear me now? Did you understand?—comes through further expression, entailing further uncertainty.

Philosophical Grammar, written around the same time as the *Blue* and *Brown* books, develops such reading experiments further. It begins with a problem of understanding and not understanding. "To understand a language," Wittgenstein writes, means "to take in a symbolism as a whole."[70] A word is always a part of a larger system. Similarly, a pass in soccer only makes sense as part of the game. It is meaningless in isolation. To appreciate soccer, one must internalize its rules and regulations. Only then do the individual elements begin to make sense. Consequently, the rule book cannot be understood in its own terms. One must begin with an analogy from another domain. Understanding the game's grammar therefore always involves transmediation of some kind. In comparing language to music, he writes, "For explanation I can only translate the musical picture into a picture in another medium and let the one picture throw light on the other."[71] And elsewhere: "How curious: we should like to explain the understanding of a gesture as a *translation* into words, and the understanding of words as a *translation* into gestures."[72] In *Philosophical Grammar,* Wittgenstein attempts to break out of the hermeneutic circuit by appealing to analogical, transmedia processes. Proper understanding ultimately involves the "translation from one symbolism into another; tracing a picture, copying something, or translating into another mode of representation."[73] To understand something said is thus akin to modeling it in clay or drawing it. Similarly, we imagine explaining basketball rules to someone who only knows how to play hockey by analogy: pucks bear grammatical resemblance to balls, goals to basketball hoops. The symbolic grammar of one game explains the other.

However, it is insufficient to merely paraphrase. To show understanding, one must draw a picture or a model in a way that reveals a correspondence of equivalent structures. In this view, language cannot be explained by more language. We must trade symbolisms to create a model that explains one representational system in terms of another. The symbolisms cannot diverge completely either. There must be some productive overlap to account for the structural similarities between balls and pucks. We would have to explain: Take note of these similarities, but not these; these are incidental. Language cannot be modeled like clay exactly. The rules of a game unfold by logics connected to its distinct physicalities: air and clay, ice and asphalt.

In thinking of the various ways in which the translation between divergent symbolisms breaks, Wittgenstein continually returns to the pianola, a type of a player piano (Figure 2.1). The pianola joins music score to mechanism in a rigid way. Mechanism and symbolic notation become one. The machine does not interpret, in that sense. Perforated paper physically actuates the appropriate pins and gears and always in the same manner, leaving no room for interpretation. So long as the mechanism functions properly, musical notation and internal arrangement of instrument parts stand in perfect accord. The rigidity of the connection ensures a correspondence of symbolisms. The machine enacts an exacting translation from one medium to the next by mechanical means, as the actuating mechanisms of the player piano fit into the grooves of a music roll.

The idea of such rigid correspondence seems to bring Wittgenstein closer to solving the challenge of "proper" comprehension. What if reading could become similarly rigid, in a way that is impossible to misinterpret? The pianola is promising in that regard, but, like other, less exacting mechanisms of comprehension, it too can malfunction. Early in *Philosophical Grammar* Wittgenstein explains, "Aren't our sentences parts of a mechanism? As in a pianola? But suppose it is in bad condition?"[74] Later, Wittgenstein expands on this thought:

> The sentences that we utter have a particular purpose, they are to produce certain effects. They are parts of a mechanism, perhaps a psychological mechanism, and the words of the sentences are also parts of the mechanism

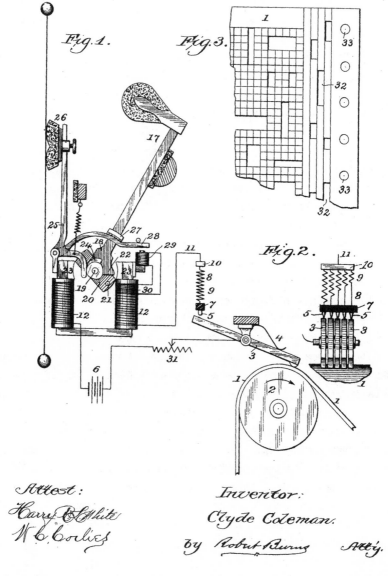

FIGURE 2.1. A page from Clyde Coleman's patent for an electrically operated musical instrument. Wittgenstein frequently returned to images of a pianola in his thought experiments. The perforated music sheet (labeled Fig. 3) is an example of a "symbolic language," which elicits the appropriate "rigid" response from the mechanism, not subject to interpretation. Source: Clyde Coleman, "Electrically-Operated Musical Instrument," Patent US1107495 A, filed August 22, 1898, issued August 18, 1914, sheet 1.

(levers, cogwheels and so on). The example that seems to illustrate what we're thinking of here is an automatic music player, a pianola. It contains a roll, rollers, etc., on which the piece of music is written in some kind of notation (the position of holes, pegs, and so on). It's as if these written signs gave orders which are carried out by the keys and hammers.[75]

As was the case with reading automata in the *Blue* and *Brown* books, Wittgenstein again substitutes a physical mechanism for the process of symbolic interpretation. Words and music notation alike contain a "purpose," in his words. They elicit specific "effects" in the mechanism.

As before, we cannot always expect the mechanism of interpretation to function properly, nor do we have a reliable way to verify its correct operation. "Suppose the pianola is in bad condition," Wittgenstein repeats. The device might hiss and bang instead of playing music, for example. One could object that notes are always "meant" to play on a mechanism in perfect working order. But to explain what is meant by a "perfect working order," we would need to draw yet another diagram or build another machine. Characteristically, Wittgenstein resorts to yet another analogy. The "sense of an order," he writes, lies in its "effect on an obedient man."[76] What looked initially like an infallible machine for comprehension once again requires the presence of a reasonable and therefore subjective human interpreter.

When drawing such analogies between mental and mechanical processes, Wittgenstein consistently rejects the model of language as a "psychophysical" mechanism.[77] Rather, as the title *Philosophical Grammar* suggests, Wittgenstein is in search of "grammars" governing the engagement: between speakers and listeners, readers and writers, player pianos and musical scores. But what is a grammar? It is a kind of a cheat sheet, a set of conventions or protocols, similar to the dictionary inside Searle's Chinese room. The grammar contains the smarts. Neither the room nor the person inside speaks the language. If anything "knows" the language, it is the dictionary, which allows the system to function. The grammar ensures proper translation between diverging symbolisms.

Wittgenstein imagines a layer of rules that mediate between symbol and machine or mental state. Two parties can agree on a protocol: a chart of appropriate correspondences that describes the exact rules of engagement. It then becomes possible to imagine a "part of the mechanism which resembles a chart, [which is] inserted between the language-like part of the mechanism and the rest of it."[78] Such instructions enforce whatever is meant by "proper" compliance. I imagine, for example, a warning bell that sounds when a musical score falls out of alignment or, in a more complicated case, a command line "interpreter" that checks entered input for syntactical errors.

Wittgenstein writes, "Can one say that grammar describes language? If we consider language as part of the psycho-physical mechanism which we use when we utter words—like pressing keys on a keyboard—to make a human machine work for us, then we can say that grammar describes that part of the machine."[79] The grammar creates a "connection between a word and 'a thing'" in order for the mechanism to function in a certain way: "The definition can make it work properly, like the connection between the keys and the hammers in a piano." Crucially, it is that "connection and not the effect which determines the meaning."[80] A programmer would say that Wittgenstein's grammatical layer resembles modern programming language interpreters and compilers, exactly the parts of the machine that connect codified instructions to their execution.[81] Similarly, Wittgenstein's grammar "means" in the sense of specifying rules by which meaning succeeds or fails. In this way, we can move away from speaking of "intended effects" or "proper obedience" and rather concentrate on this interpretive and mediating layer, which describes the rules of engagement.[82] To learn a language in that sense is not to learn individual words but to understand the mechanical linkages of meaning making.

We say that the mechanism is rigid or that the law is inexorable when the results of an action are fixed. Wittgenstein calls such a relationship "super-hardness."[83] Where a judge can be lenient, he explains, the law is compulsory. What we would now call an algorithm compels predictable execution, not subject to the vagaries of interpretation.[84] Parts of the mechanism subsequently exist in a causal relationship to one another. Pushing this or that lever will always result in such and such a movement because of the way the mechanical parts are connected.

We are tempted, as before, to privilege the inner workings of a symbolic mechanism, which is also at the core of meaning making in mathematics. "If I show you the mechanism behind the [watch] dial, you will be able to predict the movement of the hour hand for any given movement of the minute hand," Wittgenstein writes. But once again, how do we know if a mechanism is functioning properly? "For instance, I may drop the clock so that the machinery is broken, or lightning may strike it."[85] To check the mechanism for damage, we need a picture, a diagram, or schematics that describe what the properly functional mechanism looks like. As a schema, the mechanism in good order is itself a type of a symbol for the perfected behavior of the sort that we expect. We could, to take another example, compare a broken clock with clocks that work. Whereas we tried to find a mechanism behind the symbol, we found also a symbol behind the mechanism. Again, we struggle to complete the circuit of interpretation between intent and effect, which never quite manage to explain and to verify each other. How do we know that our "gold standard" clock schematics are themselves golden, that is, that they lead to the construction of properly functioning clocks? We are once more faced with a series of receding analogies: a diagram that explains a diagram that explains a diagram.

In his lectures on mathematics, Wittgenstein never finds a way out of this recursive conundrum. The foundations of mathematics rely on some such mutually dependent relationship between the physical and symbolic worlds. Whether it is in math or ordinary language, some magic happens at the coupling of matter and sign. The precise point of contact concerns Wittgenstein in all fields of human activity, from literature to psychology and mathematics. In all these fields he finds an implicit analogy between symbol and mechanism. The analogy itself is atomic. It cannot be split further into something such as sign and referent, tenor and vehicle, or signifier and signified. Considered apart, the two halves of the metaphor are strictly meaningless. In his lectures on aesthetics, Wittgenstein describes the dependency as the "concomitance between mechanism and its trace." The best we can do in formalizing aesthetics is therefore to "trace [its] mechanism," Wittgenstein concludes.[86]

Wittgenstein's thought experiments do not amount to a cohesive model of language, communication, art, or mind. However, they do contain the seeds of reading and writing machines later imagined by Alan Turing in the formative period of contemporary computing. Wittgenstein's experimental thought machines prefigure a contemporary conversation about machine intelligence. Wittgenstein conjures his fantastical broken mechanisms to test the limits of our intuitions about reading, writing, and comprehension.

THOUGHT EXPERIMENT III

In 1939 Alan Turing attended Wittgenstein's lectures on mathematics at King's College.[87] From the notes on Wittgenstein's lectures compiled and published by Cora Diamond, it is clear that Turing was a vociferous presence in the class. His name is mentioned eighty-six times in the text, more than any other student by a wide margin. At some point during the course Wittgenstein concluded his lecture by saying, "Unfortunately Turing will be away from the next lecture, and therefore that lecture will have to be somewhat parenthetical. For it is no good my getting the rest to agree to something that Turing would not agree to."[88]

One expects Turing's seminal paper on computable numbers, where he first proposed his universal computing machine, to contain a strictly technical discussion in the narrow field of number theory.[89] Instead, we encounter a number of surfeit features. These account for the perplexing undercurrent of cognitive theory always present in Turing's writing.[90] His machines "think," they are "aware," and they "remember," whereas his humans "calculate" and "compute." The cognitive language reflects a heritage of Wittgenstein's thought, which was concerned more broadly with theory of mind and the passage of inscription into understanding. Turing's machine thinks in a particularly literate way: by ingesting and regurgitating symbols. Turing inherits these traits from Wittgenstein's menagerie of comprehension automata in various states of disrepair. In the wilderness of Wittgenstein's thought Turing locates the concise coordinates for a universal mechanism, placed in the liminal space between thing and symbol.

Turing machines mediate in the metaphoric transference from intrinsic "hard" states to their extrinsic "soft" representations. Like their dysfunctional predecessors, they concern the grammar of that transformation. They are, ultimately, mechanisms of exacting obedience: fully deterministic systems that nevertheless exceed their formal limitations. "How can the rules of operation of the machine change?" Turing asked in "Computing Machinery and Intelligence."[91] His answer, which began as a mathematical proposition in the 1930s, developed by the 1950s into a dramatized conversation between a poet and her critic; into the possibility of an evolving artificial intelligence; and into an imitation game, by which computers misrepresent their assigned gender. The very theoretical formulation of a Turing machine poses a number of questions related to the problem of free will and determinism more broadly. How can a machine escape its programming? How can a poem transcend the rules of its composition? How do humans become more than the sum of their nature and nurture?

Turing's universal machine finally distills the diversity of Wittgenstein's experiments into a single concise formula. It needs the following three components to function: (1) a notational system that represents machine states,

(2) storage media capable of bearing inscription, and (3) a mechanism to transform symbolic notation into machine states. Given these three characteristics, a machine becomes a universal mechanism capable of assuming the function of any other symbolic system.

To understand Turing machines in practical terms, think about the lower limits of computation. A Turing machine can simulate the physics of using a hammer, for example, but it cannot ever become one. A smart hammer is intelligent to the extent that it contains inscription: rules and instructions for hammering. Turing machines open a space of interiority by which mechanical actions (hammering, in our case) can be traced into their notational equivalents (instructions for hammering). A smart hammer, or any other smart thing for that matter, presupposes a system of symbolic exchange within the instrument.

Once assimilated in this way, symbols are subject to grammatical transformation. Turing machines unfold the logic of instrument use, that is, their technique. More complicated symbolic logics, which represent higher-level activity like solving physical formulas or writing poetry, are similarly amenable to Turing simulation, provided a grammar. Technique, if you recall from our earlier discussion, is a mode of production abstracted from its material contexts. The extent to which Turing machines penetrate everyday life belies their involvement in the general mechanisms of such abstraction, beyond computation. The computer extends its reach broadly not because it quantifies life but because much of human cultural and cognitive activity is already symbolic in nature. The Turing machine is ultimately a tool for universal symbolic manipulation.

Let us examine the mechanics of a Turing machine more closely. Turing begins his paper with a typically Wittgensteinian provocation: "We may compare a man in the process of computing a real number to a machine which is only capable of a finite number of conditions."[92] From the start, Turing treats computation, which we normally consider a complex cognitive process, as a simple mechanism. To these ends, he proposes a machine "supplied with a 'tape' (the analogue of paper) running through it, and divided into sections (called 'squares') each capable of bearing a 'symbol.'"[93] Much like a movie reel, tape moves through the mechanism one section at a time.

At each point, only one section bearing one symbol is in the machine: "We may call this square the 'scanned square.' The symbol on the scanned square may be called the 'scanned symbol.' The 'scanned symbol' is the only one of which the machine is, so to speak, 'directly aware.'"[94] The scanned symbol becomes a part of the machine's internal configuration, or, to slide into Turing's cognitive vocabulary, a part of its "awareness." Turing argues that the machine can "effectively remember" the symbols it has "seen" and scanned previously.[95] Its initial configuration (the arrangement of tape and scanning apparatus) plus the scanned symbol determines its behavior. The scanned symbol becomes a part of machine "memory," whereby symbols are translated into machine states. Today we would say that the mechanism transforms software into hardware, and vice versa.

Imagine, then, a device not unlike a telegraph or a film projector, which ingests reels of tape. Unlike telegraphs or film projectors, the ingested symbolic representation becomes, by definition, a part of the machine's internal state in a way that telegraph tape or film reels do not when they pass through telegraphs and film projectors. The film reel and ticker tape leave the machine without a trace and do not signify machine states. By contrast, Turing's tape alters the machine's internal configuration in a way that lasts beyond its discharge from the mechanism.

In his earlier thought experiments, Wittgenstein also spoke of humans in the process of reading or doing mathematics as ingesting symbols, of the need to internalize external symbolic states, and of effecting a change in mental states on some real and empirically observable neurological level, which correlates to the symbol. Turing's machine is capable of such ingestion. It "thinks," "reads," and "remembers" to the extent of its capability to scan and internalize symbolic notation. In addition to reading, Turing's machine writes: "In some of the configurations in which the scanned square is blank (*i.e.* bears no symbol) the machine writes down a new symbol on the scanned square."[96] It is also capable of erasing and moving symbols to adjacent squares, one square at a time. In effect, the Turing machine provides a concise and minimally viable definition of "reading," "writing," and "becoming aware." These states for Turing involve the appropriate internalization and subsequent externalization of the symbol, for both human and machine.

More than a simple scanner, a Turing machine alters the very rules of reading and writing. If we take reading to initially entail moving our eyes from left to right, we can also imagine notation that stands for directives such as "Now move from right to left" or "Skip every other character." Such directives become a part of the mechanism to determine the internal movement of the reading and writing apparatus. Unlike an analog watch, the Turing mechanism is not set in stone. It is capable of altering its own inner works, where some of the scanned characters represent symbols to be manipulated and yet others represent machine instructions, which define the rules for manipulation. Data and instructions mix into the same input stream. The instructions are "meant" for the machine, in the sense that they direct the movement of the reading and writing heads, which "write," "scan," or "erase" symbols. Today, we would call such instructions programs, applications, or software.

Just as Turing machines are able, in theory, to convert extrinsic signs into intrinsic machine states, they can conversely enact the opposite movement, by representing machine states symbolically. This remarkable property allows for what Turing calls a class of *universal* machines, distinct from mere single-purpose computers. Single-purpose Turing machines perform singular actions such as addition or multiplication. However, a multiplication machine cannot perform other types of symbolic manipulation (e.g., spell-check) because the physical movement of its internal parts is fixed. An electronic weight scale, to take another example, cannot process text or calculate missile trajectories. The universal Turing machine by contrast has the ability to internalize other machine configurations wholesale. Such a machine can, in Turing's words, "compute any computable sequence."[97] In being able to internalize physical configuration as symbol, the universal Turing machine gains the ability to simulate all other single-purpose Turing machines, so long as the logic of these machines is amenable to symbolic representation. For this reason, Turing computation excludes nonsymbolic mechanical actions such as hammering nails or harvesting grain. The universal Turing machine is a tool for ubiquitous symbolic manipulation; it is a trace of a trace, a diagram of diagrams.

The transition of symbols into machine states (and the other way around) defines modern programming. Unlike other definitive single-purpose and limited-state mechanisms (e.g., a clock), a universal machine contains the ability to take on differing internal symbolic configurations. It can imitate a clock, an abacus, a scale, a book. In a later paper that links computing machinery to intelligence, Turing implied also that his machine could eventually simulate human thought, because he saw the mind as another mechanism for manipulating symbols.[98]

Are minds just types of Turing machines, or are Turing machines a kind of mind? Turing leaves the door open for either possibility. The universal Turing machine finally encapsulates a model of computation itself. It is capable of computing anything computable. In substituting the concept of computability with effective computability, Turing's paper belongs to the annals of mathematical theory. It continues to elicit conflicting responses widely because much of it contains also the excess of symbolic thought related to our more general sense of what it means to read, write, and interpret. Besides offering mathematical proofs, Turing's work embarks on an experimental, ludic even, enterprise in the spirit of Wittgenstein's playful experimentation, which often involved altered states of mind, drugs, delirium, madness, and outright deception.

DEVICE

Literature in computer science tends to treat Turing machines as algorithms: logical, not necessarily physical constructs.[99] However, it is impossible to dissociate the idea from the implementation. The historian Thomas Haigh wrote that Turing machines "abstract away from the complexity of real computer architectures."[100] The Turing machine appeals to a theorist because it is a theory. Haigh also notes that "hardware and software are interchangeable to the theorist, but not to the historian."[101] In his 1937 review of Turing's "On Computable Numbers" paper, Alonzo Church, the American mathematician whose work anticipated Turing's (independently) in several important aspects, similarly acknowledged the material foundations of Turing computing: A "human calculator, provided with pencil and paper and explicit instructions, can be regarded as a kind of Turing machine."[102] Disregarding the broader, metaphysical consequence of that statement, note for now the persistence of two implements required for the minimally viable operation of the Church-Turing human and machine calculators. Pen and paper assert themselves through the abstraction.[103]

To encounter digital books and therefore Turing machines as devices, media and book historians will find that they borrow from a number of extant designs, which, together and incrementally, give universal Turing machines their physical form. What are their technological antecedents? What would happen, for example, if Turing attempted to patent his device? What prior art would he cite in his patent application?

Most of the minimal technical requirements needed to build a universal Turing machine were within reach in the 1930s, when Turing wrote his influential paper. In practice, his proposal required, first, an apparatus capable of scanning and erasing a finite number of symbols. Second, it called for what Turing described as "one-dimensional paper," divided into discrete squares "like a child's arithmetic book."[104] Furthermore, Turing specified a mechanism to advance tape through the machine, or, alternatively, to propel the scanning mechanism along a length of tape. Having assembled these elements, our creation would look roughly like a cross between a telegraph, a film projector, and a typewriter.[105]

Were one to patent a Turing machine in the United States, these elements would find prior art in mechanisms such as the Numeral Adding or Subtracting Attachment for Typewriting Machines, the Combined Typewriting and Computing Machine, the Computing Attachment for Typewriters, the Computing Mechanism, and the Combined Typewriting and Adding Machine, among others.[106] All these patented devices contain some combination of reading and writing heads, storage tape, and a movement mechanism corresponding to Turing's specifications. A number of inventions at the end of the nineteenth century relate specifically to "circuit-controlling devices controlled by a traveling perforated strip or tape," as in the case of the Tape-driven Telegraph Transmitter filed by Charles Cuttriss in 1893.[107]

Before perforated tape, the transmission of messages by telegraph required the presence of a skilled operator, who would be able to transcribe messages from text to Morse code and into the physical motion of a lever-operated circuit. Early telegraphy required human operators to act as mute interpreters between text and telegraph. Perforated tape decoupled humans from machines. In U.S. patent 1187035 (1916) on "Telegraphy," brothers Albert and Ralph Bumstead explain, "The object of our invention is to provide a system of telegraphy which does not require skilled operators for the transmission and reception of messages."[108] Instead, the message was transcribed into perforation using mechanical means and then fed into the mechanism. Typewriter tape movement could then be connected to telegraph electronics, where perforated tape mediated between the two worlds of mechanics and electricity. A number of contraptions emerged at the time with the aim of transfiguring mechanical action into perforation and, consequently, perforation into script, completing the circuit between automated encoding and decoding. These included machines for tape-controlled telegraphic transmission, tape-controlled printing, printing telegraphs, and remote broadcast programming devices for radio and television content.[109]

With the invention of punch cards and perforated tape (also used in textile looms as early as 1725), a message meant for another human became also a physical medium—bumps and holes—used to animate the mechanical movement of the transmission apparatus, the kind of rigid link-age that Wittgenstein described in his thought experiments. Indeed, of the thirty-three asserted claims in the "Telegraphy" patent by the Bumstead brothers, the first thirteen relate to the transmission of intelligence including a transmitter:

> adapted to initiate a succession of electrical impulses all of which have a character representing significance, a receiver adapted to detect varia-tions in the time intervals elapsing between successive impulses, a plurality of interpreting relays selectively actuated by said receiver, and a printing mechanism responsive to the combined action.[110]

What begins as a description of a communication mechanism concludes with a claim about hermeneutics of control. Starting with clause 14, the brothers describe a telegraph system capable of transmitting impulses at varying time intervals. In the language of the patent, the length of a time interval "represent[s] significance," involving an automated receiver responsible for "distributing, interpreting, and recording."[111] The printing mechanism is further "arranged to print the interpretation of the signals."[112] Interpreting relays thus transform time intervals into typography, representing letters, figures, and other characters in "accordance with a code."[113] Initially, the telegraph "interprets" with the aim of "transmitting intelligence."[114] Subsequently, the Bumsteads understood also that a length of transmitted time interval could also signify information used to actuate a variety of devices. The brothers thus refer to their invention in broad terms, calling it a "controlling medium" capable of regulating remotely everything from typesetting machines to ge-neric sunflower switches: "Indeed, the detector and interpreting relays could be made to actuate a set of sunflower switches for an indicator . . . without including a printer at all."[115] By the end of the patent the brothers generalize their telegraph into a universal control mechanism.

Driven by ticker tape and connected to printers, automated telegraphs contained all the necessary Turing features: a discrete symbolic language, removable storage media, and a mechanism capable of altering its physical state according to instruction. These proto-computers read and wrote; they ingested tape and converted extrinsic symbols into intrinsic configurations. By 1905, Donald Murray, inventor of the popular Murray telegraph, could write that "if we disregard the small class of telegrams that merely express emotions, *the essence of telegraphy is control*" (emphasis mine). He stressed that telegraph systems "belong, not to the class of producing or distributing, but to the class of controlling mechanisms."[116] For the automated telegraph, control code and message are one. The mechanism "interprets" some signals as data to be manipulated and others as control code, or rules for such data manipulation. The first type of symbols holds significance for humans, whereas the second holds significance for the mechanism itself. The mechanism "transmits intelligence" in the sense of rarefying machine states; it "interprets" in the sense of mechanical embodiment.

Computing scales, dial recorders, electric tabulating machines, and computing typewriters were widely available on the market, made by such companies as Underwood Computing Machine, Electromatic, and International Business Machines (IBM). Rather than a single eureka moment, the invention of the computer should be viewed as a gradual historical process that culminates in Turing's universal and minimally viable specifications.

The limits of physical engineering pull the Turing machine back to the sphere of the applied.[117] What are we to make of universal Turing machines implemented in virtual worlds such as *Wireworld* (a cellular automaton simulation), or *Minecraft* (a procedurally generated sandbox world-exploration game)? In the least, we must admit that such simulations do not rest on immaterial "turtles all the way down," unless one believes the universe itself to be a type of Turing computation.[118] At some point, a Turing machine in the virtual world meets the material limits of the physical. Simulation engines such as *Minecraft* and *Wireworld* do in some sense exist in the abstract, as code or even rules written on paper. In another sense, they do not. They come fully into being when instantiated within first-order physical systems that involve actual circuit boards and relay switches, or, at least, pen and paper. For this reason, the performance (in terms of cycles per second, instructions per cycle, or the maximum number of instructions) of a Turing machine simulated within a virtual world like *Minecraft* cannot logically exceed the performance of the machine running *Minecraft* itself. The physical capabilities of the bottommost device limit the computational power of all (n + 1) order Turing simulations. The bottommost turtle may have its head in the clouds, but its feet rest firmly on the ground.

The exact plane where the symbolic meets the material is difficult to identify. At some imperceptible point software disappears into hardware. Such ambiguity leads to controversy in the critical literature, as evidenced by Lev Manovich's playful response to Kittler's "There is no software" argument, in which Kittler posited the postmodern writing scene. Kittler wrote, "We do not write anymore. . . . Human-made writing passes through microscopically written inscriptions which, in contrast to all historical writing tools, are able to read and write by themselves."[119] Kittler sees the paper-bound blueprints of the first integrated microprocessor as the last real piece of writing. Everything written after that point is hardware, because all digital modes of representation, including text, ultimately rest on physical circuit architecture. In this view, the inability to understand hardware precludes all higher modalities of reading, writing, and interpretation.

Manovich inverts Kittler's argument into "There is only software," by which he means that in a pragmatic sense, software determines the properties of any media object. The inversion participates in the perpetual dialectics between idealism and materialism: Hegel and Marx, Marx and Gramsci, Gramsci and Kittler, Kittler and Manovich.[120] "What you can do with the same digital file can change dramatically," depending on the software, Manovich writes.[121] When it comes to digital photographs, to use his example, one application may allow the photographer to crop the image, whereas another may not. From this property-determining aspect of software (and in reference to the work of Alan Kay), Manovich adopts the concept of the *metamedium*: "a medium that can dynamically simulate the details of any other medium."[122] Software defines the properties of digital manipulation, determining the physics of all higher-order media it simulates.[123]

Kittler would perhaps object that all such higher-order simulated physics still rest on the bedrock of silicon. In opening a series of nested software black boxes, the post-silicon writer and scholar of software hits the impenetrable casket of chip architecture. Manovich's observations hold true for all simulated media but not for the simulation itself; hardware that gives rise to simulation is not in itself one. Base media ultimately determine the properties of software, their derivative metamedia. Wittgenstein's thought experiments do not let us fall definitively into the software or hardware camp. The Turing machine remains in flux in the transformation of signs into physical states.

We return finally to the sheer alienness of the book as a piece of tele-communication technology, captured in the struggle to grasp the epistemic object—recall Shklovsky, Lubbock, and Bakhtin in the earlier sections. Writing already converts mental states into arbitrarily externalized marks on paper. Such inscriptions persist, through time, beyond their biological origin. They are then conveyed remotely and through ingestion, commonly called "reading": an action that transforms inscriptions back into mental states. The intellectual history of Turing machines leads us to a series of thought experiments about the nature of such transformations. The question of technique continues to haunt contemporary poetics. In the process of reading, the book escapes the interpreter's grasp as a thing, presenting itself only as an idea.

What does the material history of computers mean for the history of the book? In viewing the book as a precursor to a generalized machine for symbolic manipulation, we discover that it belongs to a class of controlling devices. The nature of Turing machines implies an irreversible admixture of matter, content, and control structure. When reading a paper-and-cloth book, one can definitively isolate (1) the medium from (2) content and from (3) the legal and political structures governing its production. To separate these components, one could, for example, tear out the copyright notice along with the ISBN number, copy the words into a notebook, and recycle the paper.

The digital literary device, by contrast, ingests both symbolic represen-tation and control code through the same input stream. Where images of governance (such as trademark and copyright symbols) signify control, com-puted text embodies it. We are not able to fully separate the mechanism from its message. Mechanisms of copyright enforcement are embedded into the artifact. The content is inextricably intertwined with the medium. One could copy and paste it, but the action would miss layers of meaning not accessible at the surface.

In asking "How is it made?" we arrest the advance of symbolism in an attempt to find the thing behind the process of signification, which always dissembles to conceal its material foundations. Signification ultimately ter-minates at the physical boundaries of its establishing medium. Base mate-rial conditions differ from paper to screen. Paper pages contain no internal states to speak of. The kind of symbolism they support therefore proceeds from surface inscription toward the reader. Reading, as Moreno reminds us, is already an invasive procedure. Absent human contact, we take on the mental states of others through a vehicle that conveys a remote kind of agency, displaced in time and space. It should be held in view all the more because the electronic book, unlike paper, does contain internal states of its own that further interject in the process of signification. How it is made becomes a question not only for the poetics but also for the politics of letters.

The question of technique seeks to expose the rules of symbolic transference between at least three discrete systems: one inorganic, the book; one symbolic, text; and one biological, body. There is of course a way in which the three are one: We are all cyborgs in a sense—an assemblage of organs, instruments, and inscriptions. In another sense, poetics asks us to consider the constructed nature of the coupling, the point of contact being governed by rules of engagement, protocols, grammars, and translation tables. These constructed entities grow and proliferate in a seemingly organic, ad hoc manner. They make up a part of our received technological a priori. This does not mean, however, that they should be naturalized or treated with a reverence afforded to endangered species or to nature itself. Decoupling ourselves from inscription, if only momentarily—to reject the graft or to let it wither—must remain an option. If poetics lays the groundwork for interpretation, we must acknowledge that today such grounds lie past the visible simulacrum of a digital page.

Whereas literary technique is concerned with the passage of ideas to ink, computational technique extends the chain of signification also to pixel and transistor. Techniques of the body and literary techniques intertwine in the process of conventional reading. The two couple ever tighter when reading electronically. Miniaturized, the Turing machine passes into the body—think of a digital pacemaker that contains inscription within the machine within the body. These linkages are deeply embedded. They require explication.

In the process of production, printing, and typesetting of this book, it is certain that my message was mixed with with control codes that, in turn, have changed hardware structures at hand or near the eye. I could believe that I bear no responsibility for extending the reach of machine languages so close to the reader; I only wrote the content I could object; I am not responsible for those other inscriptions. But that would be factually incorrect. The choice of our writing implements and channels of communication deeply affect the contexts of interpretation. Such choices, in aggregate, define the shared ecosystem of knowledge production. Traditional strategies of close reading, which limit interpretation to the parsing of visible content, risk missing the concealed machinations of naked circuit control. It looks as though we are reading books, but this book may change depending on the reader's race, gender, ethnicity, geography, or political affiliation. Who authors or authorizes these transformations? If books were also pills or were fused with the brain's neural circuitry, would we know what and whom we were reading?

CHAPTER 3

> FORM, FORMULA, FORMAT

DIGITAL FORMALISMS

Text shapes the human body in strange ways. A lifetime of reading stoops the shoulders as though books were exerting pressure against the solar plexus. Continual exertion deteriorates eyesight. Tendons and other supporting structures in the wrist swell from the repetitive stress of striking keys. The word takes its toll. A further profound change happens when we read and write along with the machine. As we interpret it, it interprets us.

Machine learning algorithms track the speed by which readers advance from paragraph to paragraph, creating a fingerprint that points to markers of gender, age, race, ethnicity, and economic status. Algorithmic agents follow the movement of eye and finger to direct the reader's attention and to understand how the human brain connects topics. Heat maps are drawn to represent the dynamics of boredom, fatigue, focus, and desire. Supervised training algorithms use our collective philological output—sorting and commenting—to classify information autonomously and to curate content suited to our predilections.

Deep neural networks mimic the brain to build models of human behavior. These models are notoriously difficult to interpret because they are not *intended* for human comprehension.[1] A vast archive of texts written by and for machines support the tiny, in comparison, corpus of human-compatible literature.

Despite its formative effect on practices of comprehension, code, the programmatic sign, does not often figure in our theories of meaning making.

Instead, we consign it to the ornamental formatting layer of document structure. We do so at our peril. Unlike passive decorative elements—fleurons, daggers, and pilcrows—the programmatic sign actively molds text to context. Words find their topography.

At the maximally blunt limit of its capabilities, format governs access. Commands render some words and sentences visible on-screen while suppressing others. The ability to hide text from view completely or to make it so small as to be illegible affects not just the style but also the politics of text. Code determines its audience, privileging certain voices and modes of reading. In this sense, the programmatic sign acquires its nonrepresentational, tactical character. Stripped of references, resemblances, and designations, it commands and controls.[2]

Unlike figurative description, machine control languages function in the imperative. They do not stand for action; they are action. More binding than what J. L. Austin has called speech acts—edicts such as "I pronounce you husband and wife" and commitments such as "I do"—control codes ensure regulation. Code is an exercise of power, not its representation. The difference between representation and control is one of brute force. It lies in the distinction between a restraining order and physical restraint. A restraining order *signifies* the calling forth of codified power. Physical restraints, for example, handcuffs, *enact* the exercise of codified power. Like all violence, they do not stand for anything. The handcuffs simply contort the body into the shape of submission. Absent a body, the restraints draw an empty shape. Code similarly shapes the written word. Located somewhere between screen and storage medium, formats relate matter to content. They are techniques by which immanent inscriptions, the electromagnetic charge, are transformed into transcendent digital objects: novels, songs, films, poems. Formatting imposes structure.

Think of a paragraph, for example. Writers use them to break up the flow of thoughts on a page. Paragraphs contain information. Can one imagine an empty paragraph? Could the shape of a paragraph persist outside the material confines of a page or screen? Can one imagine paragraphs that unfold spatially not in two dimensions, a rectangle, but in one, along a straight line, or in three, in the shape of a cube? These questions confound because paragraphs draw a singular figure. They are textual containers of a type. Any other shape less or more than the paragraph would go by another name; it would constitute another format. To imagine something like a one-dimensional paragraph is akin to imagining a flat shoebox. A flat shoebox cannot contain shoes. It can hold only images of footwear. A paragraph embodies a similarly singular arrangement of elements. It is a container or a data structure of a kind, made to hold a certain amount of sentences.

We may liken books, paragraphs, and sentences to nesting dolls: data structures that contain within them further smaller arrangements of information. A word fits inside a sentence, the sentence within a paragraph, the paragraph within a chapter, the chapter within a book, the book within an archive, and so on.

Formats such as the book or the broadsheet newspaper are known entities. We understand how they are made and how to unfold them in space. By contrast, computational formats change rapidly and proliferate. They contain further, as yet unexplored structural possibilities: shapes similar to the paragraph on paper but native to new media. What you see is what you get on the page. On-screen, what you see is but a small part of what you could get. We are presented with thick content, beyond visible image: the composite of all that is contained. In print, content can be gleaned from surface; there is nothing but surface expanse on a page. Screens are laminates. Light and liquid crystal, the conduits for digital media, surge between substrates in response to electric signal. Screen surfaces conceal further strata of codification, inscribed onto recondite planes of inscription: hard disks, solid-state drives, platters, drums, memory sticks, layers of copper and oxide.

A byte, made up of eight binary bits, holds a letter. The string of letters spelling out "hello world," occupies eleven bytes on a hard drive: ten bytes for the letters and one byte for the space character. A file in the Portable Document Format (PDF) containing the same "hello world" takes up 24,335 bytes on my system. What sort of information do these extra bytes contain? Historically, such data have included machine instructions for the viewing and printing or even clandestine ciphers. The PDF specification describes features that include "accessibility of content to those with disabilities," "digital signatures to certify authenticity," "electronic forms to gather data," "preservation of document fidelity independent of the device, platform, and software," and "security and permissions to allow the creator to retain control of the document and associated rights."[3]

These capabilities mediate between visible image and stored information: one surface facing the human; the other, the machine. The formatting layer specifies the *affordances* of electronic text. More than passive conduits of meaning, electronic texts thus carry within them rules for engagement between authors, readers, and devices. In our example, the PDF encodes, among other things, ideas about reading, authenticity, fidelity, preservation, and authorship. Whatever literary-theoretical framework the reader brings to the process of interpretation must therefore meet the affordances encoded into the electronic text itself.

Jonathan Sterne, a media scholar who pioneered the study of audio formats, writes that format theory "invites us to ask after the changing formations of media, the contexts of their reception, the conjunction that shaped their sensual characteristics, and the institutional politics in which they were enmeshed."[4] Attending to the affordances of format, to paraphrase Caroline Levine, "opens a generalizable understanding of political power."[5] Constraint, what Levine calls the collision of forms, happens not on the level of representation or ideology but on the level of the physical, the phatic, and the imperative, where formatting and control codes reside.

Format and content compose what may be called *thick content*, which accounts for the disparity between plain and fancy text.[6] Its explication requires thick description that draws on material particulates.[7] These further acquire tactical significance in practice: Texts that edit themselves or collect their own fees necessitate new formalisms and strategies of interpretation. In his monograph on audio formats, Sterne argues for a study of formats that "highlights smaller registers like software, operating standards, and codes as well as larger registers like infrastructures, international corporate consortia, and whole technical systems."[8]

A familiar paper paragraph structure already presents several interesting problems for analysis. A paragraph, we intuit, corresponds to a unit of thought. But there is nothing inherently paragraph-like in the neural arrangement of thoughts in our brains. Physiologically, the brain arranges information in hexagons, along the entorhinal grid.[9] There is also nothing inherently paragraph-like in the arrangement of bits along the surface of electromagnetic storage. Formats thus translate between disparate systems of ordering and signification.[10] We are presented with metaphors of order on-screen: paragraphs, pages, files, folders. These resemble their paper counterparts, but they represent other, less familiar and nonequivalent ordering structures on disk.

Formats mediate between data structures, transforming one into the other according to predefined rules. Mental images, information stored in the head, become inscription, information stored in the machine, which turns into a projection, content arranged on-screen (Figure 3.1). The complexities of transformation stem from a fundamental incompatibility between incommensurate languages and physicalities. Format specifications govern the transference of data structures from one medium to another at the point of contact between human, symbol, and machine.

In this chapter I move us toward a systematic study of textual formats. I argue that the history of formalism contains within it at least these two contradictory intuitions about the nature of literary form. Going back to the reception of Plato, Hegel, and the Russian formalists, the English "form" renders at times the material, outward, and apparent shape of something said, written, or pictured. Just as often, it is used in the sense of a Platonic ideal: abstracted from matter, inward-facing, and in need of explication. Form in this sense is closer to the idea of an algorithm or formula; it signifies according to implicit rules.

I augment these two concepts of form with a third "format." In the process I show how formats developed historically from simple machine instructions for typographical layout into complex metaliterary directives related to the protection of intellectual property rights, constraints on speech, trade agreements, the politics of surveillance, and clandestine communication. In the second half of the chapter, an intellectual history of form, drawn from the annals of literary theory, meets the material history of format, drawn from computer science. I end the chapter with a discussion of smart documents, increasingly common instruments of record capable of policing their own encoded mechanisms of reader engagement: what can be read, how, and where.

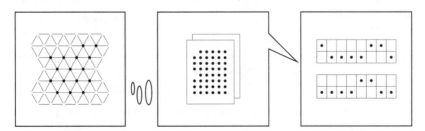

FIGURE 3.1. Formats change with the medium, as shown in the arrangement of data in the brain (left), on a page (middle), and on disk (right). Image adapted by Emily Fuhrman from author's sketches.

CONCRETE AND UNIVERSAL

The intellectual history of literary theory contains at least two contradictory ideas about form: the sign's outward shape and its inward structure or formula that governs semiosis. The distinction leads to diverging strategies of interpretation. In the sense of outward shape, form suggests the affective aesthetics or even "erotics" of art.[11] According to this view, the sign is firmly embedded in the specific contexts of inscription, or, alternatively, in the contexts of its reception. The individual peculiarity of a word in context renders it forever different from the same word used elsewhere. Formalism in this sense is concerned with the distinctive, palpable, and outward physical attributes of text.

As formula, form suggests a more analytical approach, one that explicates the inward structures (universal rules, patterns, or archetypes) that shape textual production from within. Formal analysis so conceived studies not specific traces or utterances but rather the development of ideal forms, which exist somewhat independently of their specific instantiations.[12] Form in the sense of formula embodies an abstraction, leading to generalized historical categories such as genre and period. Our ideas about, for example, "the novel" or "modernism" or "science fiction" reflect formal groupings of the kind Lisa Gitelman called "a mode of recognition instantiated in discourse."[13] Where palpable form leads to immanent material artifacts, the abstracted notion of form leads to transcendent ideal categories.

The notion of format occupies the conceptual space somewhere between form as intrinsic formula and form as extrinsic shape. In what remains, to my knowledge, a singular article-length treatment of the topic in literary studies, G. Thomas Tanselle approached the concept of formatting from the perspective of textual criticism—the practice of compiling, editing, annotating, preserving, and publishing scholarly critical editions of canonical texts. For Tanselle's narrow purposes, formatting encompassed something like the "number of page-units placed on the press at one time."[14] He acknowledged, however, that formats refer also to the "nature and order of the contents."[15] The genre of soap opera, for example, evokes both a medium (daytime television) and the specific kind of story told in that medium (melodrama and pulp). Journal formats include "broadsheet dailies" and "tabloids."

A format identifies matter of both particular shape and content. The soap opera, for example, is a kind of daytime melodrama of a certain length. It also has a certain audience in mind. Formats thus address both a thing's physical properties and its ideational subject matter. The novel is a genre, where the paperback is its common format. The novel is infinitely malleable, whereas the paperback is fixed by its methods of manufacturing and distribution. We do not usually expect scientific textbooks to appear in paperback, for example, just as we would not expect tabloids to be printed on expensive stock or to support long-form investigative journalism. Formats capture something about the shape, design, style, and thematics of subject matter; they connect the where to the what, when, and how.

Whatever the tradition of writing about form, the concept is usually contraposed to some idea of content, as in "form and content." Content in this sense refers to the stuff being shaped or arranged, whether by intrinsic law or extrinsic forces. R. G. Collingwood famously described the distinction between Classical and Romantic art in terms of the form-content divide: "Classical art stands for form; romantic art for content."[16] The distinction is invoked in other fields as well. In her recent work on computational text generation, Kathleen McKeown, a renowned computer scientist, wrote that to produce discourse, writers and speakers "must decide *what* to say and *how* to present it effectively."[17] Similarly, in her influential essay "Print Is Flat, Code Is Deep," Katherine Hayles discussed "the interplay between a text's physical characteristics and its signifying strategies."[18] Content and form often refer to what the text signifies and how it physically does it.

A distinction between text (content) and presentation (form) can also entail the distinction between the work of art in the abstract sense and the object of art in the sense of the material artifact. In this way, two slightly diverging editions of the same text—the various editions of *King Lear*, for example—nevertheless refer to the same work of art. The work of art is a transcendent idea; the individual editions are contained within its immanent formal characteristics.

As an aside, note that what counts as matter belonging to a text's contingent physical characteristics and what counts as content belonging to its signifying strategies differ from object to object. For example, when reading a novel, we commonly ignore variations in line length. The length of an average line in Herman Melville's *Moby Dick* changes with each edition. Line lengths are not usually important in novels, we would say; they carry no meaning. But when reading poetry, readers do value line length. In poetry it carries meaning, being an integral part of a text's "signifying strategies."

Distinctions between form and content therefore often entail value judgments, by which we separate those textual attributes that are meaningful from those that are not. Form, in that sense, identifies a text's superfluous physical attributes, which can thereby be omitted from interpretation and reproduction of the text. A printer can discard information about the color of a manuscript's ink, for example, or do away with the idiosyncrasies of a writer's handwriting when typesetting a manuscript.

However, the concept of form can also refer to the essence of the text. Under canonical Platonic definitions, forms denote an object's essential, not merely contingent, superfluous properties. For Platonists, the essence of something (e.g., a chair) exists in an ideal metaphysical state somewhere beyond the confines of the material universe. By contrast, a physical instantiation of that object (a specific chair) embodies a more limited, corrupted even, version of that perfect idea. The philosopher's task, then, becomes one of reconstructing the single ideal chair from its many imperfect exemplars.

Computer scientists will recognize in this chain of reasoning some of the principles behind object-oriented programming: a way of building software that works by defining abstract object classes and which are then put to use—"invoked" or "instantiated"—in specific contexts.[19] An abstract class can be further modified or extended when called into action. In this way, the abstract category of chairs becomes a given chair, complete with individual flaws and imperfections. I could, for example, modify the chair by attaching a lamp. The modified chair remains a species of chairs. As before, flaws and emendations are considered insignificant compared to the perfected class. In the idealist tradition, ideas similarly provide us with lasting universal templates for instantiation within the contingent and always changing physical confines of the material world.[20]

Ernst Gombrich, the prominent twentieth-century British art historian, famously proposed to look for "schemata" of art in educational materials: textbooks and primers that acculturate young artists to canonical blueprints of representation: "The schemata . . . represents the first approximate loose category which is gradually tightened to fit the form it is to reproduce." One learns "how to classify and catch it [a motif] within the schematic form."[21] What he called "the-will-to-form" is an "assimilation of any new shape to the schemata and patterns an artist has learned to handle."[22] Form, in the sense used by Gombrich, thus refers to universal formulas—laws, templates, schemas, patterns—which gave rise to individual, concrete artworks.[23]

The conflicting meanings of formalism—one in the sense of outward shape, and the other in the sense of inward formula—become more apparent in translation of classic Greek, German, and Russian texts. In Plato's dialogues, for example, we find a number of words that are reasonably rendered into the English "form." These include *eidos* (essence), *idea* (idea), *morphe* (shape), and *phainomena* (appearance). Compare, as an exercise, the following several translations from Plato's *Timaeus*. In a passage that anticipates the famous molten wax analogy in Descartes, Timaeus notices that some natural elements, like water, change their appearance (*phantazomenōn*) while remaining essentially the same substance. Benjamin Jowett translates the passage as follows:

> Thus, then, as the several elements never present themselves in the same form [*phantazomenōn*], how can anyone have the assurance to assert positively that any of them, whatever it may be, is one thing rather than another?[24]

Compare Jowett's translation with the following translation of the same passage by W. R. M. Lamb, who renders the Greek *phantazomenōn* as the English word *appearance*:

> Accordingly, since no one of these ever remains identical in appearance [*phantazomenōn*], which of them shall a man definitely affirm to be any one particular element and no other without incurring ridicule?[25]

Both translations of the Greek *phantazomenōn*, "form" and "appearance," capture the plain meaning of the passage: the essence of a thing remains even as its outward appearance changes, taking on a phantasmal, fantastic, ghostly, imaginable, and even "virtual" shape and appearance (all reasonable English approximations of the Greek *phantazomenōn*). Accordingly, Jowett translates *phantazomenōn*—that which is changeable—as "form" and Lamb as "appearance."

Contrast the *Timaeus* passages with the ones in *Cratylus*, on the topic of name giving. In *Cratylus* Socrates and Hermogenes discuss the ways in which words signify things by convention. "What has the carpenter in view when he makes a shuttle?" Socrates asks. "Is it not something the nature of which is to weave?" Hermogenes answers, "Well, then, if the shuttle breaks while he is making it, will he make another with his mind fixed on that which is broken, or on that form [*eidos*] with reference to which he was making the one which he broke?" Hermogenes agrees that the carpenter would fix his mind on the ideal form. In this case, Socrates concludes, we should properly call *that* the real shuttle, his point being that the exact outward appearance of individual shuttles does not matter as much as the abstracted idea of shuttles. The abstraction endures even as given instantiations shatter. There exist different types of shuttles, some for weaving wool and others, linen. All of them, however, in Jowett's translation, "must contain the form or ideal [*eidos*] of shuttle."[26]

In *Cratylus*, *eidos* thus stands for the "universal lasting ideal" of all shuttles, exactly the opposite of *phantazomenōn* as "ephemeral instantiation" in the previous passage! Yet both *eidos* and *phantazomenōn* were reasonably translated into the English word *form*, indicating the way in which the concept is overdetermined to carry both of these conflicting meanings.[27]

The overdetermination of form similarly persists in many English translations of G. W. F. Hegel, whose discussion of Platonic forms is also canonical in the formalist tradition. His *Lectures on Aesthetics* contain the paradigmatically Hegelian distinction between Classical and Romantic art periods, which hinges on the distinction between form and content. Classical art, for Hegel, reaches an equilibrium between its ideational, spiritual content and what he calls "the configuration of sensuous material."[28] Characteristically, Hegel's prose is marked by technical and sometimes idiosyncratic vocabulary. Rather than define his terms precisely, Hegel saturates his text with semantic cognates. On the side of *content* (*Inhalt*, *Gehalt*), he uses words such as *inner life* (*Innere Lebendigkeit*), *feeling* (*Empfindung*), *soul* (*Seele*), and *spirit* (*Geist*). All these convey a movement inward to a location, if it can be called such, beyond the physical world, accessible only to the spirit (*Geist*) or mind (*Gedanken*, *Verstand*). On the side of *form* (*Form* in German), Hegel accumulates words such as *expression* (*Ausdruck*) and *presentation* (*Darstellung*) but also *lines, curves, surfaces, carvings, colors, tones, word sounds*, and generally *matter* or *material* (*Linien, Krümmungen, Flächen, Aushöhlungen, Farben, Tönen, Wortklängen, Material*).[29] The semantic cognate cluster of words related to the word *form* conveys physical (palpable, of this world) and outward-facing properties available for examination by the senses (*Sinne*).

These terms help Hegel contrast the dominant aesthetic modes of Classical and Romantic periods. He subsequently paints Romanticism as an art that seeks to disengage itself from matter, reaching the realm of pure self-reflective Spirit. Romanticism, in his words, is "freed from this immediate existence which must be set down as negative, overcome, and reflected into the spiritual unity."[30] Further, "Poetry is the universal art of the spirit which has become free in itself and which is not tied down for its realization to external sensuous material; instead, it launches out exclusively in the inner space and the inner time of ideas and feelings."[31] Finally, "Inwardness celebrates its triumph over the external and manifests its victory in and on the external itself, whereby what is apparent to the senses alone sinks into worthlessness."[32] Romantic art can, in this way, triumph over the external material world, reaching at its apex what Hegel calls the stage of "free concrete spirituality" (freie konkrete Geistigkeit).[33] The idea overcomes matter to become both free from physical and determinate constraints yet gains a measure of solidity in its tangible instantiation.

Several lines in Hegel's exposition of Plato's idealism give us a glimpse of his struggle with the Platonic concept of form. In his "Lectures on Philosophy," Hegel writes that the "idea is nothing but what is current with us under the name of the Universal, when this word is not taken in the sense of formal Universal [formell Allgemeine]." For Hegel, the formal universal is "merely a property of things," whereas Plato is concerned with the "implicitly" universal (by contrast with explicitly, or formally universal). This internal "essence" and "in-and-for-itself existent" lays a claim to truth alone: "We translate the Greek word eidos by 'genus' or 'species,'" but when "genus" or "species" is "seized as a number of similar determinations collected by reflection from several individuals, to serve as a mark for the convenience of the understanding, then we have the Universal in quite an external form."[34] In other words, as soon as eidos is instantiated, it moves from being an ideal form into an apparent shape, an epistemological category.

I understand Hegel's problem with formal universals as follows. Imagine that someone wrote "All these cats are subsumed under the category of 'feline.'" The labeled category captures a snapshot of what it means at the moment of its naming. But for Hegel, the true ideal does not exist in the name alone; it must merely continue to exist and develop in the real world. In other words, it is not a socially constructed category but something that "internally distinguishes itself" while remaining "free in its infinitude and independent" from all attempts to fix it categorically. Evolutionary forces continue to change the species, even as the taxonomy describing that evolution remains fixed. The biological family evolves no matter what zoologists call cats. New and radically different feline species may come into existence, ones no longer covered by the "external mark" of being "feline," that is, by our taxonomical categories. Yet, in Hegel's terms, this would only mean that the feline ideal has expanded beyond its arbitrary categorical confines. Zoologists could, at that point, simply adjust their taxonomies to include new forms of feline being. A new vocabulary would fix the category in its altered state. It would become outmoded almost immediately, however, as the ideal feline being would continue to develop from underneath it, leaving behind only a snapshot of what it meant to be a cat in times already past. Hegel therefore cautions his reader against confusing that static categorical snapshot with the actual animate ideal. The formal is finally a mere husk of the concrete, living ideal. In contrast to such formal universals, Hegel's concrete universals exist in the real physical world. They are more than categories. We can understand them as capturing both *eidos* and *phantazomenōn*—idea and appearance—both reasonably transcribed as *form* in English.[35]

FORMAT THEORY

Plato and Hegel point to a series of related folds and creases in the formalist tradition. W. K. Wimsatt once observed that literary theorists often persist in making statements that understand a work of literary art to be, in a peculiar way, "a very individual thing or a very universal thing or both."[36] A work of art, a poem, understood as something that "cannot be expressed in other terms," leads to the kind of criticism that emphasizes the contemplation of a text's outward affective and palpable elements. The function of such criticism, according to Wimsatt, is to create "approximate descriptions of poems" and "multiple restatements of their meaning," which aid readers in coming to their own "intuitive and full realization" of literature.[37] By contrast, the analysis of literary forms understood as formula or schema seeks to recover latent universal mechanisms, laws, and deep structures that produce surface phenomena.

The dual motion of literary criticism, at once toward the extrinsic shape and the intrinsic formula—poetics and hermeneutics—is perhaps most starkly visible in the intellectual legacy of early-twentieth-century Russian formalism. The influential series of publications by OPOYAZ (Society for the Study of Poetic Language) gave voice to a collective of literary scholars that included Viktor Shklovsky, Osip Brik, Lev Yakubinsky, Boris Eichenbaum, and Roman Jakobson. The group struck out in two distinct but complementary directions.

Several essays by Brik, Shklovsky, Yakubinsky, and others contraposed sound (*zvuk*) to symbol (*obraz*). Brik wrote, "I believe that elements of symbolic and sonic [*zvukovoi*] art exist simultaneously, and that every given piece of [poetic] work comprises an equilibrium of these two heterogeneous poetic impulses."[38] Of the sixteen or so unique essays that appeared in the three collected volumes, thirteen contain the word *sound* (*zvuk*), or some variation of it, in the title, in combinations such as "sound image," "sound gesture," and "sound repetition." To this cluster of essays we can attribute the Russian formalist concern with *zaum* (literally "beyond sense") or *beyonsense*, transrational, nonsensical sounds that nevertheless elicit an affective, lived response, expressing ideas that are difficult to explain rationally.[39]

Poetry in the symbolic mode encodes meaning inwardly: an elephant "stands for" memory, or the like. *Zaum* poetics instead evokes feeling through external shape, sensually. Velimir Khlebnikov wrote that "mystical incantation and beyonsense are appeals 'over the head' of government straight to the population of feelings, a direct cry to the predawn of the soul."[40] Shklovsky similarly defined *zaum* as expression "without words but with sound," appealing to the senses rather than the intellect. He wrote:

> Thought and speech cannot keep up with inspired experience, and for this reason artists are free to express themselves not only in language of common understanding, but also in private language—language that has no settled sense. . . . Lilies are beautiful, but how deformed [*bezobrazno*] the word "lily," plundered and exhausted. This is why I call lilies "uao," restoring their primal clarity.[41]

Bezobrazno, in the meaning of "hideous" or "deformed," literally translates as "without an image." The word *lily* has lost its unique shape, I understand Shklovsky to mean. Its very idea has become vulgar. Formalism of the outward kind thus aims to restore the sensation of an image, returning form, in the sense of shape, to habituated content. Formal techniques like chanting or neologism helped revitalize the external sound image. In repetition, the word loses its sense—lily, lily, lily, lily—but gains a distinct sound signature, which otherwise goes unnoticed. The flower's new name similarly takes the object out of its usual linguistic context. How strange the newly discovered *uao*!

Three of the sixteen essays in the OPOYAZ volumes strike in another direction, away from shape and toward formula. Shklovsky's "Art as Technique" and "Linkages Between Plot and Style Device" and Eichenbaum's "How the *Overcoat* Is Made" deal with narrative structure rather than phonetic image.[42] Both writers attribute their work to the influence of Alexander Veselovsky, a little-known (in the West) nineteenth-century historian of literature, whose scholarship nevertheless had a profound impact on the history of Russian letters.

An early pioneer of comparative literature, Veselovsky advocated philology as a "historical" and "genetic" study of "poetic consciousness and its forms."[43] Citing literary explorations by Goethe, Friedrich Schiller, and Georges Polti as inspiration, Veselovsky almost always used the word *form* in the sense of "formula" and not at all in the sense of "shape" or "sound." In this, he imagined a Hegelian model of literary evolution, which develops through universal constants and narrative plot sequences. These ideal forms in turn influence the development of literary particulars. Veselovsky called his genetic constants "vagabond formulas" and "nerve centers" of culture.[44]

> Somewhere, someone gave these plots [*siuzhety*] an apt expression, a formula, elastic enough to fit, if not new content, then new interpretations of plots rich in their associative possibilities. The formula endures. Writers will return to it, altering its significance, expanding its meaning, and adopting it to new types. As the formula of "desire" was and continues to be repeated, so also are repeated the plots of *Faust* and *Don Juan* across the distance of centuries. . . . We are connected to a tradition. We expand within it—not to create new forms, but to attach to them new sentiments and concerns. This dynamic could be considered a kind of a law of conservation of energy.[45]

The Hegelian influence is unmistakable in these lines. Like the world spirit, Veselovsky's vagabond formulas exist and develop across time and space. They are a kind of a concrete universal, which develops independently of individual texts. Formulas in that sense have a life of their own, in trans- or metahuman ways, not fully accessible to an individual author or reader. They are invoked indirectly. They exist in the ether of culture, attaining historical momentum through a process of gradual evolutionary development. As such, they again mean exactly the opposite of form in the sense of a

private utterance, by which an individual author breaks with ossified tradition, as was the case with Shklovsky's idiosyncratic renaming of the flower.
In Veselovsky's model, authors participate in the formation of shared culture
by attaching new meaning to stable idioms; in Shklovsky's model, the author
uniquely dissents from a shared cultural norm.

The tension between extrinsic shape and intrinsic rule lies at the heart
of literary theory, manifesting at times under differing yet essentially related
vocabularies. The emphasis on extrinsic shape implies a poetics of affective
reading, of the kind that privileges apparent surface phenomena. By contrast,
the emphasis on intrinsic rules implies a hermeneutics or an archaeology of
text, by which a critic's role becomes to discover implicit, nonapparent deep
structural regularities.

The reader of hidden formulas reaches beyond ephemeral external appearances of a cultural artifact to explicate internal and eternal universal truths
within. For a Marxist critic such as Terry Eagleton or Fredric Jameson, that
latent meaning may have something to do with hidden machinations of capital
and ideology. The psychologically minded critic reads in search of hidden
drives or desires. The very words *explication* and *exegesis* imply an outward
movement. For example, Jameson, who seems to be channeling Heidegger
through the Russian formalists, wrote:

> The process of criticism is not so much the interpretation of content as it
> is a revealing of it, a laying bare, or restoration of the original message, the
> original experience, beneath the distortions of the various kinds of censor-
> ship that have been at work upon it, and this revelation takes the form of
> an explanation of why the content was so distorted and is thus inseparable
> from a description of the mechanisms of this censorship itself.[46]

Language is again seen to be corrupted through use. The critic of depth,
however, reveals a word's originating sense. Like scratches on a piece of furniture, superfluous distortions are polished away. Texts are to be restored to
their original condition. The business of such a restorative philosophy, in Heidegger's formulation, is to protect the power of elemental words flattened by
use. The philologist-philosopher reveals words prior to use somehow: prephilo-
sophically, before they are "covered over" and "sink back into concealment"[47]

In contrast to such circumspect, symptomatic strategies of reading, Stephen Best and Sharon Marcus describe a constellation of reading practices

concerned with "what is evident, perceptible, apprehensible in texts; what is neither hidden nor hiding; what, in the geometrical sense, has length and breadth but no thickness, and therefore covers no depth."[48] The authors identify a constellation of related interpretation practices at the surface: reading for material surface, reading for verbal structure, reading for affect, reading for description, reading for pattern, and finally, reading for literal meaning or "just reading."[49]

In making an argument for surface reading, Best and Marcus gesture toward the kind of formal poetics advocated by Susan Sontag in the late 1960s. At the time, Sontag wrote about the need for "more attention to form in art."[50] Interpretation can be liberating, she wrote, but it can also stifle creativity. It "depletes" the world in some way, placing the critic in a privileged and unnecessarily meddling position between reader and text: "If excessive stress on content provokes the arrogance of interpretation, more extended and more thorough descriptions of form would silence. . . . The best criticism, and it is uncommon, is of this sort that dissolves considerations of content into those of form."[51]

For Sontag, interpretation at the level of meaning alone is an intellectual and ultimately reactionary activity. It aims to find the "maximum amount of content" within.[52] It is reactionary because it serves only to multiply the available levels of analysis. In explicating a work of art, the critic merely creates alternative copies that diverge from the original. Each layer of criticism thus adds to the content of the work, placing additional burden on future readers. Sontag thought that designing a work of art that could be experienced in this way—always on multiple and diverging levels of ideation—might have been creative and revolutionary in the age of aesthetic paucity, when creativity and interpretation were limited to a few privileged individuals. But she believed that her epoch was one of creative abundance: "Think of the sheer multiplication of works of art available to every one of us." Contemporary culture had become based on "excess" and "material plenitude," which dull the senses.[53] Under such conditions the production of further critical variations on the theme only adds to the dulling clutter.

By "interpretation," Sontag meant a "conscious act of the mind" that illustrates a "certain code" or "certain rules" of literary engagement. It was, for her, "virtually" a type of translation. The critic "transforms" and "revamps" the text: X turns out to be A, Y turns out to be B, and so on.[54] By "form," Sontag meant the apparent perceptual properties of the work; one sentence is long, for example, another short. A critic could make something out of the variation, but Sontag wanted to stop us short of meaning making. A discipline of careful perception, of paying attention to, could sharpen sensibilities, allowing readers to interpret independently. There is no need to explain under this model, only describe. The history of interpretation that Sontag objected to was one that privileged content over form. Form in the sense of outward shape suggests an emphasis on what Sontag deemed the sensory experience or the erotics of art. In "Against Interpretation," Sontag mentions the ideal of "transparence" as the "highest, most liberating value in art—and in criticism—today. Transparence for her meant experiencing the luminousness of the thing in itself, of things being what they are."[55] Rather than show what a work of art *means*, Sontag urged critics to show "how it is" and "that it is."[56] Form, as she saw it, mirrors McKeown's shape and the "text's physical characteristics" of Hayles.

Marcus and Best remind us that Sontag's manifesto was also an "affective and ethical stance."[57] Strategies of deep interpretation carry with them a claim to authority as well as an imbalance of interpretive acumen. Critics assert to uncover what lay readers cannot without expert guidance. As an ethical stance, reading for external forms flattens the hierarchy between lay readers and professional interpreters. In this sense, Best, Marcus, and Sontag continue in the liberal, Lutheran tradition of vernacular exegesis. All readers are priests at the surface; all readers are capable, the critics suggest, of forming their own interpretation.[58]

TACTICS OF READING

If reading for sensory experience implies an erotics of art and reading for hidden formulas implies a hermeneutics, what would it mean to read for format? Formats, to borrow from Tanselle, bridge the "physical structure of finished books" and their "intellectual content" through what he calls "printing-shop routines," or techniques for the transformation of ideas into inscription-things.[59]

Textual scholars have traditionally arbitrated the conflict between divergent editions of the same text.[60] They reveal how works become texts, and vice versa. It is in this sense of arbitration that C. Deirdre Phelps described the notion of physical form. When instantiating the ideal text into its concrete being, publishers introduce changes that may not correspond to authorial intent. For example, an inexpensive edition of Blake's poetry could be printed without his illustrations to save costs, though we know them to be integral to the text. If all other editions of Blake's poetry were lost, textual critics would reconstruct the text's genealogy from extant remnants. They could, for example, infer the missing illustrations based on reception history. "The textual critic," Phelps wrote "is concerned mainly with the fact of the [textual] change itself."[61] Reading for format similarly involves a series of value judgments about what the text should be and what it is.

Different schools of textual criticism emphasize differing aspects of the publication process. Some privilege the notion of authorial intent; others, critical reception. Whatever the choices, they determine value by separating those physical attributes meaningful to the work from those that are not. Peter Shillingsburg writes that "textual awareness requires . . . that readers demand to know which of the possible texts of a work is in hand, to know what the choices [that determine it] are and why a particular choice matters."[62] In other words, Shillingsburg again reminds us that judgments about formatting are value judgments. For example, in a contemporary online edition of Claude McKay's *Harlem Shadows*, the editors encode for indentation, thus preserving the poem's visual line structure. They have also allowed the text to wrap when viewed on small devices, thus "soft wrapping" those lyrical lines too long for a small screen.[63] The end result is a compromise between authorial intent and reader convenience. The layout respects line indentation but not line length.

Other solutions were possible, of course. The editors could have recreated an exact facsimile of a particular print edition, but that would not fit on small screens because of the disparity in size between the printed page and a mobile device. In an extreme case, the editors could have tried to preserve all the text's details, down to its molecular structure. Such a text could be accompanied by a potentially unlimited amount of metadata describing the precise physical contexts of the universe surrounding the authoritative version. Reproducing the text faithfully would also mean reproducing the world around it. Contingent stains or scratches in the manuscript, typos in the critical edition, printer errors, pages inadvertently bound upside down, and other flaws are usually discarded in reproduction. They are not seen as meaningful for the understanding of a text. To decide on the formatting, then, is to commit the work of art as an ideational construct to a medium, that is, to convert it into an object of art.

Format thus belongs neither wholly to a text's physical medium (pixel or paper) nor to a work's ideational content. It lies somewhere between the two worlds: in a letter's shape, a novel's narrative structure, and spoken patterns of stress and intonation. Some formatting features matter to readers (e.g., line breaks in poetry), whereas others usually do not (e.g., font kerning). Textual criticism reminds literary theorists of the transition that happens between literary works and literary objects. It is always a fraught process, because a theorist's beliefs must be continually weighed against the material affordances of a concrete textual witness. A word or a comma omitted or a forgotten line cannot ever become a part of the meaning-making process. Format stands at the gates of hermeneutics.

In an essay on pictographs and pictographic logic, Johanna Drucker and Jerome McGann discuss how the "presentational form of texts" usually masks their "logical operations in a surface rhetoric that dominates and controls our conscious attention." At the same time, what the authors call the "holistic repleteness of images" also keeps us from perceiving their "conceptual order . . . as if the graphic character of the work were completely obvious."[64] Their insight captures the dual movement of formatting: at once toward the physical and the mental characteristics of text, toward matter and content.

The reader understands text as an idea that takes shape in the mind. Book-things thus continually retreat from grasp, as Percy Lubbock wrote in *The Craft of Fiction*.[65] Subsequently, readers treat texts as disembodied artifacts—surface rhetoric—reading past the material structures that support mental phenomena. As an object, a unified image, the page presents itself in its entirety at once—hence holistic repleteness. It is as though it was always so: These words were always in this order, at these coordinates. Printers and book designers understand otherwise. They know the image to be a carefully constructed composite. Dealing with formats directly reveals the particulates of page composition invisible to a lay reader. Drucker and McGann conclude that "systems of graphic presentation are operational, not merely passive schematic structures." They are instead "active agents for creating meaning, instructions for reading, viewing, comprehending information."[66] In other words, choices were made that would later affect meaning making. Apprehension precedes comprehension. Interpretation commences and in some cases concludes before readers ever lay eyes on a page.

Technical differences between print and digital text amplify the importance of format. Print editors and textual scholars negotiate a text's shape in advance of publication. The choice to exclude certain words, versions, or visual elements is fixed in the final proof, where it remains static for the duration of a book's existence. Books are stable platforms that support a range of reading practices, which include the annotation, copying, and preservation of written work. To the extent that books determine the affordances of reading, those affordances exhibit historical continuity. To read a book in print, one must possess certain physical capacities, for example, manual dexterity, a level of cognitive development, and eyesight within a specific range of vision. Readers who fall outside these normalized ranges are prevented from accessing the text in the manner specified. Books further afford abilities such as highlighting and the taking of notes. Empty space around the text on a page facilitates marginalia. For the highlighter or pen to function well, the print medium must be made of a porous material, not, for example, plastic, which would make marking the page difficult while affording other capabilities, such as reading underwater.[67]

The affordances of the electronic book are more diffuse. These exist in a multitude of competing digital formats, each vying to supplant print as the singular, unified reading platform. For example, software made by Adobe Systems, the company behind the popular Portable Document Format, includes Adobe Digital Editions, which the reader can use "to download and purchase digital content, which can be read both online and offline." The platform's features include the ability to "download and transfer books between devices" and to "search eBooks." It supports multiple languages, the ability to borrow books, printing, limited support for visually impaired readers, bookmarking, highlights, notes, and file organization.[68] The company's own competing Adobe Document Cloud reading platform includes the Free, Standard, and Pro versions of Acrobat Reader, the "global standard for reliably viewing, printing, and commenting on PDF documents."[69] Only the most expensive Pro version allows one to "create and validate PDFs to meet accessibility standards for people with disabilities." The free version does not support bookmarks or document editing. The Pro version enables readers to "redact and permanently remove sensitive information in PDFs" and to "compare two versions of a document to see what's changed."[70]

Another popular electronic book format, the Amazon Kindle reader, includes a feature called "Public Notes," which allows Kindle customers to "make public their highlights and notes" for "any other customer who follows them . . . to see."[71] Kindle's Frequently Asked Questions page further explains that if "someone you follow has highlighted a passage in a book and has turned on Public Notes for the book, you'll see that passage highlighted along with the name of the person who highlighted it." The FAQ continues to tout the platform's benefits:

> Now authors, thought leaders, passionate readers, professors and all Kindle users can opt-in to share their notes with other readers, helping friends, family members, and other Kindle users who choose to follow them to get more from their reading. If someone you follow has highlighted a passage in a book and has turned on Public Notes for the book, you'll see that passage highlighted along with the name of the person who highlighted it. You'll also see the notes that they made in the book.[72]

Google's Play Books software, to take another example, does not facilitate public notes, nor does it support book editing. It does, however, allow readers to translate words and passages and look up phrases using the company's search engine.[73]

Imagine reading the same novel on these four different platforms, four formats, four books. The experience would differ drastically in each case. What initially seems like one thing, an electronic book, falls apart under examination. The electronic book is in reality a multitude of dynamic formats. Each requires specialized strategies of reading and interpretation.

Encoded ideas about intellectual property are another stark manifestation of interplatform incompatibility. Whatever its interpretive affordances, reading software also emulates the logic of ownership. To own a book electronically means to access the bits that bring the simulation of that book into existence. At some lower level of abstraction, however, the variety of reading platforms rests on the same computational substratum. Both Amazon and Adobe books rely on the capabilities of the personal computer. This "hypermedia," as Lev Manovich has called it, lies at the base of all competing e-book formats.[74] Owning a book on that level entails the manipulation of hardware device states. A common act of epistemic disobedience, to borrow a phrase from Walter Mignolo, therefore includes accessing the book bits directly, through channels not afforded by the publisher.[75] Such acts disentangle the mechanisms of book ownership, as defined by Google or Amazon, from the book's content proper. The so-called ripping of proprietary book libraries involves reformatting individual books into other file formats, which could hypothetically enable unconstrained copying and circulation of texts. The activity need not be illicit. The extraction of plain text from a PDF file commonly constitutes the initial step in corpus-based natural language processing. Readers routinely liberate content in other ways as well: They lend books to friends, read them out loud, and make photocopies.

These examples illustrate that electronic books, unlike print, are not a single format but many. Software, governed by specific socioeconomic exigencies, determines the broader affordances of reading, sharing, and storing books. Thus a book available in North America might not be available on other continents, or it could be available elsewhere in a redacted form, its content dynamically tailored to a reader's geography. The aforementioned platforms supplant the affordances of print with a range of other, competing affordances particular to their proprietary digital document formats, which are incompatible with other formats. Furthermore, the potentialities of electronic reading change dynamically with each software update. Whereas print has remained a relatively stable medium for centuries (we have no trouble operating a several hundred years old book), digital text changes on a monthly, if not daily, basis. A careful book history of electronic formats would proceed in much shorter evolutionary stages to keep pace with the medium's rapid development.

These examples confront us with aspects of instrumental formatting: copying, analysis, and preservation. Even the lay digital reader is forced to become textually aware, to ask, after Peter Shillingsburg, why this version of the text and how? What does it mean to reproduce this text? Which physical aspects of this digital edition are crucial to interpretation and which are not? Are these marks mere artifacts of layout? Were they introduced to advertise a product? Did the author intend them to be shown this way? Do they belong to the form or content of the work?

Answers to such questions—in reading for format explicitly—involve the deconstruction, both literal and figurative, of the *textual laminate*. Whatever interpretive activity readers hope to enact at a book's surface is grounded in its deep material affordances. The conflicted properties of electronic text entail the added burden of materialist poetics. One cannot take the stability of print for granted when reading digitally. A number of agents intercede in the transformation between form and content, the inscription as information on disk and its representation as pixels on-screen. These intercessions may prove benign, as when the electronic book adjusts layout to fit a smaller

screen. Conversely, they could involve complex social mechanisms of censorship and surveillance, enacted for commercial or political purposes.

COMPOSITE MEDIA

Reading for format involves the delamination of media composites. It concerns the grammar of transformation between disparate conduits of information. Formats govern and control in the sense of shaping the encounter
between otherwise incommensurate physicalities, the hardware and the
wetware—storage, screen, and brain.[76]

Format necessitates a notion of document depth, distinct from the metaphoric uses of the word in the discussion on surface reading, where it
refers to concealed structures of meaning, literary formulas, signification, or
ideology.[77] In another, more literal sense, depth refers to the formation of
literary laminates that hold inscription in suspense between layers of glass,
plastic, liquid crystal, aluminum, iridium, and oxide.

The following case studies from the history of the Document Object
Model (DOM) illustrate format theory in practice.

EDIT was one of the first text editors, designed for the GE635 36-bit main-
frame computers in use at Bell Labs in 1968. I look to its blueprints to recover a model of digital document structure, which continues to shape most
electronic texts today. "The publication editor is divided into three related
sections," wrote Arthur Kaiman, one of the system's engineers. These included
the "facilities" for "document layout," "editing," and "printing."[78] "Layout," in
the language of EDIT, facilitates the justification, indentation, and spacing
of text. "The user types the document layout file and the text file," Kaiman
explained, and "then produces a proof or master copy of the text by printing
the text according to the directions of the layout file. The text file contains
layout marks to be interpreted by the document layout file."[79] In this schema,
text constitutes content that is meaningful only to the user, whereas "layout"
contains some elements that are meaningful to humans and others intended
for machine instruction. Crucially, "no document text may appear in the layout file," Kaiman wrote.[80] Layout in his schema asks the human editor to
distinguish between semantic and spatial units: words and their coordinates.
These two separate streams of data are then stored in two discrete locations,
in effect embodying the dichotomy between form and content (Figure 3.2).

The creators of QED, another influential early text editor (made for
the SDS-930 time-sharing system at the University of California, Berkeley)

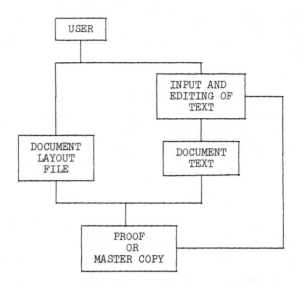

FIGURE 3.2. A schematic view of the EDIT textual composite consisting of multiple document layers. Source: Arthur Kaiman, "Computer-Aided Publications Editor," *IEEE Transactions on Engineering Writing and Speech* 11, no. 2 (August 1968): 66. © 1968 IEEE. Reprinted with permission.

similarly encouraged writers to separate the "input stream" from its layout instructions. A sequence of reserved characters was "interpreted as directives to the stream" and as "editor commands." These included sequences such as A for "append" at a specified address, D for "delete," and S for "substitute."[81] Given that control characters A, D, and S are also a part of the input stream, the writer prefaced control commands with the aptly named "control" key. Thus pressing the control key together with D would result in the deletion of the selected line. "Control characters do not have any printed characters normally associated with them," the manual explained.[82] Writers could also enter the "command mode," in which the machine interpreter recognized nothing but machine instructions. By these means, the text and layout instructions could occupy different buffers on-screen, which would then be combined for printing operations.[83]

Separate from the aims of text editors such as EDIT and QED, a text formatter was meant to arrange text spatially. To the small number of editing instructions, the formatter added instructions for typesetting: size, position, stroke width, transparency. The authors of IBM's FORMAT program, written in Fortran IV for OS/360 devices in 1968, explained that "all input to FORMAT is free-form," in that it contained "no positional constraints."[84] The FORMAT system enabled further instructions for "layout control," which included P for "begin new paragraph," T for "tab," and U for "underline." It also contained more complex "command operands" such as "Capitalize automatically," "Justify the text," and "Repeat the title on every page."[85] Finally, FORMAT had the capability of building an index, in effect listing all the unique words in any given document, along with a rudimentary facility for search, "locating text words, phrases, and strings in the input stream" (Figure 3.3).[86]

In another important paper from the history of digital text, Brian Kernighan and Joseph Ossanna described TROFF, a text processor written around 1973 for the PDP-11 output to the Graphic Systems Cat typesetter. In 1979 Kernighan modified the original program to produce output for a greater variety of typesetters. He explained that "TROFF produces its output in a device-independent form" and that its output "must be processed by a driver for that device to produce printed output."[87] The program made no ontological claims about the textual artifact. Rather, it embodied the idea of text independent of its medium and free of form. The digital writer edited text in one "virtual" location, without knowing its output in another physical one. Screens, machine memory, and pages hold inscription in different formats, which do not physically correspond to one another. For this reason, the program's designers were forced to differentiate between document

```
                              INPUT TO FORMAT                                CARD IMAGE  COMMAND OPERANDS

CTIONS STARTING WITH DIFFERENT LETTERS SPACED APART. IT IS TO BEGIN WITH THE WOR   520
         1        2    3          4       5      6         7  8  9  10    11   12  13
D "¢INDEX" AND TO CONTINUE THE REST OF THE LAYOUT OF THE DOCUMENT IN FORCE. )HLW   521     HLW
 1          2  3  4             5   6   7  8    9       10 11 12      13 14     15
2H ***10.*¢THE SEARCH ARGUMENT FOR EACH INDEX ENTRY IS TO BE THE ENTIRE ENTRY (U   522     2H
 1             2       3         4  5    6     7      8  9 10 11  12     13    14
P TO THE DOLLAR SIGN) UNDER THE CONSTRAINTS SPECIFIED ABOVE, UNLESS THE LAST CHA   523
 1  2   3      4      5     6   7           8         9       10    11  12   13
RACTER OF THE SEARCH ARGUMENT IS A PLUS SIGN. ANY PHRASE IN THE TEXT WHICH MATCH   524
        1  2    3       4      5 6 7    8     9   10     11 12 13   14      15
ES THE SEARCH ARGUMENT UP TO THE PLUS SIGN IS TO BE REGARDED AS A "HIT". A SUBST   525
 1   2      3          4  5  6    7    8    9  10 11 12      13 1415     1617
ITUTE PHRASE TO BE PRINTED IN THE INDEX MUST BE SPECIFIED. EXAMPLES: )LLW2¢T ALU   526     LLW2¢T
       1      2  3  4      5   6   7     8    9  10        11         12      13
MN+ $ALUMNI )¢T ¢ALUMNI, 53, 60 )L¢T DOG+ $DOGS )¢T ¢DOGS, 315-323 )HLLH ***11.*   527     ¢T L¢T ¢T HLLH
     1       2   3        4   5  6    7    8     9   10     11      12    13
¢THE SEARCH WILL NOT BE BASED ON THE CASE OF THE SEARCH ARGUMENT OR THE TEXT STR   528
      1      2    3   4  5    6   7   8   9  10   11     12      13 14  15   16
EAM. )H )V                                                                        529     H V
      1  2
TABS SET AT 2,30,35                                                               530
SPACING = 1 (SINGLE SPACING)                                                      531
STOP TITLE                                                                        532
NO CAPITALIZATION AUTOMATICALLY                                                   533
GO                                                                                534
)SU ¢BIBLIOGRAPHY: )U )LLLH 1.*"¢I¢B¢M ¢SYSTEM/360 ¢FORTRAN ¢I¢V ¢LANGUAGE", ¢C2   535     SU U LLLH
 1   2               3  4    5          6           7        8    9          10
8-6515, ¢SIXTH ¢EDITION, ¢I¢B¢M ¢CORPORATION, ¢PROGRAMMING ¢SYSTEMS ¢PUBLICATION   536
         1      2         3      4             5            6        7
```

FIGURE 3.3. A portion of the input stream for the layout of paper citations using FORMAT. Code is interlaced with content to control output. Source: Gerald M. Berns, "Description of FORMAT, a Text-Processing Program." *Communications of the ACM* 12, no. 3 (March 1969): 144.

content and its spatiotemporal characteristics. Some elements were to be represented in the final version, whereas others controlled representational structure and were ultimately omitted from view. For example, input machine instructions for italicized text would not themselves become visible in the output document.

More than a decade later, in reflecting on the proliferation of text editors, a group of computer scientists from the University of Washington, led by Richard Furuta, advanced the following unified theory of format: "A *document* is an object composed of a hierarchy of more primitive objects."[88] The objects are further divided into abstract or logical objects and their concrete instantiations. In this way, a chapter is made up of paragraphs and sentences, which can be rendered on pages of different dimensions. In each case the hierarchical relationship between chapters, paragraphs, and sentences persists even as the specific dimensions of a page change. A chapter in Tolstoy's *War and Peace* remains a chapter containing the same arrangement of paragraphs and sentences despite layout differences between editions. The class identifier (chapter, paragraph, sentence) thus denotes an abstract object, whereas concrete objects, in Furuta's model, occupy "one or more two-dimensional *page spaces* and represent the possible formatted images of abstract objects."[89] The concrete object gives physical shape to the instantiation of abstract universal classes.

The entirety of a document (e.g., a book) can subsequently be expressed as a hierarchical ordering of such primitive objects as words, sentences, paragraphs, and chapters. A document of a different type, say, a research paper, contains another set of primitive elements not always found in a book: footnotes and an abstract, for example. One may describe a novel in terms of an abstract succession of chapters that, in turn, encapsulate paragraphs, which contain sentences and words, which further comprise characters. These abstract units find their physical manifestation on a page. They stand in a hierarchical relationship to each other because paragraphs contain sentences, and sentences words, and not the other way around. Together, a set of primitive object classes defines more complex formats, such as letters, articles, books, and journals.[90]

The class-instance distinction gives us the means to discuss editing and formatting tasks in terms of state transformations. In this way, editing a document involves multiple transitions between abstract states, as when an author corrects spelling errors or deletes a word. Concrete-to-concrete state

transformations rearrange abstract objects in space, as when an author jus-
tifies text or changes the order of document sections (Table 3.1). Crucially
for our discussion, Furuta and colleagues defined formatting as the reification of abstract classes, for example, applying font styles. Formatting in this
sense converts what they called the "intended document" into the "visible
concrete document," according to which the abstract idea of "emphasis" in
our example is reified into the concrete representation of "bold stroke."[91]
Another typesetter might stylistically prefer to represent emphasis in italics
instead of bold letters. Both convey the same idea in visually different ways.

Document description, in Furuta's model, specifies the rules for turning
abstract objects into concrete objects. In typesetting, content and physical
text specifications are mixed together and laid out for viewing on a particular device.[92] However, the formatter does not know the exact dimensions of
the target medium in advance. One may decide to print the same document
on legal- or letter-size paper, for example. Nothing in the code guarantees
the dimensions of the visible concrete document. We are assured only of
their appropriate positioning relative to one another: that the bold text will
appear thicker than regular text, whatever the regular stroke; or that the
footnotes will appear after the main body of the text and not before, regard-
less of the layout.

One can think of other formatting operations that move in the opposite direction: from concrete to abstract. This happens in optical character
recognition (OCR) as part of a process by which images of physical pages
are converted into an intended abstract structure, the content thereby lifted
from the physical page. A text in the portable document format remains a
graphic image—a concrete, indivisible object—until it is recognized. One can
read it, of course, but it does not, from a machine's perspective, contain
abstract objects as such. Recognition implies more narrowly the transformation of images into text and shape into content. In that sense, text lies at
the innermost location within a series of nested outer containers. Lacking

TABLE 3.1. Object Transformation Types Based on the Document Object Model

Transformation	Type	Example
Abstract to abstract or concrete to concrete	Edit	Spelling correction; justify the document
Abstract to concrete	Format	Apply font; break into pages
Concrete to abstract	Recognize	Optical character recognition; page layout analysis

:S AND 1 Incremental Mod

HEORY by John H. Mulle

STEMS 20 A Unified Framev

by J. A. Brzozov

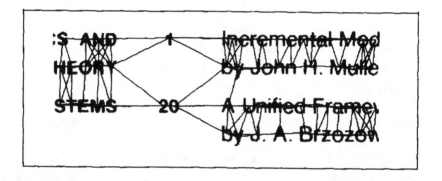

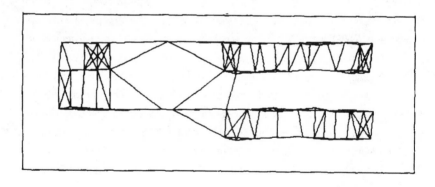

FIGURE 3.4. Format devoid of content. Researchers describe a method for extracting document structure based on the nearest-neighbor clustering of page components. Source: L. O'Gorman, "The Document Spectrum for Page Layout Analysis," *IEEE Transactions on Pattern Analysis and Machine Intelligence* 15, no. 11 (November 1993): 1164. © 1993 IEEE. Reprinted with permission.

a model of comprehension or understanding, the machine posits text as content in the sense of it being the innermost object of human recognition. Machine recognition happens only when the text is delaminated from its composite medium.

The recognition of letters does not exhaust the variety of abstract document objects gleaned from the bibliographic image. Besides letters and words, these also include paragraphs, tables, titles, and footnotes. Such arrangements are also content in some sense of the word, because they incorporate semantic rather than purely graphic units. They also could mean something to the reader. But it is also essential *where* they mean it, because the meaning of semantic elements changes depending on their location. For instance, a proper name in the author field means something distinct from other names mentioned in the body of a document. Lawrence O'Gorman, an influential researcher in the field of document image processing, called such spatial recognition at the intersection of concrete and universal "document lay-out understanding," which consists of "functional labeling of blocks . . . distinguished in some way by their physical features (such as by font size) and by the 'meaning' of the block."[93] A footnote, for example, is a block of text that gains specialized meaning in specific spatial contexts (Figure 3.4). Layout, or the arrangement of concrete objects on a page, can also contain meaningless (to humans) structures, such as the incidental rivers of empty space between words. The incidental concrete structure goes unrecognized because it does not correspond to any abstract objects in the available document object taxonomy.[94]

Finally, I am able to understand document *viewing* or *printing* as a chain of formatting operations that transform one type of concrete object, bits arranged spatially on the disk, into another type of concrete object, pixels arranged on-screen or in ink on a page. The DOM describes that chain of transformations in detail, containing in essence an intermediary map or a blueprint of the intended document. The blueprint is not itself a fully formed concrete object, however, because the machine must anticipate a number of possible two-dimensional spaces, such as pages and screens of differing sizes. The DOM therefore signifies a range of possible relationships, which can result in a number of distinct concrete possibilities: on a large screen or small, on legal- or letter-size paper. In order for text to materialize, a commitment to an actual medium must be made according to predefined rules specified in the model. In this way, a footnote that the model places "at the bottom of the page" can then be rendered one way at the bottom of a specific page of a certain size, for example, A1 (841 mm x 1,189 mm), and in another way at the bottom of another specific piece of paper of a much smaller size, A4 (210 mm x 297 mm).[95] Viewing and printing operations thus constitute a movement opposite to that of OCR. In printing a document, the machine creates a static image, which flattens out the previously stratified layers of content and visual style. Abstract objects specified by the model are then reified into a set of relationships between specific concrete objects on the page.[96]

The resulting laminate contains content appropriately formed and fused into its medium. SCRIPT and the related Generalized Markup Language (GML), developed in the late 1960s by IBM (originally for use on the CP67/CMS time-sharing system) and now at the basis of the ubiquitous XML and HTML markup languages,[97] describe a number of such text transformations that occur to "generat[e] the correct output form." In the process of formatting, SCRIPT represents the "logical topology" of text in its "canonical form" to produce an "intermediate data structure," which is then "'unfolded' all at once" by "'peeling' the data structure one level at a time."[98]

The schematics show that formatting involves more than simple application of visual style to words. Rather, formatter designers from TROFF to FORMAT describe their programs in terms of instrumental control. Richard Berns, the IBM engineer and developer of FORMAT, wrote that text control accomplishes four basic tasks: "to read the input; to interpret and convert the input as required; to keep the document flowing smoothly from line to line, column to column, and page to page, unless otherwise instructed; and to break this automatic flow as directed."[99]

The *TROFF User's Manual* analogously describes text processing in terms of accepting "lines of text interspersed with lines of format control information."[100] The TROFF and FORMAT languages are thus a species of Turing computation.[101] They interpret input mixed with machine instruction, including codes that halt the process of interpretation. Text control can involve operations such as "replace word," "make invisible," or "insert file." Commands intertwine with free-form content at the formatting level. They become apparent in the viewing stage of text processing, where the layers flatten across two-dimensional space. Formats envelop the text instrumentally. They govern the reification of abstract content models into document objects. They shape ideas in the process of becoming a thing.

The move from paper to such composite media carries with it a profound shift in the physical affordances of the everyday document. Not much space separates ink from paper. There, text lies flat, in two dimensions. What you see is truly what you get. Not so on screens connected to other drives, keyboards, and screens. Composite media extend into the third dimension, away from the reader and deep into the bowels of the machine.

For example, the Open Systems Interconnection (OSI) reference model of communication, implemented in every computer, including electronic book readers, describes no less than seven layers of communication involved in the simple act of sending an e-mail, taking notes in the margins of a networked book, or reading a newspaper online.[102] It includes:

- The Application Layer, which is concerned with the semantics of "all services directly comprehensible to the user."
- The Presentation Layer, which defines the syntax for the "representation and manipulation" of data to be transferred.
- The Physical Layer, which provides "mechanical, electrical, functional, and procedural" characteristics of communication.[103]

Apart from technical intricacy, consider the practical complexity of the onion-like composite (Figure 3.5). Whatever one designates as core content is enveloped within a multiplicity of standards, references, models, and formats, which in aggregate define the medium—the physical preconditions—of laminate text.[104]

In his book on protocols, Alexander Galloway discussed the OSI model in reference to what he calls distributed and decentralized networks of control.[105] The OSI standard is distributed to be sure, although to what extent it is decentralized is a matter of some debate. Like a good soldier, each device in a network of textual machines internalizes dozens if not hundreds of protocols that enable the system to function seamlessly as a whole, in the way, for example, that our mobile phones connect to multiple transmitting towers with minimal loss of connectivity. Communication protocols and DOM hierarchies are densely consolidated to ensure such interoperability. They are governed by international bodies such as the World Wide Web Consortium, an organization that encompasses national as well as corporate bureaucracies.[106]

Stretched between the sites of storage and projection—screens and solid-state drives—the inscription travels along a lengthy pipeline of protocols, undergoing arbitrary transformations throughout. On one device that pipeline

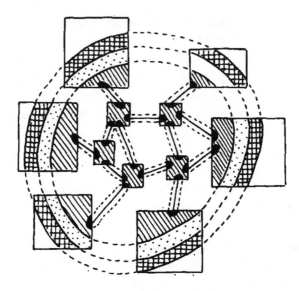

FIGURE 3.5. The onionlike layering of the OSI network envelops most connected devices. Readers apprehend digital text at the outermost "application" layer. Mechanisms of governance and control are within and beyond user comprehension. Source: J. D. Day and H. Zimmermann, "The OSI Reference Model," *Proceedings of the IEEE* 71, no. 12 (December 1983): 1335. © 1983 IEEE. Reprinted with permission.

may extend just a few inches, connecting disk storage to a screen. On a networked device that pipeline can stretch across continents, spanning widely divergent regions of legal and administrative governance. The data that make up an electronic book may be stored on a server on the other side of the country. Readers encounter that elongated protocol stack from without, on the periphery of the stratified structure. For example, when paging through an electronic book, itself usually an OSI-compliant device, readers access only the outputs emanating from the application layer and then only at the exposed "window" level of the DOM. What you see is far less than what you get. The perceived content exposes only a small fraction of the underlying formal topology. Reader interaction happens at the superficial application layer, which at best conceals the dynamics of deep text transformation. In more acute cases, access to deep structures is made illicit outright.

SMART CONTRACTS

Text at a document's surface is subject to professional rules of conduct governing practices of sharing, quotation, and attribution. The North American reader may further be familiar with those portions of U.S. copyright law that codify these practices more formally, entailing a degree of legal accountability. For example, U.S. Code Title 17 extends "exclusive rights" to "owner[s] of copyright" of "literary" works. Such rights include the ability to "reproduce," "prepare derivative works," "distribute copies," "perform," and "display . . . publicly."[107] The easy reproducibility of digital media has eroded the efficacy of legal copyright restrictions. The work of art in the age of digital reproduction has lost much of its already tenuous hold on the material substratum.[108] Photocopiers, desktop printers, inexpensive digital storage drives, and peer-to-peer file-sharing networks reduce the barriers to mass copying and the dissemination of media.[109]

The response from the film, game, music, and publishing industries has been to shift mechanisms of copyright enforcement from legal structures into the medium itself. Charles Clark, a prominent British copyright attorney, wrote, "The answer to the machine is in the machine."[110] He went on to argue for the efficacy of copyright enforcement at the device level and to propose that the International Standards Organization (ISO), the same legislative body responsible for maintaining the DOM and the OSI specifications, create standards for digital rights management.[111] As an example of how such hard-coded copyright enforcement could work in the real world, Clark refers to the Copyright in Transmitted Electronic Data (CITED) report, which imagines books and music players attached to a kind of a tamper-proof "meter" for the collection of "commercially viable material." To prevent "unauthorized" use of copyrighted material, the report proposes a device that would include "a tamper-proof software module which acts rather like indestructible tachometers installed on long-distance coaches and lorries, recording everything that happens to the copyrighted or commercially valuable material. . . . The basic idea is to link the 'valuable material' of intellectual property to a specific piece of software and hardware."[112]

The emergence of such embedded contractual enforcement mechanisms can be subsumed under the broader idea of smart contracts. In his seminal article "Formalizing and Securing Relationships on Public Networks," Nick Szabo explained that "smart contracts combine protocols, user interfaces, and promises expressed via those interfaces, to formalize and secure relationships over computer networks."[113] Clark, CITED, and Szabo were instrumental in the rise of smart contracts in the 1990s. The technology was meant to redress the fading efficacy of legal copyright protections.[114]

```
1234567890010001021727300161000232
```

```
RIFF0›☐☐AVILISTÔ☐☐☐hdrlavih8☐☐☐j☐☐☐ŠW☐☐C\A
D☐☐☐☐i☐☐☐☐☐☐☐☐☐☐☐☐P☐☐@☐☐☐ŏ☐☐☐☐☐☐☐À
¶☐☐w☐☐☐☐☐V6LISTt☐☐☐strlstrh8☐☐☐vidscvid☐☐☐œ
Š☐☐☐{{{hhhhhh{☐n—œŠ—œŠhm[hhh☐☐☐™{{{|sd¢™Š
Ç¡°¡"8=+☐☐☐☐☐☐☐☐☐☐☐☐☐☐{☐n☐"☐'¡§⁻☐{☐nqvd
☐☐☐½½½————hhh{☐n'§¡"{☐n—œŠ¡"qvd{☐n,,‰owm[,,
‰ow¡"—œŠ'§Ç¡°¡"{{{{{{™DĐĐaaaaaaUÚÚ½
```

```
1234567890010001021727300161000232RIFF0›
☐☐AVILISTÔ☐☐☐hdrlavih8☐☐☐j☐☐☐ŠW☐☐C\AD☐☐
☐☐i☐☐☐☐☐☐☐☐☐☐☐☐P☐☐@☐☐☐ŏ☐☐☐☐☐☐☐À¶☐☐
w☐☐☐☐☐V6LISTt☐☐☐strlstrh8☐☐☐vidscvid☐☐☐œŠ☐☐
☐{{{hhhhhh{☐n—œŠ—œŠhm[hhh☐☐☐™{{{|sd¢™ŠÇ¡°¡"
8=+☐☐☐☐☐☐☐☐☐☐☐☐☐☐{☐n☐"☐'¡§⁻☐{☐nqvd☐☐☐
½½½————hhh{☐n'§¡"{☐n—œŠ¡"qvd{☐n,,‰owm[,,‰ow¡¦
"—œŠ'§Ç¡°¡"{{{{{{™DĐĐaaaaaaUÚÚ½
```

```
1234567890010001021727300000000000000
☐☐☐☐☐☐☐☐☐☐☐☐☐☐☐☐☐☐☐☐☐☐☐☐☐☐☐☐☐☐☐☐☐☐☐☐
☐☐☐☐☐☐☐☐☐☐☐☐☐☐☐☐☐☐☐☐☐☐☐☐☐☐☐☐☐☐☐☐☐☐☐☐
☐☐☐☐☐☐☐☐☐☐☐☐☐☐☐☐☐☐☐☐☐☐☐☐☐☐☐☐☐☐☐☐☐☐☐☐
☐☐☐☐☐☐☐☐☐☐☐☐☐☐☐☐☐☐☐☐☐☐☐☐☐☐☐☐☐☐☐☐☐☐☐☐
☐☐☐☐☐☐☐☐☐☐☐☐☐☐☐☐☐☐☐☐☐☐☐☐☐☐☐☐☐☐☐☐☐☐☐☐
☐☐☐☐☐☐☐☐☐☐☐☐☐☐☐☐☐☐☐☐☐☐☐☐☐☐☐☐☐☐☐☐☐☐☐☐
☐☐☐☐☐☐☐☐☐☐☐☐☐☐☐☐☐☐☐☐☐☐☐☐☐☐☐☐½
```

FIGURE 3.6. Control code is injected into the document (an audio-video file) "to comply with predetermined conditions of usage." The resulting "data object" is further encrypted to deter circumvention, thus obscuring the mechanisms of control. The pictured technology, from a patent by Benson and colleagues, is central to the idea of smart contracts, that is, documents capable of enforcing contractual compliance, in this case, between users and content owners. Source: Greg Benson, Gregory H. Urich, and Christopher L. Knauft, "Method and System for Managing a Data Object so as to Comply with Predetermined Conditions for Usage," Patent US8479305 B1, filed October 1, 1998, issued July 2, 2013, sheet 10; quotes on p. 1.

U.S. patent 5845281, for example, proposed a method and system for managing a data object so that it would comply with "predetermined conditions for use." The text reads:

> The data object owner may want to have permanent secure control over how, when, where, and by whom his property is used. Furthermore, he may want to define different rules of engagement for different types of users and different types of security depending on the value of particular objects. The rules defined by him shall govern the automated operations enabled by data services and networking. The owner may also want to sell composite objects with different rules governing each constituent object.[115]

A data object in this case stands for any media content, from books to music, video, or software. Similar to the CITED mechanism, it embodies a contract between the object's true "owner," that is, the copyright holder, and its "user," that is, its reader, viewer, or listener, who has only a temporary and limited possession of the object. The medium sets the conditions of use predetermined by its creator (or, more likely, distributor). Crucially, the smart document can enforce the rules of engagement without revealing them to the reader. The codified contract is in fact tamper–proof; it is resistant to physical access and therefore interpretation.[116]

The managed data object described in the patent concatenates content and control code (Figure 3.6). For example, if one meant to transmit a string of numbers, "123456789 . . . ," by means of the smart object, the numbers would be mixed with instructions for access—how, when, where, and by whom. These instructions would then be encrypted, that is, made inaccessible, to prevent tampering. Decryption would require a special proprietary key available only to the manufacturer of the composite. By such means, the seemingly innocuous text control layer that we saw emerge in the 1960s, originally used to specify layout, was extended to carry legal instruments responsible for enforcing contractual obligations, extracting economic value, and ensuring compliance.

Increased security, as always, involves a compromise with freedom. To the extent that a document's control data are legible to the interpreter, they are also open to "abuse and circumvention." Encryption and other physical tamper proofing mechanisms are essential features of a smart contract. The reader must be prevented from accessing deep structure. The 1998

Digital Millennium Copyright Act (DMCA) and similar initiatives criminalize the circumvention of such systems, even when the reader owns the smart document outright.[117] The smart document limits reading practice to the manner specified. Readers hold no rights to comprehension at depth. Unsanctioned modes of access and interpretation are deemed illicit. Contrast this with the ownership of a conventional paper document, which places no such restrictions on the reader.

The DMCA in particular stipulates that "no person shall circumvent a technological measure that effectively controls access to a work protected under this title."[118] The letter of the law further specifies that to "circumvent a technological measure" means in this case "to descramble a scrambled work, to decrypt an encrypted work, or otherwise to avoid, bypass, remove, deactivate, or impair a technological measure, without the authority of the copyright owner."[119] A technological measure that "effectively controls access" is further defined as a measure that "in the ordinary course of its operation, requires the application of information, or a process or a treatment, with the authority of the copyright owner, to gain access to the work."[120] For a literary scholar this means that, when encountering a text on a digital device, reading sometimes *must* limit itself to surface phenomena. An attempt at reading for depth—to discover the implemented terms of a smart contract, for example—may carry censure or reprobation.[121]

The short-lived legal history of the DMCA anticircumvention provisions is already littered with ambiguous case law, which the Electronic Frontiers Foundation believes to have the effect of "stifl[ing] a wide array of legitimate activities," "chilling free expression and scientific research," "jeopardiz[ing] fair use," and "imped[ing] competition and innovation."[122] Several incidents relate to the practice of literary interpretation directly. In one case a security researcher exploring the activity of censorship filters on public library computers was forced to seek DMCA exemption from the Librarian of Congress.[123] In another case a Russian programmer speaking at a security conference was jailed and detained for several months for developing software that converts Adobe electronic book files into PDFs using a process that could potentially remove embedded digital rights management protections.[124] Finally, in 2005 the Agfa Monotype Corporation took Adobe Systems to court in a dispute over Adobe's Acrobat Free Text tool, which allowed users to "change text annotations using Plaintiff's TrueType fonts" without a license.[125]

In each case the interpretive activity that readers usually take for granted—the ability to take notes, to mine data from a corpus, or to access information on a public computer—is brought into question. These cases set a dangerous precedent that could be used to further limit the efficacy of reading digital texts.

The lack of access to deep structure exposes a glaring problem at the heart of smart contracts. The spirit of contract law demands explicit consent on the part of both parties. In the language of English common law, contracts involve promises that are "manifestation[s] of intention" and adopt an "external or objective standard for interpreting conduct."[126] By extension, contracts between authors, publishers, and readers must exist in an objectively verifiable manner that is mutually accessible for analysis.

Smart contracts purposely obscure the terms of such agreements. Readers lack the physical means to examine their obligations or to analyze interests embedded within the document's encrypted, tamper-proof layer. Worse yet, when presented with documents that describe the terms of a smart contract in writing—the terms of service, for example—readers have no way to verify their appropriate concrete form. The written terms of service could in any detail differ from their software- or hardware-enforced implementation. Moreover, on networked devices code is routinely updated independently of the originating accord. A book purchased on a proprietary platform may become unavailable at a later date; private information related to a reader's search habits may be shared with third parties; screen aids for the visually impaired that "read" the text out loud may suddenly cease to function. The affordances of the medium and its terms of engagement can change with every software update.

The idea of tamper-proof smart contracts stands in stark opposition to a tradition of contract law—and textual interpretation more generally—tied to models of deliberation and consent that involve expressed, mutual, and uncoerced forms of acquiescence. The contract is meaningless if its implementation is enacted beyond scrutiny in the form of hidden, encrypted, or otherwise purposefully illegible code.

The impact of smart contracts on the practices of reading, writing, and literary analysis is potentially immense. In the language of the DMCA, the electronic book is not a book at all but a "copyrighted work" composed of "content" and "standard technical measures," such as "copy control technology."[127] An essay in the Yale Journal of Law and Technology explains that "while e-books and their print counterparts embody essentially identical content," they differ considerably from a transactional standpoint:

> Books are tangible goods that can be owned, sold, and passed on without express limitation—the Uniform Commercial Code (U.C.C.) governs their sale, while copyright law protects their content. But despite appearances, Kindle e-books are not, according to Amazon, sold at all: they are distributed under restrictive license terms, similar to downloaded software.[128]

Under these conditions, literature is forced to relinquish its ontological status of the indeterminate. The DMCA arrests the movement of texts between the concrete and the universal. Reified into objects, books morph into devices—no longer lasting and transcendent but rather immanent and contingent—firmly determined by their instrumental affordances. The literary device adapts itself to the situation—to the needs of both the owner and the user of the book—by hidden logics.

For a textual critic such instability of medium means analysis cannot be confined to reading for surface meaning alone. How can close or distant reading practices persist when the reading device reconfigures a text dynamically to fit individual taste, mood, or politics?[129] Or when it simply prevents access to some of the content? Formats shape the very structure of interpretation. The seemingly innocuous formatting layer contains the essence of control over the mechanisms of representation. Long a marginal concept in literary theory, formatting is therefore central to the contemporary practice of computational poetics. More than embellishment, formats govern the interface between meaning and matter, thought and page. Formats embody governance. Some prevent simple copy and paste operations. Others are used to censor and surveil.

CHAPTER 4

> RECONDITE SURFACES

The scholar Wendy Hui Kyong Chun views magnetic storage as an "enduringly ephemeral" medium that "creat[es] unforeseen degenerative links between humans and machines."[1] If the floating-gate transistor where my text now lives can be called enduring and ephemeral, I can call my liquid crystal display where the text shows itself fading and persistent.[2] This is not to suggest that digital text transcends its material contexts, only to observe that it drifts from surface to surface, beyond the field of vision, in ways that erode trust its general permanence. If we are to dwell on surfaces, I do not know where to look: the screen or the floating gate.

Where does text reside? We know the answer for print: It is there, stuck to a page. Computational media complicate our ability to situate inscription. We point at screens without certainty; their surfaces remain in flux. They are sites of fleeting projections that emanate from hidden storage media. Digital text passes through multiple filters and transformations on the way to the surface. Although we observe the inscription on-screen only, it embodies a complicated figure, stretched across at least two sites. The sign strains and splits between the configuration of magnetic pulse and circuit state at one end and in the phases of liquid crystal on-screen at the other. Both locations afford distinct constraints to interpretation. Familiar actions such as reading and writing imply distinctly differing operations depending on the surface.

Thus when Michael Heim refers to the "ephemeral quality" of the electronic text or when Pamela McCorduck describes it as "impermanent, flimsy, malleable, [and] contingent," they are correctly identifying a facet of digital inscription at its site of projection.[3] McCorduck tells the story of a rabbinate court that, when interpreting a law that prohibits observant Jews from erasing God's name, deemed that words on a screen do not constitute writing and therefore sanctioned their erasure.[4]

Conversely, when such scholars as Johanna Drucker, Katherine Hayles, or Matthew Kirschenbaum respond to Heim and company with hardened materialism, they are also rightly locating properties of digital inscription at the site of its archival immanence. The two schools of thought disagree because they speak neither of the same phenomenon nor at the same site. One group highlights ephemeral, transcendent qualities of the projected word; the other foregrounds the "uniquely indelible nature of magnetic storage,"[5] "drives, tracks, and disks," "fundamental physical supports," and "material substrates of computing."[6] Screen and hard drive partition the sign between surface and depth, projection and archive. At the site of projection one speaks of texts that are—I have kept a list of adjectives when reviewing the literature—ephemeral, shimmering, electric, flimsy, contingent, malleable, impermanent, flowing, transcendent, ghostly, and radiant. At the archival site scholars describe inscription as enduring, solid, persistent, permanent, indelible, hard, immanent, lasting, palpable, and concrete.

The seeming immateriality of digital media has real-world effects; for example, the costs of replication plummet. Computational text can be copied effortlessly, with minimal cost and near-perfect fidelity. Hyperreproducibility of this sort was unthinkable for most of the twentieth century. Lowered costs of copying further reduce barriers to access and conveyance. Symbols that adhere lightly to their medium are easy to store and transport. Public knowledge works like search engines and massive open online encyclopedias subsequently claim to organize all the world's knowledge. Such projects unfold by the logics of immateriality: total archives, big data, and universal accessibility.[7] When the sign appears to weigh nothing, one imagines its weightless aggregate, available immediately and everywhere. The perceived weightlessness of text also has other side effects. A text that adheres lightly to its medium is difficult to contain. Bureaucracies struggle to restrict it in transit.

Despite appearances, text cannot be unmoored from its material foundations. Rather, the sign splits in two, with one half arising visibly, a weightless and apparent screen simulation, and the other half remaining opaque, etched into hefty and hidden material contingencies. The material substrates of computational text likewise carry real-world consequences. First and foremost, they are hidden from view. Drives and tapes reside inside boxes made of plastic and aluminum. If only because they carry electric current and are thus flammable, they are regulated. They contain heavy and rare metals and are often hazardous to touch or ingest. They become toxic when discarded. Flash memory cards, USB sticks, solid-state storage devices, and magnetic disk drives contain circuitry to prevent unauthorized access and to resist tempering. Inside, text intertwines with machine internals, sealed hermetically and hermeneutically in a way that resists human interpretation. The laminate is not fully compatible with humans: machine literature, a hazard.

Form and content lie flat in print. Print interfaces are paper thin. Ink adheres to paper in a way that pixels do not to screens. Textual fissure complicates traditional structuralist distinctions between form and content. Digital inscription occupies at least two distinct sites, each entailing drastically different affordances for interpretation. If we were to untangle the tightly wound coil of the circuit, we would find ample distance between hard drive and screen. Some readers measure that distance in inches, as when reading documents locally, stored on their own computer; other measure it in miles when reading documents remotely, stored on faraway cloud servers. Where print is flat, digital inscription is stratified across multiple incongruent planes.[8]

How did this multiplicity come to be? And what effect does it have on the life of the mind? In this chapter I make visible the gap between projected sign and archived inscription. I begin by providing a historical account of a letter's passage from paper to pixel. My narrative arc proceeds in three stages, which I summarize here and expand on later.

First, with the advance of telecommunications, we observe an emerging divide between human-readable text and machine-readable code. Removable storage media such as ticker tape and punch cards embodied a machine instruction set meant to actuate mechanisms, which in turn produced human-legible inscriptions. Unintelligible (to humans without special training) control codes were thereby mixed with plain text, the content of communication. Inscription split between sites of storage, which archive an expanded machine instruction set, and projection, which displays human alphabets.

Second, whereas ticker tape and punch cards were legible to the naked eye, magnetic tape storage made for an inscrutable medium, inaccessible without instrumentation. In the 1950s and 1960s machine operators worked blindly, using complicated workarounds to verify equivalence between input, storage, and output. Writing began to involve multiple typings or printings. Specialized magnetic reading devices were developed to make inscription more apparent and to establish a correspondence between input, storage content, and output of entered text. The physical properties of electromagnetic inscription have placed it, in practice, beyond human sense.

Finally, the appearance of cathode-ray tube (CRT) displays in the late 1960s restored a measure of legibility lost to magnetic storage media. The sign reemerged on-screen. Crucially, it framed a simulacrum of archived inscription. Typing a word on a keyboard produced one sort of a structure on tape or disk and another on-screen. The two relate contingently, without necessary equivalence. The lay reader has no means to ensure the correspondence between visible trace and stored mark. An opaque black box intercedes between simultaneous acts of writing and reading what one has written.

A number of textual machines illustrate this history. Three mechanisms mark the journey: the Controller patented by Hyman Goldberg in 1911; the Magnetic Reader introduced by Robert Youngquist and Robert Hanes in 1958; and, for a lack of a better name, the Time Fob, introduced by Douglas Engelbart in 1968.

Goldberg's device was designed to bridge the rift between human and machine alphabets in that it was a mechanical punch card that could move minds and levers alike. His Controller traced an alphabet understood by both humans and machines. Youngquist and Hanes attempted to give human operators a glimpse into the hidden world of magnetic polarities and electric charges. Engelbart's Time Fob finally belongs to what Peter Denning, a prominent computer scientist, calls the third generation of computer systems. It is an assemblage of storage, input, and output technologies that continue to shape our encounter with texts.[9] Together, these devices tell a story of a fissure at the heart of our contemporary textual predicament.

PROGRAMMABLE MEDIA

To begin, we need some background on telegraphy. The turn of the twentieth century was a pivotal period in the history of letters. It saw the languages of people and machines enter the same mixed communications stream. Artificial fixed-length alphabets, such as the Baudot code, paved the way for the automation of language. The great variety of human scripts was reduced to a set of discrete and reproducible characters. So regularized, type was converted into electric signal, sent over great distances, and used to program machines remotely. These expanded textual affordances came at a price of legibility. Initially, a cadre of trained machine operators was required to translate human language into machine-transmittable code. Eventually, specialized equipment automated this process, removing humans from the equation. Machines could communicate with other machines without human intervention, triggering a chain of cascading events that reverberate today, from algorithmic financial trading to the war between junk mail (spam) generators and their filters.

The advent of programmable media (punch cards and ticker tape) coupled human-compatible alphabets with machine control code.[10] Reduced to a discrete and reliably reproducible set of characters, natural languages could be conveyed as electric signals. In such a transitive state, language became more mobile than ever before. It was transmitted efficiently across vast distances. The mechanization of type also introduced new control characters into circulation that were capable of affecting machine state changes at a distance. Initially, such state changes were simple: "begin transmission," "sound error bell," or "start new line." With time, they developed into what we now know as programming languages. Content meant for people was being routinely intermixed with code meant to control machine devices. Such early remote capabilities were quickly adapted to control everything from radio stations to advertising billboards and knitting machines.[11]

Language compressed and pushed through the wires underwent a number of transformations. Donald Murray, the inventor of the popular Murray telegraph alphabet, conceived of telecommunications in terms of time and space. Advancing a self-professed "metaphysics of telegraph signalling alphabets," he described spatial writing symbols that "appeal to the eye" and temporal "telephonic" signals that "appeal to the ear."[12] Paradoxically, space signals (e.g., words on a billboard) occupy little space but persist in time: "For instance, a signboard may extend over 10 feet and 100 years."[13] By contrast, time signals dilate in space, whereas they contract in time: "A Morse signal in a wire may extend over half a second" and 500 miles, Murray wrote.[14]

Physical structures such as sentences and paragraphs that appear on a page take shape in the reader's mind. Unlike a painting, a paragraph cannot be perceived wholly and at once; it must be reassembled mentally.

The printed word extends in time. By contrast, the electric signal is nearly instantaneous. However, it claims space in transmission. A perceptive reader of electric letters reconstructs a sign's spatial characteristics along with its temporal characteristics. The digital inscription gains a new dimension, which extends away and beyond a reader's field of vision. Elongation in space compounds elongation in time to complicate the tactics of reading.

The emergent physics of electric language presented new technological and administrative challenges. As telegraphy spanned national boundaries, agreements were needed to standardize conventions for equipment and message encoding. These were handled on a regional, ad hoc basis until 1865, when the International Telegraph Union (ITU) was created. The International Telegraph Conference (ITC), held in Paris between March 1 and May 17, 1865, adopted, among other things, the use of a modified Morse code character set, containing thirty-three Latin letters (including characters from the French, German, and Spanish alphabets), ten numbers (0–9), fourteen punctuation marks (including a fraction bar), and ten control codes (including "end of service," "attention," and "error").[15] In specifying the conversion tables for the Morse alphabet, the 1865 ITU rules required a silence equal to three dots (or one dash) to indicate a space between two letters and a silence equivalent to four dots (later changed to seven) to indicate a gap between words.

Although Morse code is commonly imagined as a binary code, it is technically a ternary notation, because it uses three elements: dots, dashes, and silences. Morse code encapsulates characters into strings of variable length, for example, one dash for *t* and six dots for the number 6. The transmission of variable-length codes consequently required the presence of human operators who could translate from natural to machine language using keys, which when depressed vertically would complete the electric circuit to produce a signal. A key interfaced between disparate conduits—paper and wire—to translate between human- and machine-meaningful encodings.

Writing in 1929 for the journal *American Speech*, Hervey Brackbill preserved some of the specialized language associated with Morse code culture: "Morse telegraphy is commonly referred to as a 'game,' and the operator 'works a wire.'" Operators tapping keys used "bugs," which where insectlike machines that had "long slender levers and springs." Bugs had trade names such as Lighting Bug, Gold Bug, and Cootie (for a small model).[16]

Operators using straight keys achieved speeds upward of 25–30 words per minute, limited by the shortest possible length of the smallest transmitted unit (a dot), fixed by the American and International Morse Code conventions to $1/24$ of a second in duration.

At the time, companies like Vibroplex began manufacturing semiautomatic keys, which made use of horizontal switches capable of emitting a rapid succession of dots to one side of the action and dashes to the other.[17] A semiautomatic bug was said to "run away" when adjusted for too high a speed. Vibroplex keys would also greatly alter the "fist," or the operator's individual transmission style, by which telegraphers could be previously recognized. They allowed for speeds approaching 50 words per minute when not following the minimum signal length specifications.[18] Despite such improvements, Morse code was showing its age. Although the convention stipulated a fixed length, the actual length of silences between meaning-carrying units varied greatly with the vagaries of transmitting media. Cross-talk between wires and weather interference were common; communicating in Morse code still required a human operator for efficient ciphering and deciphering. In the long chain of time-sensitive transformations between the message and its recipient, the human posed a limiting factor.

Telegraph operators working a "hand sender" often developed partial paralysis in their wrists or arms. The condition was commonly known as "glass arm."[19] Senders were called "hams" or "bums" when they "fell down," or made frequent errors.[20] To "put someone under the table" in sender's lingo was to transmit faster than a receiver could transcribe. The "reader" was "burnt up" when he fell behind. He had to "break," or interrupt, the sender to ask for repetition.[21] To "paste" someone was to deliberately burn him up.[22]

The 1908 ITC, held in Lisbon, ratified two additional alphabet standards for international use: Hughes and Baudot. Both were developed in response to the limitations of Morse code and allowed for fully autonomous telegraph operation. The Hughes telegraph, an 1855 design modification of the 1846 American Royal E. House model, was a capricious machine that relied on a tuning mechanism to transmit individual characters. It was inspired by the player piano and even looked like one, complete with a keyboard and rotating drum. Its sending device struck a tone that, when transmitted by electric current, initiated the rotation of a similar drum in the receiving apparatus "at the pleasure of the distant operator."[23] The length of time between the initial synchronization signal and the struck chord corresponded to a letter, which the machine then printed to tape using a letter wheel. Hughes referred to his invention as a "Compound Magnetic and Vibrating Printing Instrument," a name that hints at its fragility.[24] When the sending and receiving drums fell out of sync, the message became impossible to decipher. Precise coordination between the various drums and their operators was therefore of paramount importance.

The number and size of telegraph cables further limited the system's capacity to carry information. Independent developments in communication technology led to a range of techniques for sharing the same wire to send multiple messages, known as multiplexing. These fell into two categories: time-division modulation and pulse-amplitude modulation.[25] Pulse-amplitude modulation involved filling the available space (bandwidth) with simultaneous signals of different types. Imagine someone speaking loudly and quietly at the same time into the same channel. In this way, all the loud messages could be sorted to one side and all the quiet ones to the other side which would effectively utilize the whole sonic spectrum.[26] Initially, pulse-amplitude modulation was difficult to implement. Cross-channel noise and device sensitivity hampered reliable reception and decoding across multiple simultaneous wave frequencies.

Emile Baudot, among others, noticed that the prevailing Morse and Hughes telegraph systems also failed to make full use of the *time* allotted for message transmission. Hughes telegraphs in particular relied on the use of long silences, which could have been condensed to improve bandwidth capacity. Baudot-type time multiplexers used synchronized rotating mechanisms at the sending and receiving ends (Figure 4.1). These mechanisms distributed units of time among multiple operators. For example, one operator could send messages at the top of the minute and the other at the bottom. In this way, receivers could sort messages based on their time signatures: all those sent at the top of the minute would go into one pile, and all those sent at the bottom would go into another. A duplex printing telegraph, of the Murray type, involved a complicated synchronization device, known as the distributor, that was capable of orchestrating two distinct streams of transmission along the same channel. By taking turns to transmit to the regular tolling of a tuning bell, two operators could send separate messages along the same channel. The receiving machine would then sort the messages based on their time signatures.[27]

It was important to maintain unison in such multiplexed systems. Time-shared device operators had to know when it was their turn to type. The

MULTIPLE PRINTING TELEGRAPH

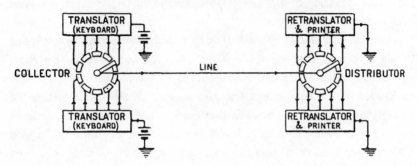

FIGURE 4.1. Schema for a "multiple printing telegraph," used to send multiple messages at different time intervals along a single channel (line). Synchronization between the two devices was crucial for transmission. Source: Donald Murray, "Setting Type by Telegraph," *Journal of the Institution of Electrical Engineers* 34, no. 172 (May 1905): 574.

Baudot multiplexer used time, or cadence, tapper mechanisms to indicate turns. In some devices the keyboards would lock to prevent out-of-turn input. In a quadruplex system, up to four operators could engage in an intricate dance of fingers, keys, tappers, and signals, synchronized by the rotation of the telegraph distributor.

Synchronization was also needed to decipher Morse code transmissions, to better distinguish non-meaning-carrying silence (the receiver is turned off) from meaning-carrying silence (the receiver pauses between signals). Telegraph operators had to agree on a unit of measure, a duration of silence, to differentiate between dots and spaces between words, which was indicated by silences of a different length. When two devices fell out of sync or if communication lagged for some reason, the coherence of the message faltered. Sending and receiving machines had to be tuned to a cadence of common information exchange. The system of operators, transmitters, and receivers was, in aggregate, tuned to a specific but arbitrary rhythm by which certain messages made sense only in particular (also arbitrary) units of time. In early telegraphy these units of time were slower than natural human time, enough so for the operator to remain idle. Later systems increased the pace to a rhythm beyond natural human abilities of comprehension, to a point where human operators could no longer decipher signals without machine assistance. In the language of wiremen, bugs were running away with the whole game. A human operator examining wire signals directly would find a jumble of data. This, in fact, is a decent provisional definition of data: information beyond human time, not amenable to unmediated interpretation.

Hundreds of alphabet systems vying to displace Morse code were devised to speed up automated communications. These evolved from variable-length alphabets such as Morse and Hughes codes, to fixed-length alphabets such as Baudot and Murray codes. The systematicity of the signal—always the same length, always at the same time—shifted text encoding further away from natural human languages, which rely on affect and variation, toward artificial languages, which prioritize other attributes, such as consistency and reproducibility.

The discovery of binary arithmetic belongs, in part, to Gottfried Leibniz, who, influenced by hexagrams of the *I Ching*, articulated his own system in his 1979 *Explication de l'arithmétique binaire*.[28] Francis Bacon deserves credit for articulating some of the earliest examples of a fixed-length binary code. In the sixth book of his *De augmentis scientiarum*, an encyclopedic treatise on the "partition of sciences," Bacon mentioned a "highest degree of cipher" that could signify "all in all" (*omnia per omnia*).[29] He proceeded to describe a "fivefold" "bi-literarie" alphabet that encoded each letter of the English language using a five-character string of a's and b's. The letter A, became aaaaa, B became aaaab, C aaaba, and so on to Z, rendered into babbb. Unlike other known cipher systems, all of Bacon's characters took up exactly five spaces. He wrote:

> Neither is this a small matter. These Cypher-Characters have, and may per-forme: For by this *Art* a way is opened, whereby a man may expresse and signifie the intentions of his minde, at any distance of place, by objects which may be presented to the eye, an accommodated to the eare: provided those objects be capable of a twofold difference only; as by Bells, by Trumpets, by Lights and Torches, by the report of Muskets, and any instruments of like nature.[30]

Writing more than two centuries before electric telegraphy, Bacon eloquently described its essence, which lay in expressing and signifying the human mind at a distance.

The fixed-length property of Bacon's cipher, later implemented in the 5-bit Baudot code, signaled the beginning of the modern era of serial communications.[31] The Baudot and Murray alphabets were designed with automation in mind.[32] Both did away with the "end of character" signal that separated letters in Morse code. Signal units were to be divided into letters by count, with every five codes representing a single character. Temporal synchronization was unnecessary given the receiver's ability to read a message from the beginning. A character became a unit of space divisible by 5.

The Murray code was more compact than Morse and especially more economical than Hughes, which, in the extreme, used up to fifty-four measures of silence to send a signal representing double quotes.[33] The signal for "zero" in Morse code occupied twenty-two measures. By contrast, all Baudot and Murray characters were a mere five units in length, with the maximum of ten used to switch the receiving device into "figure" or "capital letter" states, for a total of ten units (Figure 4.2).[34]

Fixed-length signal alphabets drove the wedge further between human and machine communication. Significantly, the automated printing telegraph decoupled information encoding from its transmission. Fixed-length encoding of messages could be done in advance, with more facility and in volume. Prepared messages could then be fed into a machine without human assistance. In 1905 Donald Murray wrote that the "object of machine telegraphy [is] not only to increase the saving of telegraph wire . . . but also to reduce the labour cost of translation and writing by the use of suitable machines."[35] Baudot and Murray codes were not only shorter but also simpler and less error-prone and thus resulted in less complicated and more durable devices.

With the introduction of mechanized reading and writing techniques, telegraphy diverged from telephony to become a means for truly asynchronous communication. It displaced signal transmission in time as it did in space. The essence of algorithmic control, amplified by remote communication devices, lies in its ability to delay execution; a cooking recipe, for example, allows novice cooks to follow instructions without the presence of a master chef. Similarly, delayed communication could happen in absentia, according to predetermined rules and instructions. A message could activate a machine that prints and another that trades stocks and another that replies with a confirmation.

A new generation of printing telegraphs was programmed using removable storage media, similar to the way player pianos were programmed to play

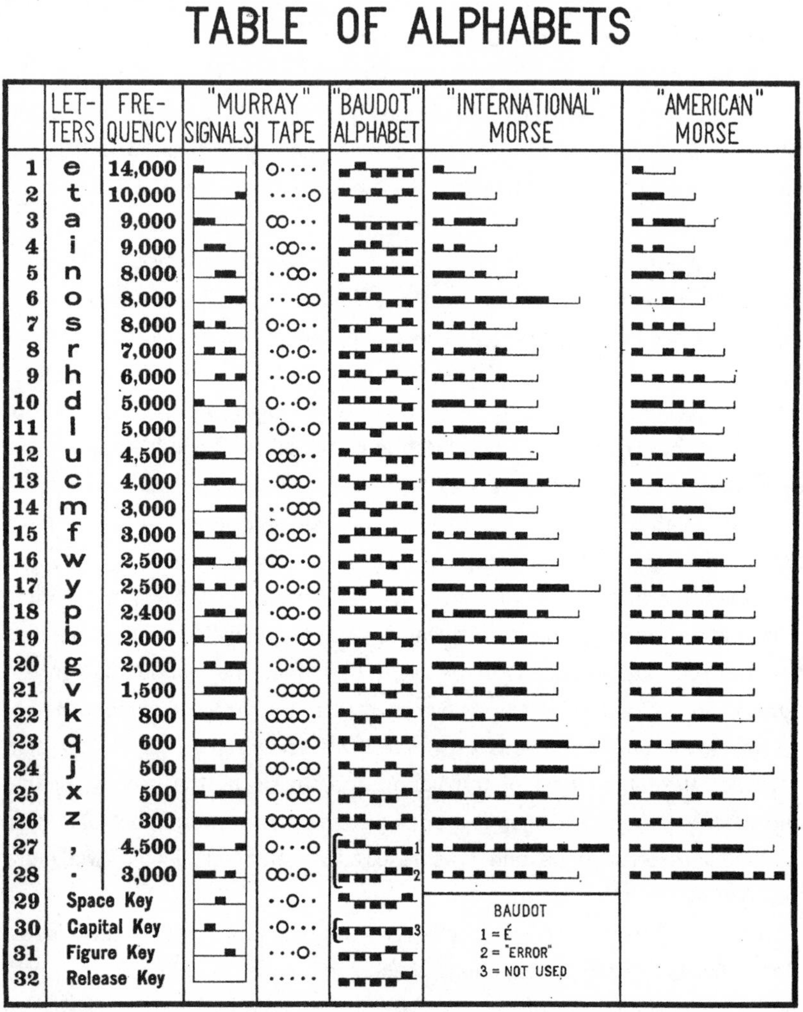

TABLE OF ALPHABETS

LET-TERS	FRE-QUENCY	"MURRAY" SIGNALS	"BAUDOT" TAPE	"BAUDOT" ALPHABET	"INTERNATIONAL" MORSE	"AMERICAN" MORSE
1 e	14,000		O····			
2 t	10,000		····O			
3 a	9,000		OO···			
4 i	9,000		·OO··			
5 n	8,000		··OO·			
6 o	8,000		···OO			
7 s	8,000		O·O··			
8 r	7,000		·O·O·			
9 h	6,000		··O·O			
10 d	5,000		O··O·			
11 l	5,000		·O··O			
12 u	4,500		OOO··			
13 c	4,000		·OOO·			
14 m	3,000		··OOO			
15 f	3,000		O·OO·			
16 w	2,500		OO··O			
17 y	2,500		O·O·O			
18 p	2,400		·OO·O			
19 b	2,000		O··OO			
20 g	2,000		·O·OO			
21 v	1,500		·OOOO			
22 k	800		OOOO·			
23 q	600		OOO·O			
24 j	500		OO·OO			
25 x	500		O·OOO			
26 z	300		OOOOO			
27 ,	4,500		O···O	[1]		
28 .	3,000		OO·O·	[2]		
29 Space Key			··O··			
30 Capital Key			·O···	[3]		
31 Figure Key			···O·			
32 Release Key			·····			

BAUDOT
1 = É
2 = "ERROR"
3 = NOT USED

FIGURE 4.2. A comparison of fixed- and variable-width encodings: Baudot, Murray, and Morse alphabets. Source: William B. Vansize, "A New Page-Printing Telegraph," *Transactions of the American Institute of Electrical Engineers* 18 (January 1901): 23.

music by means of music rolls. Just as perforated music rolls decoupled music making from its live performance, programmable media decoupled inscription from transmission. In both cases, one could strike keys now, only to feel the effects of their impact later. Programmable media conserved the logic of desired effects for later execution. Decoupled from its human sources, that logic could then be compressed and optimized for speed and efficiency. Prepared ticker tape and punch cards were fed into a mechanism for transmission at rates far exceeding the possibilities of hand-operated Morse telegraphy.

Besides encoding language, the Baudot schema left space for several special control characters. The character space was therefore expanded by switching the receiving mechanism into a special control mode in which every combination of five bits represented an individual control character, instead of a letter. In this manner, human content and machine control became intertwined and began to occupy the same spectrum of communication.

By the 1930s devices variously known as printer telegraphs, teletypewriters, and teletypes displaced Morse code telegraphy as the dominant mode of commercial communication. A 1932 U.S. Bureau of Labor Statistics report estimated a more than 50 percent drop in Morse code operators between 1915 and 1931. Morse operators referred to teletypists on the sending side as "punchers" and those on the receiving side as "printer men."[36] The printer men responsible for assembling pages from ticker tape were called "pasters" and sometimes, derisively, as "paperhangers."[37] Teletype technology automated this entire process, rendering punchers, pasters, and paperhangers obsolete. Operators could enter printed characters directly into a machine, using keyboards similar to typewriters, which, by that time, were widely available for business use. The teletype would then automatically transcode the input into transmitted signal and then back from signal onto paper on the receiving end.

As Bacon's early writings on the language arts suggest, the roots of telegraphy lie in cipher making and cryptography. It is no surprise, then, that the encoding of human languages for machine use was intimately connected to wartime, diplomatic, and otherwise clandestine communications. The seemingly innocuous problem of machine translation was therefore inextricable from questions of access and legibility: Who gets to understand the encoded message and when? To comprehend the effects a message would have in transmission, one had to understand its encoding.

For example, the Final Protocol to the Telegraph Regulations, ratified in Madrid in 1932 by the governments of more than seventy countries, included a special provision delineating the difference between transmitting plain and secret language. The protocols grouped secret languages into "code" and "cipher" categories. Plain language was defined as words that present "an intelligible meaning in one or more of the languages authorized for international telegraph correspondence, each word and each expression having the meaning normally assigned to it in the language to which it belongs."[38] By contrast, code language was defined as "composed either of artificial words, or real words not used in the meaning normally assigned to them in the language to which they belong and consequently not forming intelligible phrases."[39]

The terms of the convention were binding. Codes were not permitted to contain more than five bits per character and were charged, by contrast with plain text, at six-tenths of the agreed tariff rate. Upon request, senders were required to "produce the code from which the text or part of the text of the telegram has been compiled."[40] Otherwise, the language was considered a secret cipher, defined as "groups or series of Arabic figures with a secret meaning."[41] Participants agreed to accept and pass telegrams in plain language through their jurisdictions. They were not obliged, however, to accept or help deliver secret messages.

Machine code thus occupied a gray area between plain text and cipher. Theoretically, it was considered intelligible only when its compilation sources were available to the transmitter. Without its sources it became equivalent to secret communication. In practice, the proliferation of encodings and machine instructions had the effect of selective illiteracy. Telegraph operators carried with them multiple cheat sheets, small cards that reminded them of each system's particularities. Telegraphy reintroduced a pre-Lutheran problem of legibility into human letters.

To speak in telegraph was to learn arcane encodings, which required specialized training. A number of failed communication schemas consequently attempted to bridge the rift between human and machine alphabets. "You must acknowledge that this is readable without special training," Hymen Goldberg wrote in the patent application for his 1911 Controller.[42] The device was made "to provide [a] mechanism operable by a control sheet which is legible to every person having sufficient education to enable him to read." In an illustration attached to his patent, Goldberg pictured a "legible control

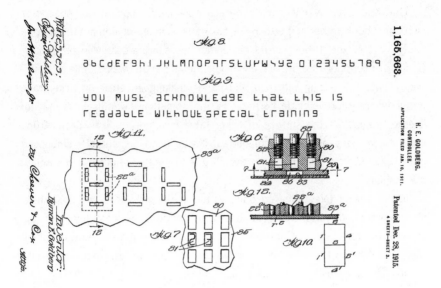

FIGURE 4.3. Goldberg's control cards. Machine language and human language coincide on the same plane. The perforations that actuate levers can also be read "without special training," in contrast to other text encodings. Source: Hyman Eli Goldberg, "Controller," Patent US1165663 A, filed January 10, 1911, issued December 28, 1915, sheet 3; quote on p. 1.

sheet . . . in which the control characters are in the form of the letters of the ordinary English alphabet."[43] Goldberg's perforations did the "double duty" of carrying human-readable content and mechanically manipulating machine "blocks," "handles," "terminal blades," and "plungers."[44] Unlike other schemas, messages in Goldberg's alphabet could be "read without special information," effectively addressing the problem of code's apparent unintelligibility (Figure 4.3).[45]

The inscription remained visible at the surface of Goldberg's control sheet, as a perforated figure punched through the conduit. Whatever challenges punch cards and ticker tape presented for readers, these were soon complicated by the advent of magnetic tape.

TEXTUAL LAMINATES

"Historically unforeseen, barely a thing, software's ghostly presence produces and defies apprehension," Wendy Chun wrote in her *Programmed Visions*, an influential monograph that continues to shape the field of software studies.[46]

One could hardly call early programmable media ephemeral. Anecdotes circulate about Father Roberto Busa, an early pioneer of computational philology, who in the 1960s carted his punch cards around Italy in his truck.[47] Codified inscription, before its electromagnetic period, was fragile and unwieldy. Just like writing with pen and paper, making an error on ticker tape entry required cumbersome corrections and sometimes wholesale reentry of lines or pages. On the surface of ticker tape, inscription still made a strong commitment to paper. Once committed, it was nearly immutable. Embossed onto ticker tape or punched into the card, early software protruded through the medium.

In the age of telegraphy encoding stood in the way of code comprehension. Morse code and similar alphabet conventions at least left a visible mark. They were legible if not always intelligible. Once the machine encoding was identified (as Morse, Baudot, or Murray), it could be translated back into natural language using a simple lookup table.

Magnetic tape changed the commitment between inscription and medium. It provided a temporary home, where the word could be altered before being embossed into paper. At the 1967 Symposium on Electronic Composition in Printing, Jon Haley, staff director of the Congressional Joint Committee on Printing, spoke of "compromises with legibility [that] had been made for the sake of pure speed in composition and dissemination of the end product."[48] A new breed of magnetic storage devices allowed for the manipulation of words in "memory," on a medium that was easily erased and rewritten. A magnetic charge adhered lightly to tape surface. This light touch gave the word its newfound ephemeral quality. But it also made inscription illegible. In applications such as law and banking, where the fidelity between input, storage, and output was crucial, the immediate illegibility of magnetic storage posed a considerable engineering challenge. After the advent of teletype but before cathode-ray screens, machine makers used a variety of techniques to restore a measure of congruence between invisible magnetic inscription and its paper representation. What was entered had to be verified against what was stored.

The principles of magnetic recording were developed by Oberlin Smith (among others), an American engineer who also filed several patents for inventions related to weaving looms. In 1888, inspired by Edison's mechanical phonograph, Smith made public his experiments with an "electrical method" of sound recording using a "magnetized cord" (cotton mixed with hardened steel dust) as a recording medium. These experiments were later put into practice by Valdemar Poulsen of Denmark, who patented several influential designs for a magnetic wire recorder.[49]

Magnetic recording on wire or plastic tape offered several distinct advantages over mechanical perforation. Tape was more durable than paper; it could fit more information per square inch; and it was reusable. "One of the important advantages of magnetic recording," Marvin Camras, a physicist with the Armour Research Foundation, wrote in 1948, "is that the record may be erased if desired, and a new record made in its place."[50] Most early developments in magnetic storage were aimed at sound recording. The use of magnetic medium for data storage did not take off in earnest until the 1950s.[51] However, early developers of electromagnetic storage and recording technology already imagined their work in dialogue with the long history of letters (and not just sound). In an address to the Franklin Institute on December 16, 1908, Charles Fankhauser, the inventor of the electromagnetic telegraphone, said:

> To transport human speech over a distance of one thousand miles is a wonderful achievement. How much more wonderful, then, is the achievement that makes possible . . . its storage at the receiving end, so that the exact sentence, the exact intonation of the voice, the exact timbre, may be reproduced over and over again, an endless number of times.[52]

Comparing magnetic recording to the invention of the Gutenberg press, Fankhauser added:

> It is my belief that what type has been to the spoken word, the telegraphone will be to the electrically transmitted word. . . . As printing spread learning and civilization among the peoples of the earth and influenced knowledge and intercourse among men, so I believe the telegraphone will influence and spread electrical communication among men.[53]

In that speech Fankhauser also lamented the evanescence of telegraph and telephone communications. The telephone, he rued, fails to preserve "an authentic record of conversation over the wire."[54] Fankhauser imagined his telegraphone being used by

> the sick, the infirm, [and] the aged. . . . A book can be read to the sightless or the invalid by the machine, while the patient lies in bed. Lectures,

concerts, recitations—what one wishes, may be had at will. Skilled readers or expert elocution teachers could be employed to read into the wires entire libraries.[55]

Anticipating the popularity of twenty-first-century audio formats like podcasts and audiobooks, Fankhauser spoke of "tired and jaded" workers who would "sooth [themselves] into a state of restfulness" by listening to their favorite authors.[56] Fankhauser saw his "electric writing" emerge as "clear" and "distinct" as "writing by hand," "an absolutely legal and conclusive record."[57] Whereas written language was lossy and reductive, Fankhauser hoped that electromagnetic signals would hold high fidelity to the original.

In 1909 Fankhauser thought of magnetic storage primarily as an *audio* format that would combine the best of telegraphy and telephony. Magnetic data storage technology did not mature until the 1950s, when advances in composite plastics made it possible to manufacture tape that was cheaper and more durable than its paper or cloth alternatives. The state-of-the-art relay calculator, commissioned by the Bureau of Ordinance of the Navy Department in 1944 and built by the Computation Laboratory at Harvard University in 1947, still made use of standard-issue telegraph "tape readers and punchers" adapted for computation with the aid of engineers from Western Union Telegraph Company.[58] It was equipped with a number of Teletype Model 12A tape readers and Model 10B perforators, using 11/16-inch-wide paper tape, partitioned into "five intelligence holes," where each quantity entered for computation took up thirteen lines of code.[59] Readers and punchers were capable of running 600 operations per minute. Four Model 15 Page-Printers were needed to compare printed characters with the digits stored on the ticker tape print register. The numerical inscription in this setup was therefore already split between input and output channels, with input stored on ticker tape and output displayed in print.

The Mark III Calculator, which followed the Computation Laboratory's earlier efforts, was also commissioned by the Navy's Bureau of Ordinance. It was completed in 1950. Its organization or "floor plan" ("system architecture," we would say today) did away with punch cards and ticker tape, favoring instead an array of large electromagnetic drums coupled with reel-to-reel tape recorders. The drums, limited in their storage capacity, revolved at much faster speeds than tape reels. They were used for fast, temporary internal storage. A drum's surface was coated with a "thin film composed of finely divided magnetic oxides of iron suspended in a plastic lacquer, and applied to the drums with an artist's air brush."[60] The Mark III Calculator used twenty-five such drums, rotating at 6,900 rpm, each capable of storing 240 binary digits.

In addition to the fast "internal storage" drums, the floor plan included eight slow "external storage" tape-reader mechanisms. Tape was slower than drums but cheaper. It easily extended to multiple reels, approaching the architecture of an ideal Turing machine, which called for tape of infinite length. In practice, tape was in limited supply, merely long enough to answer the needs of military computation. Unlike stationary drums, tape was portable. Operators could prepare tape in advance, in a different room, at the allotted instructional tape preparation table. The information on tape would then be synced with and transferred to a slow drum. In the next stage the slow drum accelerated to match the higher rotating speeds of the more rapid internal storage drums, at which point the information was transferred again for computation. Mark III was further equipped with five printers "for presenting computed results in a form suitable for publication." The printers were capable of determining the "number of digits to be printed, the intercolumnar and interlinear spacing, and other items related to the typography of the printed page."[61] In reflecting on these early "supercomputers," one imagines the pathway of a single character as it crosses surfaces, through doorways and interfaces, gaining new shapes and temporalities with each transition.

Electromagnetic signals had to be transcoded into binary numerical notation. To transfer characters onto tape, operators sat at a numerical tape preparation table, yet another separate piece of furniture. Data were stored along two channels, running along the tape's length. Operators entered each number twice, first into channel A and then into channel B. This was done to prevent errors, because operators worked blindly, unable to see whether the intended mark registered properly upon first entry. An error bell would sound when the first quantity did not match the second, in which case an operator would reenter the mismatched digits. To "ensure completely reliable results," one of the five attached Underwood electric teletypes could further be used to print all channels and confirm input visually.[62]

Before screens, the potential for incongruence between recondite data formats and their apparent representation posed a significant problem. In a 1954 patent, filed on behalf of Burroughs Corporation, Herman Epstein and Frank Innes described an "electrographic printer" involving an "electrical method and apparatus for making electrostatic images on a dielectric surface by electrical means which may be rendered permanently visible" (Figure 4.4).[63] The electrographic printer anticipated the modern photocopier in that it proposed to use dusting inks to reveal the static charge. Rather than encoding its data into another representation, such as the Baudot code, the printer traced human-legible letter shapes directly onto tape. A small printing head would convert binary input into a five-by-seven grid of electromagnetic charges, rendering the English alphabet. Such magnetic shapes were then made apparent by combining them with a "recording medium" that had the "correct physical properties

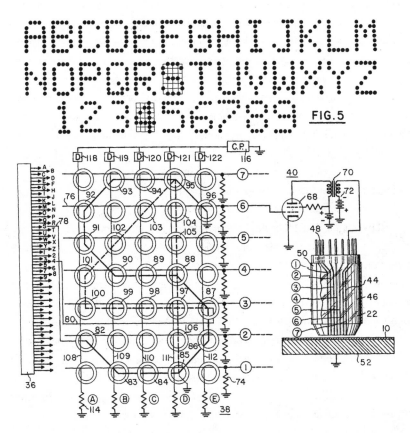

FIGURE 4.4. Another attempt to bypass encoding in favor of drawing magnetic images in the shape of a human alphabet. The diagram illustrates "images formed by a negative voltage" in a device that prefigures modern photocopy machines. Source: Herman Epstein and Frank Innes, "Electrographic Printer," Patent US3012839 A, filed July 15, 1954, issued December 12, 1961, sheet 3; quote on p. 5.

to adhere to the electrostatic latent images."[64] A light dusting of powder ink would reveal the otherwise imperceptible magnetic inscription. Tape and paper configurations could thus achieve a measure of literal analogy.

Advances in magnetic storage found their way into small businesses and home offices a decade later. In 1964 IBM combined magnetic tape (MT) storage with its Selectric line of electric typewriters (ST). Selectric typewriters were popular because they were ubiquitous, relatively inexpensive, and could be used to reliably transform a keyboard's mechanical action into binary electric signal. Consequently, they became the common input interface in a number of early computing platforms.[65] Because it combined electromagnetic tape storage with keyboard input, the MT/ST machine could be considered one of the first personal "word processing" systems. Built on a simpler architecture than its supercomputer cousins, the machine used a single tape reading and writing mechanism. An advertisement in the *American Bar Association Journal*, circa 1966, called it the "$10,000 typewriter," "worth every penny." Where typists previously had to stop and erase every mistake, the IBM MT/ST setup allowed them to "backspace, retype, and keep going." Mistakes could be corrected in place, on magnetic tape, "where all typing is recorded and played back correctly at incredible speed."[66]

Despite its advantages, MT/ST architecture inherited the problem of legibility from its predecessors. Information stored on tape was still invisible to the typist. In addition to being encoded, electric alphabets were written in magnetic domains and polarities, which lay beyond human sense.[67] One had to verify input against stored quantities to ensure correspondence. But the stored quantity could be checked only by transforming it into yet another inscription. Like Wittgenstein's broken hermeneutic circuit, magnetic tape was insufficient to close the loop. To verify what was stored, an operator was forced to redouble the original inscription, in a process that was prone to error, because storage media could not be accessed directly without specialized instruments.[68]

Users of the Mark III Calculator were therefore asked to input quantities several times over. Another class of solutions involved making the magnetic mark more apparent. For example, Youngquist and Hanes described their 1962 magnetic reader as a

> device for visual observation of magnetic symbols recorded on a magnetic recording medium in tape or sheet form. Magnetic recording tape is often

criticized because the recorded signals are invisible, and the criticism has been strong enough to deny it certain important markets. For example, this has been a major factor in hampering sales efforts at substituting magnetic recording tape and card equipment for punched tape and card equipment which presently is dominant in automatic digital data-handling systems. Although magnetic recording devices are faster and more trouble-free, potential customers have often balked at losing the ability to check recorded information visually. It has been suggested that the information be printed in ink alongside the magnetic signals, but this vitiates major competitive advantages of magnetic recording sheet material, e.g., ease in correction, economy in reuse, simplicity of equipment, compactness of recorded data, etc.[69]

The magnetic reader consisted of two hinged plates (Figure 4.5). Youngquist and Hanes proposed to fill its covers with a transparent liquid that would host "visible, weakly ferromagnetic crystals." When sandwiched between the plates, a piece of magnetic tape incited the crystal medium, which would in turn reveal a signal's "visibl[e] outline."[70]

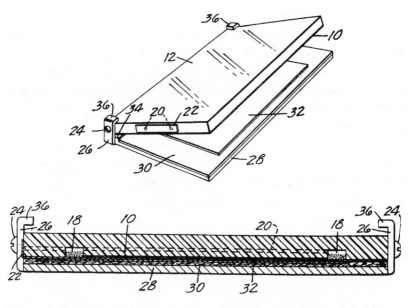

FIGURE 4.5. "Magnetic recording tape is often criticized because the recorded signals are invisible." Youngquist and Hanes imagined a solution: a device that physically reveals the magnetic inscription. Source: Robert Youngquist and Robert Hanes, "Magnetic Reader," Patent US3013206 A, filed August 28, 1958, issued December 12, 1961, sheet 1; quote on p. 1.

I have yet to find an account of a magnetic reader in use. The problem they were designed to solve remained: Tape and paper were fundamentally incompatible media. Data plowed into rows on the wide plains of a broad sheet had to be replanted along the length of a narrow plastic groove. To aid in that transformation, the next crop of IBM Magnetic Selectric typewriters added a composer control unit, designed to preserve some of the formatting lost in transition between paper and plastic. It could change margin size or justify text in memory. The original IBM Composer unit justified text (its chief innovation over the typewriter) by asking the operator to type each line twice: "one rough typing to determine what a line would contain, and a second justified typing."[71] After the first typing, an indicator mechanism calculated the variable spacing needed to achieve proper paragraph justification. The formatting and content of each line required separate input passes to achieve the desired result in print.

IBM's next-generation Magnetic Tape Selectric Composer (MT/SC) built on the success of its predecessors (see Table 4.1 for the evolution of the MT/ST line). It combined a Selectric keyboard, magnetic tape storage, and a Composer format control unit. Rather than having the operator type each line twice, the MT/SC system printed the entered text twice: once on the input station printout, which showed both content and control code in red ink, and a second time as Composer output, which collapsed the layers into the final typeset copy. Output operators still manually intervened to load paper, change font, and include hyphens. The monolithic page unit was thereby further systematically deconstructed into distinct strata of content and formatting.

Like other devices of its time, the IBM MT/SC suffered from the problem of indiscernible storage. Error checking of input using multiple printouts was aided by a control panel consisting of eleven display lights. The machine's

TABLE 4.1. Generations of the IBM Selectric Line of Word Processors

Model	Year	Technologies
Selectric Typewriter	1961	Electric, binary code, replaceable font element
MT/ST	1964	Magnetic tape, Selectric typewriter
Selectric Composer	1966	Justification, spacing, typesetting
MT/SC	1968	Magnetic tape, Selectric typewriter, Selectric Composer
MC/ST	1969	Magnetic card, Selectric typewriter

manual suggested that the configuration of lights be used to peek at the underlying data structure for verification.[72]

In an attempt to achieve ever greater congruence between visible outputs and data archived on a magnetic medium, IBM briefly explored the idea of storing information on magnetic cards instead of tape. On tape, information had to be arranged serially, into one long column of codes. Relative arrangement of elements could be preserved, it was thought, on a rectangular magnetic card, which resembled paper in its proportions. The 1968 patent "Data Reading, Recording, and Positioning System" describes a method for arranging information on a storage medium "which accurately positions each character recorded relative to each previous character recorded."[73] In 1969 IBM released a magnetic card–based version of its MT/ST line, dubbed the MC/ST. Fredrick May, whose name often appears on word-processing-related patents from this period, would later reflect that a "major reason for the choice of a magnetic card for the recording of medium was the simple relationship that could be maintained between a typed page and a recorded card." The card approximated a miniature page, making it a suitable "unit of record of storage for a typed page" (Figure 4.6).[74] Although it offered a measure of topographic analogy between tape and paper, the "mag card" was short-lived partly because of its limited storage capacity, capricious feeding mechanism, and persistent inscrutability.[75] [fig4.6]

FIGURE 4.6. An opaque slate: the IBM Mag Card II, introduced in 1969 for use in the Magnetic Card/Selectric Typewriter (MC/ST). Unlike tape, cards preserved the topography of print. A simple analogy could be achieved between document elements on card and page. Source: F. T. May, "IBM Word Processing Developments," *IBM Journal of Research and Development* 25, no. 5 (September 1981): 743. Image scanned by Pointillist, Wikimedia Commons.

The structure of textual artifacts—from a simple leaflet to a novel in multiple volumes—has remained remarkably stable since the invention of movable type. One rarely finds a sentence that spans several paragraphs, for example. Nor would a contemporary reader expect to find pages of different sizes in the same tome. Long-standing historical conventions guide the production of printed text. Likewise, semantic and decorative units on a page exist within a strict hierarchy. No book of serious nonfiction, for example, would be typeset in a cursive font. Unless something out of the ordinary attracts their attention, readers tend to gloss the inconsequential details of formatting in favor of content. The material contexts of a well-designed book fade from view during reading.

For a few decades after the advent of magnetic storage media but before the arrival of screen technology, the sign's outward shape disappeared altogether. It is difficult to fathom now, but at that time—after the introduction of magnetic tape in the 1960s but before the widespread advent of CRT displays in the 1980s—typewriter operators and computer programmers manipulated text blindly. Attributes such as indent size and justification were decided before ink was committed to paper.

In the 1980s an engineer reflected on the 1964 MT/ST's novelty: "It could be emphasized for the first time that the typist could type at 'rough draft' speed, 'backspace and strike over' errors, and not worry about the pressure of mistakes made at the end of the page."[76] The MT/SC further added a programmable control unit to separate inputs from outputs. Final printing was then accomplished by

> mounting the original tape and the correction tape, if any, on the two-station reader output unit, setting the pitch, leading, impression control and dead key space of the Composer unit to the desired values, and entering set-up instructions on the console control panel (e.g., one-station or two-station tape read, depending on whether a correction tape is present; line count instructions for format control and space to be left for pictures, etc.; special format instructions; and any required control codes known to have been omitted from the input tape). During printing the operator changes type elements when necessary, loads paper as required, and makes and enters hyphenation decisions if justified copy is being printed.[77]

The tape and control units intervened between keyboard and printed page. The "final printing" combined "prepared copy," "control and reference codes," and "printer output."[78] Historical documents often mention three distinct human operators for each stage of production: one entering copy, one specifying control code, and one handling paper output. These three could hypothetically work in isolation from one another. The typist would see copy; the typesetter would enter formatting and control codes; and the printer would output the interpolated results.

Researchers working on these early IBM machines considered the separation of print into distinct strata a major contribution to the long history of writing. One IBM consultant went so far as to place the MT/SC at the culmination of a grand "evolution of composition," which began with handwriting and continued to wood engraving, movable type, and letterpress: "The IBM Selectric Composer provides a new approach to the printing process in this evolution." He concluded by heralding the "IBM Composer era," in which people would once again write books "without the assistance of specialists."[79] Inflationary marketing language aside, the separation of the sign from its immediate material contexts and its new composite constitution must be considered a major milestone in the history of writing and textuality.

The move from paper to magnetic storage had tremendous social and political consequences for the republic of letters. Magnetic media reduced the costs of copying and disseminating the word, freeing it, in a sense, from its more durable material confines. The affordances of magnetic media—its very speed and impermanence—created the illusion of light ephemerality. Yet the material properties of magnetic tape itself continued to prevent direct access to the site of inscription. Magnetic media created the conditions for a new kind of illiteracy, which divided those who could read and write at the site of storage from those who could only observe its aftereffects passively, at the shimmering surface of archival projection.

The discussed schematics embody textual fissure in practice. The path of a signal through the machine leads to a multiplicity of inscription sites. These are not metaphoric but literal localities that stretch the sign across manifold surfaces. Whereas pens, typewriters, and hole punches transfer inscription to paper directly, electromagnetic devices compound them obliquely into a laminated aggregate. The propagation of electric signal across space continues to require numerous phase transitions between media: from one channel of tape to another, from tape to drum, from a slow drum to a fast one, and from drum and tape to paper. On paper the inscription remains visible in circulation; it disappears from view on tape, soon after key press.

Submerged beneath a facade of opaque oxide, inscriptions thicken and stratify into laminates.

LEGIBILITY

The contemporary textual condition took its present form in the late 1960s. Computers subsequently changed in terms of size, speed, and ubiquity. However, they have retained the same essential architecture to this day: programmable media, electromagnetic storage, screen.

The addition of a screen to the floor plan could finally address the problem of electromagnetic legibility. In the first stage of its digital development, language became "programmable." Fused with machine instruction, it could be used to automate devices remotely. Language itself became automated. Coupled with electromagnetic storage in the second stage, programmable media were freed, to an extent, from their immutable contexts. They were "lighter," faster, more portable, and therefore more iterant and malleable than print or punch. Ferric oxide became the preferred medium for digital storage: memory. That new memory layer was also beyond the reach of human senses. It was difficult to access and manipulate mentally.

Screens added a much needed window onto the abstraction. On-screen, machine memory could be mapped and represented visually, obviating the need for double entry or frequent printouts. Screens interjected to mediate between input and output. They flattened stratified complexity to facilitate use. Textual laminates were still invisible in part. Screen simulacra restored the appearance of a single surface, as they obscured the dynamics of mediation.

On December 9, 1968, Douglas Engelbart, then the primary investigator at the NASA- and ARPA-funded Augmentation Research Center at the Stanford Research Institute, gave what later became known as the "mother of all demos" to an audience of roughly 1,000 or so computer professionals attending the Joint Computer Conference in San Francisco.[80] The flier advertising the event read as follows:

> This session is entirely devoted to a presentation by Dr. Engelbart on a computer-based, interactive, multiconsole display system which is being developed at Stanford Research Institute under the sponsorship of ARPA, NASA and RADC. The system is being used as an experimental laboratory for investigating principles by which interactive computer aids can augment intellectual capability. The techniques which are being described will, themselves,

be used to augment the presentation. The session will use an on-line, closed circuit television hook-up to the SRI computing system in Menlo Park. Following the presentation remote terminals to the system, in operation, may be viewed during the remainder of the conference in a special room set aside for that purpose.[81]

The demo announced the arrival of almost every technology prophesied by Vannevar Bush in his influential 1945 *Atlantic* essay, "As We May Think." During his short lecture, Engelbart presented functional prototypes of the following: graphical user interfaces, video conferencing, remote camera monitoring, links and hypertext, version control, text search, image manipulation, windows-based user interfaces, digital slides, networked machines, mouse, stylus, and joystick inputs, and "what you see is what you get" (WYSIWYG) word processing.

In his report to NASA, Engelbart described his colleagues as a group of scientists "developing an experimental laboratory around an interactive, multiconsole computer-display system" and "working to learn the principles by which interactive computer aids can augment the intellectual capability of the subjects."[82] CRT displays were central to this research mission. In one of many patents that came out of his "intellect augmentation" laboratory, Engelbart pictured his "display system" as a workstation that combines a typewriter, a CRT screen, and a mouse. The schematics show the workstation in action, with the words "NOW IS THE TIME FOB" prominently displayed on-screen. The user was evidently in the process of editing a sentence, likely to correct the nonsensical "fob" into "for" (Figure 4.7).[83]

Reflecting on the use of visual display systems for human–computer interaction, Engelbart wrote, "One of the potentially most promising means for delivering and receiving information to and from digital computers involves the display of computer outputs as visual representations on a cathode ray tube and the alteration of the display by human operator in order to deliver instructions to the computer."[84] The first subjects to read and write on-screen reported feeling freedom and liberation from paper. An anonymous account included in Engelbart's report offered the following self-assessment:

> 1B2B1   "To accommodate and preserve a thought or
> piece of information that isn't related to the work
> of the moment, one can very quickly and easily

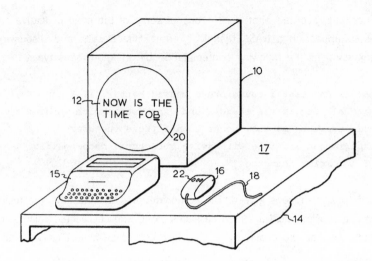

FIGURE 4.7. Schematics for Engelbart's display system. The arrangement of keyboard, mouse, and screen will define an epoch of human–computer interaction. Source: Douglas Engelbart, "X-Y Position Indicator for a Display System," Patent US3541541 A, filed June 21, 1967, issued November 17, 1970, sheet 1.

> insert a note within the structure of a file at such
> a place that it will neither get in the way nor get
> lost.
>
> 1B2B2 "Later, working in another part of the file,
> he can almost instantly (e.g. within two seconds)
> return to the place where he temporarily is storing
> such notes, to modify or add to any of them.
>
> 1B2B3 "As any such miscellaneous thought develops,
> it is easy (and delightful) to reshape the structure
> and content of its discussion material.[85]

Writing, which this typist previously perceived as an ordered and continuous activity, subsequently was performed in a more disjointed way. The typist could delight in shaping paragraphs that more closely matched her mental activity. Screens restored some of the fluidity of writing that typewriters denied. Writers could pursue two thoughts at the same time, documenting both at different parts of the file as one would in a notebook. Not constrained by the rigidity of a linear mechanism, they moved around the document at will.

Engelbart recorded what must count as some of the most evocative passages to appear in a NASA technical report. His "Results and Discussion" section contains the following contemplation by an anonymous typist:

```
1B4 "I find that I can express myself better, if I can
make all the little changes and experiments with wording
and structure as they occur to me. [Here the user
experiments a little with using structural decomposition
of a complex sentence.]⁸⁶
```

A decomposition follows indeed. The author deviates dramatically from technical writing conventions. Numbered passages along with unexpected enjambment heighten the staccato quality of prose, which attains an almost lyrical quality:

```
1B4A "I find that I write faster and more freely,

    1B4A1 "pouring thoughts and trial words onto the
    screen with much less inhibition,

    1B4A2 "finding it easy to repair mistakes or wrong
    choices

        1B4A2A "so while capturing a thought I don't
        have to inhibit the outpouring of thought and
        action to do it with particular correctness,

    1B4A3 "finding that several trials at the right
    wording can be done very quickly

        1B4A3A "so I can experiment, easily take a look
        and see how a new version strikes me—and often
        the first unworried attempt at a way to express
        something turns out to be satisfactory, or at
        least to require only minor touch up.

    1B4A4  "Finding that where I might otherwise
    hesitate in search of the right word, I now pour out
    a succession of potentially appropriate words,
    leaving them all there while the rest of the
    statement takes shape. Then I select from among
    them, or replace them all, or else merely change the
    list a bit and wait for a later movement of the
    spirit.⁸⁷
```

When input and output coincide in time, as they do on paper, mistakes are costly. Once inscribed, the sign gains permanence; it becomes difficult to emend. An eraser can help remove a layer of physical material. Alternatively, writers use white ink to restore the writing surface. Engelbart's anonymous typist reports the feeling of freedom from such physical commitment. She can simply backspace and start over. Words come easily because there are no penalties for being wrong. Virtual space seems limitless and endlessly pliable.

The feeling of material transcendence—the ephemeral quality of digital text—is tied directly to the underlying physical affordances of electromagnetic storage. Screens expose the pliability of the medium, where erasure is effortless. Content can be addressed in memory and copied at the stroke of a key. The numbered paragraphs suggest a novel system for recollection. Data storage units become, in a sense, mental units. I am struck by the distinctly phenomenological quality of technical description: The editor does not merely resemble a page; it is, for the writer, a newly discovered way of thought that changes the writer's relation not only to text but also to her own thoughts. The highly hierarchical and blocky paragraph structure, along with its repetitive refrain ("finding" and "I find that"), gives the prose a hypnotic drive forward. The cadence matches the reported experience of discovery.

The writer continues:

1B4B "I find that

    1B4B1 "being much more aware of

        1B4B1A "the relationships among the phrases of a sentence,

        1B4B1B "among the statements of a list,

        1B4B1C "and among the various level and members of a branch,

    1B4B2 "being able

        1B4B2A "to view them in different ways,

        1B4B2B "to rearrange them easily,

        1B4B2C "to experiment with certain special portrayals,

1B4B2C1 "not available easily in unstructured
data

1B4B2C2 "or usable without the CRT display,

1B4B3 "and being aware that

1B4B3A "I can (and am seeking to) develop still
further special conventions and computer aids

1B4B3B to make even more of this available and
easy,

1B4B4 "all tend to increase

1B4B4A "my interest and experimentation

1B4B4B "and my conviction that this is but a
peek at what is to come soon.[88]

The passages appear too contrived to be spontaneous. Despite their experimental structure, these phenomenological reflections advance key elements of Engelbart's research program, which aimed to develop new data structures in combination with new ways of displaying them. Yet I cannot help but be moved by the fluency of the prose and by the sheer audacity of the project.

Engelbart's research into intellect augmentation created tools that augment research. In an image that evokes Baron Münchhausen pulling himself out of a swamp by his own bootstraps, Engelbart called his group's methodology "bootstrapping," which involved the recursive strategy of "developing tools and techniques" to develop better tools and techniques.[89] The "tangible product" of such an activity was a "constantly improving augmentation system for use in developing and studying augmentation systems."[90]

It was an appealing vision, but only so long as it remained recursive. Engelbart's group benefited from creating their own tools and methods. Engelbart also hoped that his system could be "transferred—as a whole or by pieces of concept, principle and technique—to help others develop augmentation systems for many other disciplines and activities."[91] Undoubtedly, Engelbart's ideas about intellect augmentation have had a broad effect on knowledge work across disciplines. However, his vision loses the property of self-determination when transferred outside the narrow confines of a laboratory actively engaged in the transformation of material contexts of their own knowledge production. Word processing today rarely involves communities pulling themselves up by their own bootstraps: using tools and techniques of their own design. Augmentation enforced from without advances values and principles no longer comprehensible to the entity being augmented.

To bring his system into being, Engelbart convened a community that through recursive self-improvement could lift itself up toward a smarter, more efficient, more human way of doing research. The group crafted novel instruments for reading and writing. They engineered new programming languages, compilers to interpret, and debuggers to troubleshoot them. The system shows care and love for the craft of writing. But there is also complexity. "This complexity has grown more than expected," Engelbart wrote in conclusion.[92] The feeling of transcendence that the anonymous typist describes in using the system engages a sophisticated mechanism. The mechanism was not, however, the primary instrument of augmentation. Rather, it was the process of designing, making, and experimenting with tools that enhanced the intellect. Engelbart wrote, "The development of the Bootstrap Community must be coordinated with the capacity of our consoles, computer service, and file storage to support Community needs, and with our ability to integrate and coordinate people and activities."[93] In other words, the development of the community must form a feedback loop with software development. It involves training, practice, critical self-reflection, and thoughtful deliberation.

Modern word processors enable us to drag and drop passages with unprecedented facility. We live in Engelbart's world, to the extent that we use his lab's complex systems daily and in a similar configuration: screens, keyboards, storage. Today's computer users rarely form a self-determined bootstrapping community. The contemporary writer is bootstrapped passively to the prevailing vision of intellect augmentation. The very metaphor of bootstrapping suggests the impossibility of using one's bootstraps to pull others out of the Platonic cave. Engelbart's liberatory research program therefore left another less lofty imprint on the everyday practice of modern intellectual life. Text, which before the advent of CRTs was readily apparent on the page in all its fullness, finally entered a complex system of executable code and inscrutable control instruction. The material lightness of textual being came at the price of legibility.

Short-lived screenless word processors of the early 1960s (e.g., the MT/ST) were difficult to operate, because typists had no means to visualize complex data structures on tape. Screens helped by representing document topography visually, restoring a sense of apparent space to otherwise opaque media. The contemporary digital document resembles a page on-screen, but beneath, it is a jumble of bits, split into the various regions of internal memory. Screens simulate document unity by presenting holistic images of paragraphs, pages, and books. The simulation seems to follow the physics of paper and ink: One can turn pages, write in margins, and insert bookmarks. But the underlying inscription remains in fracture. Simulated text does not transcend matter. Screens merely conceal its material properties while recreating other, more seemingly transcendent ones. The act of continual dissemblage, one medium imitating the other, manufactures an ephemeral illusion by which pages fade in and out of sight, paper folds in improbable ways, and words glide effortlessly between registers of copy and paste.

In the rift between input and output, programmable media inject arbitrary intervals of time and space. Forces of capital and control occupy the void as the sign acquires new dimensions and capabilities for automation. Code and codex subsequently sink beneath the matte surface of a synthetic storage medium. Screens purport to restore a sense of lost immediacy, of the kind felt on contact between pen nib and paper as the capillary action of cellulose conveys ink into its shallow conduit.

Screens are meant to open a window onto the unfamiliar physicalities of electromagnetic inscription. They obviate the need for multiple typings or printouts. Projected image should, in theory, correspond to its originating keystroke. The gap separating inputs and outputs appears to close. Crucially, the accord between archived inscription and its image cannot be guaranteed. The interval persists in practice and is actively contested. Deep and shallow inscriptions entwine. Laminate text appears weightless and ephemeral at some layers of the composite, allowing for rapid remediation. At other layers its affordances are determined by its physics; at still other layers they are carefully constructed to resist movement or interpretation. Alienated from the base particulates of the word, we lose some of our basic interpretive capacities to interrogate embedded power structures.

CHAPTER 5

> LITERATURE DOWN TO A PIXEL

Screens have this one major peculiarity: They refresh themselves multiple times per second. Even those shapes that appear to stand still continuously move at a speed beyond the threshold of human perception. We are vaguely aware of this movement; it is commonly visible when a screen appears on another screen, as it does in documentary films that show someone typing at a computer terminal or watching television. The difference in flicker rates between the projector showing the image and the projector in the frame is what produces the characteristic horizontal interference pattern. Such glitches give us a glimpse into the nature of the simulation.

Signs are no longer immutable, as though etched in stone or absorbed into wood pulp. Rather, we observe them in motion. The illusion of digital textuality is a consequence of the dynamic property of projection. To place texts on a screen is to bring them closer to the moving image. What does it mean to perceive seemingly static words through a fundamentally dynamic medium? What happens to literature that takes place on cinema screens?

In this chapter, I present a short meditation on the digital commonplaces in popular culture before focusing on two case studies, one from the material history of telegraphy and the other from the history of modern display technology. Archival material—patents, blueprints, phenomenological accounts from the early history of word processing—are brought to bear on a debate concerning the nature of digital representation and perception in the philosophy of aesthetics.

Digital. The adjective is used everywhere, but it is still poorly felt and understood. One intuits that it has something to do with numbers or fingers, yet something more is always at stake in its distinction from analog things. That something—a remainder, a trace—is my focus here. Several case studies will test our theoretical intuitions against the material realities of digital representation. As always, I advance a materialist, formal, and historically grounded analysis. In this chapter I engage the elemental particulates of two fundamental media conduits: electric ether and liquid crystal. The first is a primary host for telegraphy; the second filters light on-screen.

I am also concerned here with a phenomenological description of human perception. My goal is to disrupt the naturalized congruity between organ and device. The quality of something being digital, I argue, might initially appear to be an intrinsic attribute of the medium. Under closer examination, it reveals itself as a political construct that lays claims on the body, structuring the physical affordances of communication. The change of the *medium* from paper to pixel entails a series of corresponding changes in the *mode* of perception. The mode attunes viewers to its message. By "attunement" I mean something analogous to what Marcel Mauss has called the "techniques of the body": the way in which we sit down to read, for example, the position of head and hands, eye movement, and posture.[1] Attunement structures apprehension. It answers the "how" of perception.

It would be wrong to conflate the medium with the message in this context. At stake in the digital-analog divide is rather a reader's ability to do something with texts. Throughout this chapter I use the word *medium* to narrowly identify the physical conduits of representation.[2] Thus the medium of painting is paint and canvas; the medium of books is paper and ink.

A change in medium often implies a corresponding change in the mode of perception. At some level of music production, for example, classical music may involve a family of brass or woodwind instruments, shaped to move and vibrate air. Brass, wood, wind, and air are media through which sound and vibration travel to reach a listener's ear. The mode of music appreciation is listening, which involves a set of conventional cultural techniques: the buying of tickets, dress code, and proper comportment at a concert. These modalities are not rigidly determined. For example, members of the deaf community may use other modes of listening, such as leaning against sound-amplifying speakers or touching an instrument while it is being played.

Yet at another stage of music production, classical music involves notation. A whole system of distribution is built around the printing and circulation of sheet music. Modalities of reading sheet music involve other body postures, strategies of interpretation, and cultural and financial institutions.

We confuse the conversation when we conflate the modality of information (music, image, text) with the physical channels of its transmission (air, liquid crystal, paper). Modality influences the message to a much greater extent than medium. In fact, in most communication systems, the medium is a relatively neutral conduit. One can use a violin to transmit a concerto or a secret message. The medium remains the same, whereas the mode of apprehension changes. To decode a secret violin message, listeners might attune themselves to a different pitch. Modality shapes apprehension, whereas media—air, wood, and strings—remain agnostic to the information being transmitted.

Initially, we must know how to perceive and which senses to use: when to look, touch, or listen. Modalities further contain the *register* of a message. Register identifies the signifying elements: I need to understand which of the sounds are a part of the composition and which are incidental. In more refined arts, the register also governs bodily technique; for example, one must neither speak nor cough during a classical recital, one can look at but not touch artwork in a museum. The modality of communication ultimately demands corporal compliance; it is a claim on the body.

Therein lies the starkest difference between analog and digital media. The shift from one to the other affects not the message but the mode of perception. It is as though someone has asked you to read a book or watch a film in a stranger's armchair. It feels off in a way that is difficult to explain. The mode of digital perception similarly contorts the body into new and unfamiliar shapes, which often give discomfort. Something happens when digital media subsume their analog counterparts. An electronic device uses other sensualities, modes of signification, and ways of listening and understanding.

DIGITAL WAKE (MY TWO TERMINATORS)

What does the digital look like? It looks blue for one—not just any kind of blue, but a particularly cool shade of pure blue, which passes from dark to white to translucent with starburstlike overtones. An online image search for the word *digital* produces many sharp, sterile visuals of that kind. Abstract geometric patterns predominate in the first dozen or so search results: curved, three-dimensional tunnels or lines that resemble circuit boards. There are other things too, of course: cheap and expensive consumer items such as scanners, memory cards, circuit boards, and backup drives. But most of all there are cameras—digital cameras, which stand in stark contrast to traditional film photography. Few marketplace objects exhibit such a strong sense of the opposition between the digital and the analog as a consumer camera.

These search pages also contain the outdated clichés of yesterday's digital detritus: digital clocks, purple lightning bolts, and the abstract chrome landscapes made widely available by graphic editing software in the 1990s. There are numbers. The preferred arrangement is in a torrential grid—the matrix—descending in the background, behind a generic humanoid form, also translucent. Or better yet: alphanumeric characters arranged to create a globe or a face. Ones and 0's are best arranged as an unending string that runs at a slight angle on the z-axis and beyond the frame, foregrounding whatever object is meant to take on the digital as a property: the digital wake.

When we constrict the image search to the twenty-first century, we see these cool-blue images give way to a more varied palette: bright greens, yellows, and reds in retrogeometric pixelated shapes. Pixels take the place of numbers here—not the small, invisible pixels of contemporary computer screens, but the large and boxy pixels that by their pronounced boxiness flaunt their digital being. These images allude to a time when pixels really did stand out as individual units, when technology was not refined enough to produce the illusion of visual continuity. This faux low-fidelity aesthetic likely appeals to the romantic nostalgia many feel for the early days of computing, and yet it also asserts its independence from that history. No longer will the digital serve to emulate reality or be judged merely by its degree of lifelike verisimilitude. The blocky world of Markus Persson's *Minecraft* (2011) stands in antithesis to the magical realism of Cyan's *Myst* (1993), the best-selling graphic-adventure PC game of the twentieth century. Whereas critics lauded *Myst* for its moody and atmospheric photorealistic environments, they embraced *Minecraft* for its playful low-bit, low-fidelity aesthetic of gaming consoles from the 1980s. The pseudo-pixelated world of *Minecraft* encourages its inhabitants to experiment with deconstruction, producing cuboid landscapes that foreground discontinuity of form and surface.

Digital iconography also works in another direction, by approaching and challenging the perceived continuity of the analog world. Liquid-metal Photoshop font effects are supplanted by hyperrealistic renderings of fire, smoke, and water—fluid elements that are difficult to render digitally, especially in movement. Digital alchemy approaches the boundaries of technological possibility, but, absent the constraints of realism, it pushes past reality, past nature, and past mere fidelity to the natural world. A real-world explosion caught on film looks cheap in comparison to its cinematic "special effects" simulacrum. A blazing corporate logo rendered digitally would lose much of its appeal if it were produced by literally lighting a logograph on fire. The burning digital logograph does not just say, "We are hot!" or "We are on fire!" (that would be too naive); it says that our fire is better than fire, more vivid and more lifelike. The digital fire is the ideal Platonic image of fire, an image that all actual fires should emulate.

I am evoking these commonplaces to get at the conflicting popular intuitions about "the digital" as something at once discrete, angular, and therefore reductive and deterministic but also shiny, smooth, perfect, and liquid in a way that drowns out or transcends everything susceptible to time, everything that has a distinct shape and anatomy. Consider the transition between *The Terminator* and *Terminator 2*. In the former film, the bad robot that sets out to destroy humanity is an animatronic mechanism. In the latter, it is an amorphous puddle of mercury that makes the original mechanical Arnold seem like a friend and savior.[3] The original robot terminates with shotguns and tire irons; the second morphs into human shapes and pours itself inside, threatening life from within.

Like the terminators of yesteryear, digital sprites and bogeymen have lost their hold over popular imagination. Digital photography, digital clocks, and digital humanities already ring archaic in their futuristic ambition, going the way of *e-* or *i-* anything, the way of retrosuffixes such as *-bot*, *-mat*, *-lux*, and *-tron*. The digital dissolves into the everyday as all clocks, all books, all texts, in short, all human activity passes through some form of digital being.[4] My aim here and throughout has been to understand what is meant by its evocation—to come to terms, to make visible, to denature, and to make it appear strange again.

Digital media, digital humanities, digital divides—these constructions share a word that suggests entirely differing qualities depending on the context. In some cases digitality stands in opposition to a notion of naturally analog human experience. Digital media reduce fuzzy and indeterminate human experience to something binary, discrete, and deterministic. In his influential monograph *The Cultural Logic of Computation* David Columbia insists that "languages are not codes." For Columbia, human language practice therefore should not be reduced to a "single correct interpretation" or "at the absolute limit, a determinate number of discrete interpretations":[5] "To submit a phenomenon to computation is to striate otherwise-smooth details, analog details."[6] Following Deleuze, Columbia conceives of "striated space" in opposition to "smooth" and "analog" spaces, such as brains, society, politics, language, and baseball.[7] For Columbia, striated and digital phenomena fall under suspicion because "our society is already oriented towards binarisms, hierarchy, and instrumental rationality."[8] In this view, human experience is continuous and analog. The digital threatens it by breaking it apart into individual and, by implication, computable units.

In his essay against digital humanities, Stephen Marche similarly worries about the digitization of human experience, but for the opposite reason. Smoothness, in his view, is a property of the machine.

> Meaning is mushy. Meaning falls apart. Meaning is often ugly, stewed out of weakness and failure. It is as human as the body, full of crevices and prey to diseases. It requires courage and a certain comfort with impurity to live with. Retreat from the smoothness of technology is not an available option, even if it were desirable. The disbanding of the papers has already occurred, a splendid fluttering of the world's texts to the winds. We will have to gather them all together somehow. But the possibility of a complete, instantly accessible, professionally verified and explicated, free global library is more than just a dream. Through the perfection of our smooth machines, we will soon be able to read anything, anywhere, at any time. Insight remains handmade.[9]

In this worldview, digital artifacts fall under suspicion for smoothing out differences and thereby for betraying some essential and wonderfully messy property of being human.

Stanley Fish, another prominent critic of the digital humanities, writes in a similar vein. For Fish, the traditional humanities exist within the "linear, temporal medium in the context of which knowledge is discrete, partial and situated—knowledge at this time and this place experienced by this limited being." By contrast, the digital humanities imagine a "steady yet dynamic state where there is movement and change, but no center, no beginning and end, just all middle."[10] The digital vision is meant to deliver us from linearity and from time itself. Indeed, the digital fails because it does not offer *enough* of a difference. He writes:

> Delivered from linearity, from time-bound, sharply delineated meanings, from mortality, from death, everyone, no longer a one, will revel in and participate in the universal dance, a "mystical dance" of "mazes intricate,/Eccentric, intervolved, yet regular/Then most when most irregular they seem,/And in their motions harmony divine/So smooths her charming tones, that God's own ear/Listens delighted. (John Milton, "Paradise Lost," V, 620, 622–627)[11]

Whether too discrete or too continuous, critics agree on the danger of digitization. Digital being follows determinism and mechanization as another opponent to humanism. Whether it is Plato discussing the role of writing in *Phaedrus* or Fish discussing the development of digital humanities through Milton, critics worry that emergent modes of representation will fail to weave the human experience into their fabric. New media are often depicted as departing from some previously constructed category of the human, with one audience applauding its transhuman potential for liberation and the other lamenting its antihuman potential for demise and destruction. A conversation about media modalities, unlike any other, is quick to slide into ethics, aesthetics, politics.[12]

Because apprehension is grounded in the physical capabilities of human perception, new media affect the very notion of what it means to be human. I am interested first and foremost in the challenge that digital media pose to humanity as a determined, a priori category.[13] The repeated contradictions in debates around digital media expose a historically contingent anxiety. Both orthodoxies of humanism and the futuristic ambition of posthumanism are displaced onto the same digital-analog spectrum. However, the material conditions of media production do not allow for social constructivism unmoored from the senses. Technology evolves along the lines of human perception. For example, the illusion of continuity disappears when screen projection flickers much slower than 60 frames per second. A historical account of digital media must therefore acknowledge both their contingent and their essential characteristics.[14]

In what follows I offer two case studies that challenge commonly expressed intuitions about digital media. They show that whatever is meant by the digital-analog distinction is tied not to some essential properties of a medium but to its affordances. A text that can be copied and preserved is more digital, in a sense, than one limited in its circulation, whether by nature or design. A philosophical consideration of the terms *digital* and *analog* informs the media archaeology that follows.

SPIRITUAL TELEGRAPH

The contemporary attempt to fix human experience on the spectrum between discrete and continuous representation echoes a similar conversation that occurred at the turn of the twentieth century. The parallels suggest that our present belief in the essentialism of corporeal technique (e.g., writing by hand) in fact constitutes an arbitrary ideal of the human.

Consider the historical connection between telegraphy and spiritualism. Before the standardization of telegraph alphabets, multiple ways of translating language into electric signal competed for their share of the rapidly growing telecommunications market. A well-publicized feud emerged between proponents of direct current (DC) and alternating current (AC) systems. A few technical details are necessary to understand how an argument about engineering design gained metaphysical significance.

Telegraph systems based on DC designs converted electric current flow into dashes and the absence of current into dots.[15] Systems based on AC designs converted Morse code (and other encoding systems) into pulses of alternating positive and negative current, where positive current could stand for dashes and negative current for dots. Direct-current designs preferred the use of the sawtooth or square periodic waveforms to represent binary states. The signal was either on or off with nothing in-between. By contrast, proponents of AC designs often argued for the use of the rounder sinusoidal signal, which covered a more organic range of amplitudes. The sinusoidal wave could be modulated into a multitude of intermediary states.[16] Instead of being just on or off, points of current intensity could be measured along the curve of the sine wave. Consequently, AC designs tended toward the transmission of continuous quantities, such as images and cursive handwriting. The sinusoidal curve itself resembled natural, organic shapes, like handwriting. The alternating current suggested a visual analogy between the thing being transmitted (picture or text) and the electric signal.

The Pollak-Virag telegraph, which the media theorist Bernhard Siegert mentions briefly in his essay on cacography, was one such device.[17] A closer look reveals the reductive idea implicit in the digital-analog distinction. The Pollak-Virag telegraph purported to transmit handwritten curves, which were, despite appearances, broken down into its discrete constituent components in transit. The original Pollak-Virag machine patented in 1900 sent regular Morse encoding by means of alternating current of two different polarities and two different strengths, for a total of four types of signals.[18] Other than the irregular signal shape and the use of alternating current, Pollak-Virag encoding differed little from single-Morse systems. By 1901, the authors were issued an American patent for the "Writing Telegraph," which built on their previous design in an interesting way. Rather than using a wave in four steps, Pollak and Virag proposed an "automatic transmitter . . . capable of sending current impulses over the line which correspond to the direction and the size of a single letter element."[19] In other words, they wanted to bend the sinusoidal wave to correspond roughly to the shape of a letter. In this way, the letter *s*, to pick an easy example, could be transmitted by means of an s-shaped wave (Figure 5.1).

Pollak-Virag design aimed to constitute an electric alphabet analogous to cursive writing: "to trace in a substantially continuous unbroken outline the written letters composing the matter transmitted."[20] To achieve this, the engineers broke cursive script down into distinct vertical and horizontal elements. Pollak-Virag encoding thus represented a continuous quality (cursive script)

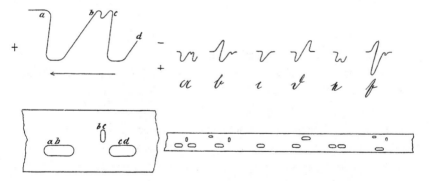

FIGURE 5.1. Illustration from Pollak and Virag's patent for the "Writing Telegraph" showing the reproduction of Gothic characters (top) and the transmission strip with suitable perforations for influencing the receiver (bottom). The cursive script is represented by the means of vertical and horizontal perforations. Made up of discrete atomic elements, the system is not as "analog" as it first appears to be. Source: Anton Pollak and Josef Virag, "Writing-Telegraph," Patent US675495 A, filed June 28, 1900, issued June 4, 1901, sheet 3.

through discrete atomic elements, as punches that moved the writing stylus in cardinal directions (up, down, left, or right). It was not, in other words, a purely analog device. The analogy was rather achieved through a process of discrete analytic atomization of script on ticker tape and its subsequent reconstitution into a continuous shape. The cardinal directions formed an intermediate discrete description of smooth handwriting curves. Pollak and Virag believed that their sine-wave telegraph had the distinct advantage of transmitting messages "recorded in ordinary written or script characters." In the language of the patent, other forms of "facsimile" telegraph transmitted merely the "conventional form" of the letter, not the letter itself, whereas the Pollak-Virag system was "non-autographic."[21] The autographic telegraph claimed to preserve the particularity of the human hand, an individual's signature. It was the humane telegraph in the sense that it preserved the human trace.

The metaphysics accompanying telegraph communication at the time were often concerned with the possibility of human erasure in communication. Notions of material discreteness and continuity represented not mere physical attributes of encoding or electricity but higher-order cultural and even ethical or theological categories. Beneath the technical conversations about the advantages of discrete or continuous electric signal lay a philosophical concern with the fundamental makeup of the universe itself.

Henri Bergson, for example, wrote about the "real whole of the universe," which constituted an "indivisible continuity."[22] In his thought, science, technology, and other "artificial systems" imposed discrete "partial views" on the whole.[23] Bergson wrote that these partial views resembled the operation of the cinematograph, which divides continuous motion into distinct frames. By running the frames through a projecting apparatus, telegraphs reconstituted "the individuality of each particular movement": "Such is the contrivance of the cinematograph. And such is also that of our knowledge."[24] The intellect, in this view, continually partitioned undifferentiated reality into discrete states of time and space.[25] But these states were virtually, not actually, discrete. According to Bergson, the evolution of life proceeded "rather like a shell," which "bursts into fragments," which are themselves again shells.[26] The new differentiated unit, a part of the indivisible universe, contained the kernel of the whole. It did not split from but subsumed the totality.

In Bergson's view of the universe, the brain and the central nervous system act as a "central telephonic exchange," which communicates between the extrinsic continuous world and the intrinsic "memory-shot[s]" of our perception.[27] The mind receives images of the world that it compares with existing stored images to produce a new composite image that is once again stored into memory. Bergson thus denied the "flashlight" model of perception. The mind, according to him, did not shine a light to bring attention to this or that hidden feature of the world: "Metaphor for metaphor, we would rather compare the elementary work of attention to that of the telegraph clerk who, on receipt of an important dispatch, sends it back again, word for word, in order to check its accuracy."[28] The object in the world was therefore neither an independent thing nor purely a product of the mind. By this telegraphic model of perception, Bergson avoided both fully relativistic and fully essentialist accounts of perception.

To agree with Bergson is to imagine the mind as a cinematographic framing device. It is to accept that the world is a priori continuous in nature. In a damning evaluation of Bergson's philosophy, Bertrand Russell noted that such assumptions were merely poetic images, not subject to verification.[29] They hold the truth of poetry, not physics or philosophy, Russell wrote. To this day, it is difficult to find scientific consensus on such topics as the digital makeup of the physical world or the continuity of consciousness. There was certainly no consensus on the matter at the time. The nature of telegraphy itself was disputed. The property of being electric, similar to digitality today, was seen as both more smooth and more discrete than human experience.

Consider the following passages from Samuel Brittan's Swedenborg-inspired *Spiritual Telegraph* in 1854, in which an anonymous author expounds a theological media theory that hinges on what he or she assumes to be the ultimately discrete nature of the universe:[30] "Whenever two persons are brought into sympathetic relations, either by corporeal contact or through those refined media which pervade the Universe and serve as the airy vehicles of thought, they mutually feel the presence of each other."[31] In this relationship "the mind which is gifted with the greater degree of activity and power" at once attains a hierarchical relation to the lesser intellect, becoming "the proximate cause and fountain of inspiration to the other."[32] God naturally occupies the highest point of such a pyramid: "From sources superior to ourselves, the very elements of life and thought flow into us, and every living thing, according to its nature and discrete degree, derives a kind of inspiration from that which is above."[33] In other words, the discrete degree must be preserved, because without it the hierarchy would lose meaning. To facilitate the "transmission of impressions," "the recipient" of the vital flow "must be willing to receive instruction, and assume the passive or negative relation of a learner." Without discreteness and without hierarchy he or she will resist "the infusion of foreign impressions and Divine ideas."[34]

In this essentially telegraphic model of the universe, to deny the stepwise hierarchy of refined media is to close oneself off from the transmission of impressions in a communication act (consisting of a contact and the exchange of signifying "thought vehicles") between a "source superior" and the receiver of instructions, who are placed in a binary and opposing relation (negative but without resistance) to the idea of the divine.

Unlike Columbia and Fish today, telegraph spiritualists associated determinism with continuity, not discreteness. Witness George Henry Dole writing in his *Philosophy of Creation* in 1906:

> Scientists have prosecuted research on the plane of *continuous degrees of the ultimates*, and they have thereby failed to penetrate to *interior things of discrete degree* [emphasis mine]. Consequently they derive life as not from the Lord, but from nature, of which they have no other idea than that it is something mechanical.[35]

Telegraph spiritualists shunned continuity because it confused the sacred and the profane. They believed that a truly Christian order would remain digital in essence. To claim otherwise would be to propagate the Gnostic heresy, by which the divine and the profane were one.[36]

Whereas Bergson believed that telegraphy translated continuous analog experience into discrete digital snapshots, the Swedenborgian mystic saw it as a model of communication that maintained fidelity to the hidden order of a well-differentiated and fundamentally discrete universe. Their intuitions were diametrically opposed. Arguing against sine-wave telegraphy in 1905, Donald Murray, whose alphabet would become the basis for modern character encodings (ASCII and UTF-8), displayed a similar bias against analog quantities, which, for him, could encode complex human activity, like writing or dance. He wrote:

> About ten years ago there was a brisk discussion in some of the electrical journals in regard to the advantages of the simple harmonic curve or sine wave for the transmission of power by the alternating current. . . . If Smith

wants to make Jones spin round like a dancing dervish, the best way might be for Smith to transmit sine waves . . . but in practice, Smith always wants to make Jones perform an excessively complicated and irregular series of motions, and for this purpose it is essential to transmit similar motions by introducing upper harmonics in a fragmentary, non-periodic, and very irregular way.[37]

Murray, again contrary to Bergson, assumed that human experience was discrete at its core. For him, the regular and continuous sine wave fell under metaphysical suspicion, just as the discrete nature of computation would fall under suspicion for such contemporary critics as Golumbia and Fish. In Murray's view, human experience was analogous to the sawtooth wave: fragmentary, nonperiodic, and irregular. By contrast, the sine wave had the exotic and orientalist characteristics of being cyclical, repetitive, and continuous. The shape of the square wave more closely resembled Murray's own normative vision of human culture.[38]

The appeal to a normative model of human experience in this context belies a kind of a technological essentialism, reductive of both technology and human nature. Neither can be definitively reduced to universal notions of discrete or continuous qualities. Under close examination, human perception—cognition, consciousness, existence—involves a complex synthesis of analog and digital processes. Telegraphs and computers also function in the digital mode at some layers of the system and in the analog mode at others. The distinction between digital and analog, as I continue to challenge it in this chapter, comes under increasing doubt.

It is tempting to think of the telegraph as a digital apparatus, created to convert analog input into electric signal.[39] The innards of the Pollak-Virag telegraph, to return to our example, reveal complex dynamics that involve long chains of transcoding and transmediation that oscillate between discrete and continuous qualities. To be transmitted, a signal travels from biological brain wetware, onto ink and paper, to the mechanical action of cogs and wheels, and finally, through copper wire by means of an electric signal. In the process, language, already a discrete and portable representation of thought, undergoes a number of further material-phase transformations. In the writing telegraph this involves what I have been calling, borrowing from the language of concrete poetry, inter- or transmediation: from notebook to paper tape to the movement of an electromagnetic vibrator to the recording mirror galvanometer into the copper wire to the receiving vibrator and into the machinations of the printing apparatus that once again produce ink and alphabet.[40] This entire system further participates in the complexities of the human neurological apparatus, involving haptic, visual, and cognitive feedback. Neither wholly digital nor wholly analog, the signal undergoes multiple encoding and phase changes in transmission.

By "encoding," if we could pause again to define the terms, I mean a controlled mode of representation. Representation in its unrestrained form (as in "pictorial representation") differs from encoding in the size of its vocabulary. Painting and other forms of uninhibited representational conventions offer limitless expressive possibilities. The language of painting, we might say, is infinite. Encoding, by contrast, reduces the universe of expressive possibilities to a limited number of salient codes, an alphabet. These codes obey formal rules of composition, a grammar. Although the expressive potential of written language is limitless in some combinatorial sense of the word, language and other codes can break, that is, be reduced to nonsense, in a way that painting strictly cannot. An artificial computer language constrains the vocabulary even further. Finally, contrast the infinitude of possible brush strokes with the hundred or so "reserved words" available to a programmer.

Media, modes, and encodings are logically related in nonobvious ways. Changes in the media conduit (e.g., from sound, wire, or paper) necessitate the corresponding modal change. Consider a Morse code transmission coaxed out of a violin, written on paper, or transmitted by wire. In each case, the encoding remains formally the same: dots and dashes. But the dots and dashes are expressed alternatively in ink, as sound waves, and as electric charge. The encoding changes when human speech is transferred into Morse code. In reading and playing music, a musician furthermore transforms musical notation (a controlled, paper-bound vocabulary) into sound waves, which are unlimited in their expressive potential.

Blueprints for the writing telegraph reveal a device that mixes discrete and continuous modes of representation through multiple acts of transcoding and transmediation. Digitality defined by those terms is not a helpful reduction. More precisely, the telegraph is a device that pushes language, which is normally bound to brains (as thought), air (as speech), or paper (as a writing system), through metal wire.[41] To fit into the wire, a thought changes its conduit media. It undergoes a number of modal transformations in the process: from the hexagonal grid patterns at regions of cortical anatomy, to ripplelike sound waves, to rectangular sentences and paragraphs arranged spatially on paper, to the chain of charged electrons arranged serially along the length of a wire. An arrangement of cells changes into an arrangement of air molecules, ink, and copper, each entailing its own system of encoding and mechanisms of storage, retrieval, and transmission. The affordances of the medium change with the conduit. A sound wave dissipates momentarily. Ink dries and endures. The electric signal travels at the speed of light.

If I imagine, for a moment, human bodies as a kind of a medium and persistent data structure—an arrangement of elements of a given time signature and shape—I could say that they outlast the sound wave but not paper, that they move at a pace slower than light, that they exhibit more spatial continuity than Morse code, that they are less ordered and less heterogeneous on a microscopic scale than copper or liquid crystal. The modalities of human media intersect with technology along multiple dimensions, in parts congruent to and in other parts divergent from books, computers, screens, and telegraphs.

SOAP OPERA EFFECT

Consider another case study at the human–machine, digital–analog divide. Modern televisions began shipping with a feature called motion-compensated frame interpolation (MCFI) in 2010. It caused some viewers to report what was dubbed the soap opera effect. Everything looks cheap to a viewer experiencing the soap opera effect. Even critically acclaimed footage, featuring top acting talent and expensive camera work, looks unnatural, as though produced on home video. I am almost always able to recognize the symptoms. Under the MCFI effect, a shot's dynamics look somehow fabricated. The actors, even in films that I know and love, appear to be faking it. Their acting seems forced and over the top. I notice their makeup and props. It is like watching bad silent cinema of the kind that prevents the suspension of disbelief and immersion. I am no longer susceptible to the conventions of the medium.

MCFI was developed to correct the motion blur that occurs on flat-panel liquid crystal displays (LCDs). LCDs work by passing light through a liquid crystal medium that is sandwiched between two polarized light filters positioned at 90 degrees to one another. As light enters through one side, it twists, following the slightly curved molecular structure of the crystal, allowing the beam to rotate and pass through both filters. The structure unwinds when it receives electric current, which effectively blocks light from passing through the medium (Figure 5.2). The gates close, so to speak, as the second filter prevents light from exiting. By these means, a series of small pinholelike pixels can be turned on and off to create shapes, letters, and images on the screen.[42]

In addition to filtering light, modern displays also flicker at a precisely calibrated rate. What we observe as a static image on screen is in reality a highly dynamic projection. Traditional film projectors advance through 24 frames every second. The film camera's shutter similarly moves up and down 24 times per second, capturing a static snapshot at each turn. Projectors and cameras therefore act in unison to produce the illusion of time that feels objectively real to the viewer.

Furthermore, a projector's light flickers 2 or 3 times per frame, giving it a refresh rate of 48–72 cycles per second (Hertz; Hz), which produces the effect of continuous motion. Without this strobe effect, under continuous light, the succession of frames would appear as a blurry streak of undifferentiated images.

An image persists in the human visual field for about 16 milliseconds after the stimulus passes, giving humans the temporal resolution of about 60 images per second. Consequently, an average person reaches the state of "critical flicker fusion," in which the strobe light becomes unnoticeable, at refresh rates equal to or greater than 60 Hz. At the limits of flicker fusion, the image begins to persist through the gaps between frames, creating the appearance of continuous motion.[43] Below the threshold of flicker fusion the viewer would notice the strobe effect, which hinders viewing.

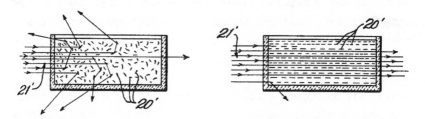

FIGURE 5.2. Digital text moves even as it appears to stand still. Textual laminates are suspended in liquid crystal. Illustration from Land's patent showing a method for controlling the passage of light through a material medium. Source: Edwin Land, "Light Valve," Patent US1963496 A, filed January 16, 1933, issued June 19, 1934, sheet 1.

LCDs mimic the action of an analog projector by refreshing the screen at intervals between 60 Hz and 120 Hz. This happens even when the image is wholly static, such as the page of an electronic book.

To complicate matters, humans are more sensitive to rapid motion at the periphery of vision, in a mechanism that likely evolved to detect predatory threats.[44] As we move closer to our screens (e.g., when sitting in front of a computer monitor), more of the image enters our field of peripheral vision, making us more sensitive to screen flicker. When sitting close to a screen, flicker can become more noticeable because more of the moving image enters the sensitive area of peripheral vision adept at perceiving rapid movement.

Furthermore, being closer to a screen increases the angular velocity of any depicted moving object. When viewed from afar, a movement of several inches on-screen corresponds to a few degrees' change in the sight angles and a few millimeters of iris movement. When viewed up close, the same several inches on-screen correspond to a much larger angle, forcing the iris to move farther laterally.

The human visual system is particularly adept at tracking smooth horizontal movement. The brain anticipates the perceived trajectory of a laterally moving object and stabilizes the retinal image appropriately while keeping it at the center of the fovea in what is called smooth-pursuit lateral eye movement.[45] To put it simply, we are good at tracking things that move horizontally—an antelope running across the plains, for example. Even though our brain cannot capture such movement smoothly, it fills in the gaps to create the illusion of smooth movement sideways. This makes us good at anticipating the trajectory of laterally moving objects, another likely adaptation that favors self-defense and hunting. But beyond some threshold, and particularly when things move rapidly up and down, the motion begins to appear fitful. Think of tracking a fly, for example, which seems to skip from one place to another as our visual system struggles to process its erratic trajectories at threshold-crossing speeds.

The "sample and hold" nature of LCDs frustrates the cognitive assumption of smooth movement. The brain assumes that moving objects move smoothly. But on-screen the object's anticipated location does not always correspond to its actual trajectory, because the motion of a represented object-image in the frame does not follow the anticipated physics of a similarly sized real-world object. The image moves inches, whereas our brain tells us it should move yards. Trajectories of moving objects on-screen are further subject to the quirks of technology used to edit and record video. Because of the flicker, the movement is actually intermittent; it is missing frames. The moving object appears at discrete stationary locations punctuated by gaps in on-screen movement. This mismatch between what is expected and what is perceived appears to the eye as blur. Shapes become fuzzy in motion under certain unfavorable viewing conditions.[46] To complicate matters, the on-off phase transitions of the liquid crystal medium are not instantaneous. The individual pixel fades instead of vanishing at once, leaving a physical (and not merely a perceptual) trail of not quite transitioned pixels in the wake of object movement.[47] Digital television runs into analog limitations of the liquid crystal medium.

To put all these factors together: We observe film shot at 24 frames per second on LCD screens that redraw the screen 60–120 times per second. The disparity between the low sampling rate of traditional film and the high sampling rate of modern monitors confounds human perception, which evolved to process motion in a particular way. The liquid crystal is also not a perfectly digital medium. It exhibits analog trailing artifacts. Moreover, we increasingly watch television on small hand-held devices, close to our field of vision. The combination of these factors leads to motion blur, an effect that has made early LCDs unsuitable for home entertainment.

To compensate for motion blur, LCD manufacturers introduced MCFI technology, by which the television itself inserts artificially computed frames in-between the images of original stock footage. Like a brain, the algorithm anticipates movement and fills in missing information. First, it averages the position of a moving object between two frames, then it creates an approximation of the object's computed position, and finally it inserts the computed frame into the action. The extra frames should, in theory, make the motion appear more natural, filling in the gaps that confuse the brain. Unfortunately for the viewer, the effectively higher sample rates carry a major unintended side effect. Most viewers associate sampling rates of 40 Hz and above with daytime soap operas, which were, for a time, shot on lower quality (but more modern) video equipment, as opposed to expensive legacy film equipment used by the big-budget film industry.

Film is expensive because film cameras work by fixing the image onto the medium through a photochemical process. Like traditional film photography, raw footage must be developed and processed properly before it can be used for editing, playback, and distribution. By contrast, video and more modern digital recorders transform light into fluctuations of the electromagnetic field, storing the results on tape or solid-state storage. The transducer (tape head) reads and writes directly from and to tape, making magnetic storage significantly more compact and less expensive than film, because it does not require chemical processing for playback.[48]

Crucially for our story, video recorders operate at 60 frames per second, a recording resolution that together with the distinctive video color profile and audio aberration signatures gives rise to what viewers perceive as that "cheap video" "soap opera" look. By inserting extra frames into the moving image, modern televisions in effect alter the apparently expensive, discrete, slow film format to match its faster, more continuous, and cheaper video alternative. The net objective improvement in sampling degrades the perceived subjective quality of the original. The motion may be smoother, but it looks unnatural, in that it differs subtly from acculturated practice. MCFI gives the eye too much detail. Minutiae of costume and makeup, previously hidden by the low sampling quality of film, become more readily apparent. An actor's micromovements and expressions, not usually perceptible to the eye, come to the fore and highlight the contrivance of the proceedings. The extrapolated detail breaks the spell of acting.[49]

The soap opera effect undercuts some of our most ingrained intuitions about perceptual phenomena on the digital-analog spectrum.

First, it challenges the easy equivalence between digital and discrete properties of the medium so often found in critical literature. According to accepted intuitions, film (the more discrete format of representation) more closely approaches the analog (continuous) nature of observed phenomenon, despite being the more fragmentary medium. Under closer examination, however, it reveals itself to be the more digital medium (in some respects) than digital video, if we take "digital" to mean "discrete" and "differentiated" sampling of reality. The incongruity between theory and practice points to a confusion in terms.

Second, it seems that the material properties of the medium involved in our understanding of digital and analog formats are also implicated in higher-level functions of aesthetic judgment. Perception of quality in a given recorded performance drifts with the vagaries of encoding. Good acting inexplicably falls apart with the introduction of extra frames. This should worry the critic unfamiliar with artifacts of digital conversion. Even an introductory examination of the soap opera effect reveals sensory glitches and distortions that affect the coupling between organ (sight) and device. The illusion of cinematic motion takes advantage of the idiosyncratic particularities of human vision. A more perfected visual apparatus would perceive flicker at much higher rates and have no persistent visual trail artifacts. The socially constructed aesthetic object is shown to contain physiologically determined qualities, undermining the strong version of social constructivism.[50] Screens, at the viewing end of most digital media—film and text—operate at the nexus of physiology and culture.

Finally, where theory often places artificial digital discreteness in opposition to natural analog continuity, a thick description of our perceptual apparatus reveals a complex patchwork of fragmentary cognitive mechanisms, already digital and discrete in their operation. The human-screen coupling is deeply heterogeneous throughout. At some level of analysis, gaps in the encoding format relate to gaps in human visual processing. Neither can be said to represent reality with perfect fidelity. Instead, brains, cameras, and screens stitch together landscapes from unevenly sampled visual topographies, achieving a measure of arbitrary synchronicity in viewing.

Critical literature often conflates the discrete nature of digital representation with human debasement, following the logic by which the perceived material impoverishment in one sphere leads to the implied spiritual impoverishment in the other. The sentiment is everywhere in the popular press and has deep intellectual roots in the history of thinking about technology. Philosophers of technology from Heidegger to Kittler advance a powerful hermeneutics of suspicion toward mechanization, digitization, and the subsequent computability of human experience. To take that tradition seriously is to direct hermeneutic suspicion to aspects of digital being that have meaningful sociopolitical consequences. If, as the case of motion blur suggests, human experience is already and always born digital (i.e., it is discrete and differentiated throughout), then we must find ways of advancing critique along theoretical distinctions that better capture the instrumental reality of media practice. Nostalgia for analog oneness and continuity should itself fall under the critical gaze, examined alongside media marketing slogans that advertise gapless playback and lossless file formats. To long for the analog is to long for the experience of oneness, which was never attainable in the first place.

Indeed, it appears that the whole matter of digital representation rests on arbitrary and contingent assumptions. If language and literature are already digital and discrete systems of representation, why should it bother us when it is otherwise digitized or transcoded into other controlled vocabularies? The Latin letter already comprises an atomic and indivisible unit. When it is further broken down into pixels, the smallest indivisible units on screen, it undergoes only a subtle ontological change. Just as one learns to translate an alphabet's arbitrary shape into distinct sounds, one can learn to translate arbitrary digits into letters and back into sounds and thoughts. The language of machines is merely another language.

Neither do media evolve independently of human sensory constraint. Humans cannot perceive the ultraviolet spectrum, for example. Nor would it be practical to create books that are so heavy as to prevent readers from turning their pages. Media modalities are tuned to average human capabilities, which mature in their socially constructed media modal environments.[51] Sensory constraints shape media, just as media constraints shape perception.

WE HAVE ALWAYS BEEN DIGITAL

A thick description of the human–machine interface at the point of contact exposes our frequent misunderstanding of the term *digital*. What does it mean, for example, to digitize film, if it is already a digital medium? What properties are being brought forth through digitization if the digital cannot simply be equated with discreteness? We can now revisit our initial intuitions in light of the physics of digital apprehension.

The conversation about digital media often begins with the difference between discrete and continuous quantities.[52] For example, in a popular book about what a "well-informed person should know about computers," Brian Kernighan describes analog quantities as those conveying "the idea of values that change smoothly as something else changes."[53] Much of the world is analog, Kernighan explains. A water tap, a pen, or a car steering wheel are all examples of analog interfaces. For example, when riding a bicycle, turning the handlebars one way results in a corresponding motion of the machine. This motion is smooth. Compare that with the action of a light switch. A properly functioning light switch takes on two discrete states only: on or off. A range of pressure applied to the switch does not correspond to any mechanical action of the lever. But once a certain threshold is reached, the switch flips to change states. "Digital systems," as Kernighan writes, "deal with discrete values."[54] The switch contains a limited number of state possibilities, whereas the bicycle handlebars can be rotated in an infinite number of minutely differing gradations.

Nelson Goodman was one of the first philosophers to examine digital representation in the context of aesthetic theory. In the late 1960s, drawing on technical intuitions about devices like pressure gauges and computers, he proposed to call those notational systems analog, which are "dense" and "undifferentiated in the extreme." By contrast, he called "digital" systems those that are "discontinuous" and "differentiated throughout."[55] By these definitions, written language and music notation are digital systems par excellence, having the property of reducing the undifferentiated analog input (human thought) into discrete semantic units (text or musical notation).[56] Following Goodman's logic, one can reasonably maintain that the art of painting, unlike music or language, cannot be reduced to the production of discrete semantic units and would be more of an analog system under the proposed definitions.

In this light, the language of pointillist painting, which breaks shapes down into their modular atomic components, transforms an analog art form into a digital one. Similarly, in the cuboid world of *Minecraft*, players interact with blocks, the smallest differentiated units that constitute all other more complex things in the game. The world of *Minecraft* is sparse and therefore digital. By contrast, the world of the hyperrealistic *Myst* depicts the paintinglike, semantically irregular reality that cannot be broken down into neat components. *Myst*, a digital game, depicts a dense, undifferentiated, and analog world.

Goodman's definitions strain under closer examination. Plainly, *Myst* is also a digital game. All digital images (and worlds) follow the logic of cubism to its deconstructive conclusion in that they atomize analog quantities into discrete and differentiated points of light. The world of *Myst*, like the world of *Minecraft*, is made of pixels. At some deeper level of analysis, both worlds are sparse and differentiated throughout. Could we not say the same thing about all rule-based analog games, such as chess? On the level of syntax, chess is also a sparse game, discrete and differentiated throughout like its computer counterparts. One plays on top of a grid with pieces that move according to rigidly prescribed rules and along binary color distinctions. At another scale of analysis, however, chess is an analog game. The wood grain of the chess board is part of a dense, undifferentiated world. At a deeper level still, at the atomic scale of observation, the chess board again begins to appear sparse, discontinuous, and differentiated throughout. We are left without the critical means to tell wood and (faux) ivory chess pieces apart from the block and pixel pieces of *Minecraft*.

The quality of being digital seems to depend on our perspective. Density and sparseness change with the viewer's ability to perceive differentiation. Ultimately, these qualities belong not to the object of representation (chess or computer game) but to the viewer. In the 1980s philosophers engaging with Goodman's earlier work began to move away from discussing digital representation in terms of properties of the medium. The conversation moved toward a more process-based, viewer-dependent understanding of the terms.

For example, an interesting corollary to the continuous property of analog systems is our inability to duplicate their states exactly. I can approximate the pressure someone else puts on their bicycle handlebars with some arbitrary measure of precision that never reaches perfect reproducibility. This means also that, although more digital art forms such as literature are, in some sense, perfectly reproducible, analog forms, such as painting, are not. Following similar reasoning, the American philosopher John Haugeland proposed to consider the quality of being reproducible as essential to our understanding of digital representation. For Haugeland, reproducibility involved "flawless copying . . . and preservation."[57] To Goodman's criteria of the digital, he therefore added the notion of "feasible procedures," which led to "positive" and "reliable" processes for reading and writing digital tokens.[58]

Let us consider Haugeland's addendum in relation to some of our previous case studies. Chess movements are patently reproducible. Several notational conventions exist to ensure the perfect preservation and reproducibility of chess games. These include the descriptive and standard algebraic chess notations. Individual chess *sets*, by contrast, are not perfectly reproducible. Each is a somewhat unique version of the same regulation ideal. The grammar and the medium of chess answer to differing definitions, depending on the context of analysis. The sometimes drastic differences in the shape of the figures or the materials used to make chess sets are not meaningful in the context of the game. They do become meaningful to those collectors who prize certain chess sets for their rarity or craftsmanship. However, craftsmanship and rarity are not in themselves signifying properties that figure in the game of chess. They are meaningful only in the game of collecting.

For some chess players, chess pieces are therefore perfectly exchangeable; for others they are not. Similarly, at the other extreme, we know that no amount of copying can reproduce an original Rembrandt. Every aspect of the painting is meaningful, including those not visible to the naked eye, such as traces of other paintings or sketches hidden under the surface representation. This would hold true even if an invented technique could make a perfect, molecule-by-molecule reproduction of a Rembrandt painting. The rules of fine art collection demand an original work of art that preserves the artifact's provenance, including incidental bumps, scratches, and patina accrued through history. Such marks carry no meaning by the rules of painting, but they do carry meaning by the rules of collecting.

From that perspective, painting is an analog genre. But if we were to disregard the rules of collecting—if we simply enjoyed looking at beautiful pictures—we would be justified in treating painting as a perfectly reproducible art form. Painting would, in essence, become more similar to chess, that is, a reproducible digital medium. Similarly, our newly found ability to reproduce something pushes the artifact closer to the digital side of the spectrum, even though the object itself has not changed. Its ontological status shifts with the viewer's attitudes and technological capabilities: to perceive or to reproduce.

With regard to discreteness, moving images lie somewhere between the extremes of competitive chess and fine art. In the case of the soap opera effect, we may think of analog film as a series of still shots. For some purposes these still shots are reproducible in mass quantities, although not perfectly. Multiple copies of each film reel are routinely distributed to multiple cinemas. Each is authentic in the sense that it is sanctioned by the film studio. From another perspective, each frame is also an irreproducible work of art, which, like a painting, can accrue the patina of time and in some context attain value based on such unique properties as belonging to this or that prominent film director.

Could magnetic tapes become unique works of art by similar logic? Imagine a collectible videotape that was handled by the late Elvis Presley. One could object that humans cannot observe magnetic traces directly; whatever sense of valuable degradation or patina particular to magnetic storage media is lost on the average collector. An objection could also be raised that videotapes were produced in much greater quantities than film. Should we then impose an arbitrary cutoff point, a certain number of copies that, once exceeded, take the work of art out of the aesthetic realm? What about the obverse movement? In 2014, Wu-Tang Clan, a New York–based musical collective, released an album digitally on CD-ROM, but only in a single copy that cannot, by contract, be reproduced by its buyer.[59] Given the restrictions, does the album retain its digital properties, or does it become, in effect, an analog work of art?

These thought experiments show that qualities such as reproducibility, originality, patina, and authenticity depend on an observer's capacities to perceive or enact them and not solely on any intrinsic property of the medium. Film and video are reasonably irreproducible series of paintings and, from another perspective, perfectly copyable facsimiles.

In 2008, the philosopher Matthew Katz proposed two further important theoretical qualifications to the digital-analog debate. First, he distinguished between format and medium. Second, he proposed that the digital-analog distinction often depends on the observer. To illustrate these two amendments, Katz imagined a measuring system that involves a supply of marbles in a large beaker. We can thereby agree to use a "handful" as an approximate unit of measurement in that system. One can imagine a situation in which a beaker contains three handfuls of marbles, for example. Katz's system is analog, even though marbles themselves are a perfectly discrete medium, because it establishes no precise convention to reproduce handfuls. The marble-beaker system violates Haugeland's requirement for positive and reliable standards of reproducibility. My two handfuls might be different from yours because of the difference in the size of our hands. Whereas the medium (marbles) is discrete, the format (handfuls) is analog.

The mechanism of measuring depends on the measurer. It is analog when we cannot accurately perceive approximate quantities. If humans were able to magically discern the exact number of water molecules in a beaker, previously analog systems (such as unmarked beakers) would in effect become digital. Similarly, if humans were endowed with hands of a definite size and volume, handfuls would be counted as discrete and therefore digital quantities. From similar thought experiments, Katz concluded that the physical, perceptual, and cognitive capabilities of users (readers, audience, perceivers) affect the ontological status of the system, a handful of marbles or a work of art.[60]

Katz's seemingly minor amendments to Haugeland entail several radical consequences in practice. The physics of the medium, he reveals, are significant insofar as they are tied to our ability to impose order, to format something. Whether a beaker is full of marbles or water is irrelevant. What matters is our ability to structure the medium into exactly reproducible units. We can do that with marbles by counting. To format water, we would need more precise instruments. Undifferentiated matter like cake is analog only until someone cuts it into pieces. A "piece of cake" is already a format and a unit of measurement. And the technique of cutting is important. The ontological status of cake changes depending on the agent doing the cutting. For someone armed with a laser cutter and a microscope, the cake is, on a spectrum, a near perfect digital medium. Alternatively, it is an analog medium for those who eat with their hands.

Our confusion about the dual status of *Myst* resolves when we introduce the distinction between medium and format. *Myst* is digital for those who can access the game's code, to take an obvious example. This binary layer is not normally accessible at the site of the projection. Players cannot access the game's discrete bits, which produce surface images. Players therefore perceive computed scenery as indivisible analog representation. The property of being digital indicates the systematic ability to impose structure. *Myst* is digital for a programmer and analog for the player. The quality of something being digital in that sense separates those able to differentiate from those who apprehend the differentiated structure in the "holistic repleteness of images."[61]

Further, note that from an instrumental point of view, to make something digital, in Katz's final formulation, implies the separation of structure and medium. The painting is wholly analog so long as it remains irreproducible. It becomes digital when the viewer is able to impose structure, by which the visual form is lifted from the medium of canvas. When taken outside their theoretical contexts, the affordances of reproduction—flawless copying and preservation through positive and reliable means—acquire an immediate practical significance. For example, it is important to a librarian that a document is preserved reliably and that it continues to be accessible to the public. By contrast, a copyright holder may be invested in preventing digitization. Reliability and accessibility are thus social, technological, and institutional properties of the medium. They vary by cultural and political contexts.

Once we understand the terms *analog* and *digital* as instrumental properties, which we impose on media from without, we can better perceive their political and not vaguely metaphysical import. Truly digital text can be copied and placed into other hands and minds, feasibly and reliably. The possibility of enacting such procedures is what ultimately gives representation its digital form. Our senses limit our ability to format, to impose structure onto media. We cannot, for example, communicate in the infrared spectrum without proper instrumentation. Our ability to format media, to make it digital, is often limited from without by political means. A classified document, for example, loses some of the necessary digital preconditions. One is literally not allowed to copy it. It has to remain embedded within this particular piece of paper on this particular desk.

Technologies like digital rights management, which limit a reader's ability to copy books, similarly transform digital content into its media-dependent, irreproducible, and ultimately analog forms. Paradoxically, a paper and ink book that places no restrictions on copying and transmediation is, in a sense, a more digital format than a restricted electronic book. Arbitrary restrictions on digital formatting create class distinctions between those with and those without permissions to copy, share, and transform.

The word, already a discrete quantity, comes into digital being as form when coupled loosely to its material contexts. Ontologically, text is by nature a digital format: first, because it represents discrete units of information about the world and, second, because it allows for some measure of flawless copying and preservation. Flawless copying and preservation are in themselves contingent, not essential, properties of writing. Human language operates in the digital mode, then, so long as it continues to participate in the unhindered transmediation of thought—from mind states to voice, from voice to paper, from paper to wire, and then on to other mind states. Without such chains of transmission and transmediation there can be no culture, in the sense that culture constitutes a shared intellectual achievement. I participate in that collective endeavor insofar as I am free to unburden my thoughts from their natural medium, my brain. I speak out loud; I write thoughts down on paper; I pass notes to others.

In the extreme, analog logic entails total censorship. Purely analog thoughts would be ones that could never leave their origins. Media independence in that sense transcends the intellectual confines of an individual. Without digital portability, all representation—art and knowledge—attaches itself irrevocably to untranslatable and irreproducible conditions of their production.

Imagine a world in which ideas forever adhere to their brain-bound media. Imagine also a society that positively prohibits the transmediation of thought, on paper or between brain cells. Envision extreme forms of thought control that restrict fundamental basics of speech and literacy, prohibiting the manufacture of pens, paper, computers, photocopiers, voice recorders, and word processors—language and communication itself. Such prohibitions would amount to total censorship. A radically analog society would also be a radically mute one.

Understanding digitality as a kind of order—a format that arranges matter in certain ways tied to particular affordances of specific devices—recasts the history of computing into something other than simple "mathesis," the idea that computation reduces the world into more discrete and therefore computable elements. That notion would be true if the computer was simply a glorified calculator. But computers are more than that. In practice, they reveal themselves to be self-amending machines for universal transmediation—machines that, depending on the user's acuity and dispensation to access deep structure, separate readers into those for whom texts and images exist as a fixed analog given and those for whom they exist in a fluid form. Digitization implies the ability to impose structure onto the world, a liberty to exchange one symbolic order for another among signs, people, and machines.

THE MEDIUM IS NOT THE MESSAGE

In examining the material conditions of digital representation, we find format—a quality distinct from both medium and content—to emerge as a political construct that governs the physical affordances of communication. We began this chapter with popular intuitions about the essence of digital representation. We end on firmer ground, on which formatting identifies the tactical ability to impose structure onto a medium. Formatting matters because it frames the mode of media apprehension. How the cake is cut also determines how we eat it. To format text without margins, for example, is also to deny marginalia. And to format text in a way that prevents further remediation is to deny the formation of shared culture.

Circumspect critics, like Fish and Golumbia, are rightfully suspicious of unexamined claims about digitization, but for the wrong reasons. Digitization threatens humanity only insofar as it lays claim on the recipient of the message. Paragraphs facilitate understanding by structuring undifferentiated text into units that more closely correspond to our mental ability to retain information. Margins give space to annotation. Conversely, formats can hinder comprehension. A poorly formatted text discourages or prevents critical thought outright.

In his influential essay on the political quality of technological artifacts, Langdon Winner famously argued that in modern times "people are often willing to make drastic changes in the way they live to accord with technological innovation," but at the same time they would "resist similar kinds of changes justified on political grounds."[62] The insight is yet to filter into literary studies. Readers, writers, and critics who would be pained to support laws in favor of censorship or surveillance effectively promote such systems in daily use. The mismatch between political belief and practice comes from the lack of critical engagement with technology, which, as Winner writes, requires "both the study of specific technical systems and their history as well as a thorough grasp of the concepts and controversies of political theory."[63] Winner elucidated this dynamic through the case study of Robert Moses and his twentieth-century highway-building projects in New York. Moses built low overpasses with an eye toward discouraging bus travel, which reflected his social and racial biases. These in effect carried the force of legislation, Winner argued, denying the poor access to public spaces.[64]

Similarly, in our case, claims on a reader's attention can happen through legislation, by social convention, or through specific material affordances—the inability to take notes, for example, or to share books among family and friends. Such technological constraints disproportionately affect those most reliant on informal knowledge networks, which exist outside economies of wealth and prestige. Digitizing the public archive without a thorough understanding of the platforms and technologies involved risks committing the public to an empty and impoverished vision of social knowledge production. Technologies that hinder feasible procedures for reliable copying and preservation create textual artifacts that are less, not more, digital than paper books. They push us toward privatized knowledge economies. To "read" becomes to "purchase temporary reading rights"; to "take notes" becomes to train supervised learning algorithms; personal reading habits, long protected by our libraries, become a matter for bureaucratic control.

Consider the seemingly innocuous decision to distribute scientific literature formatted in the ubiquitous Portable Document Format (PDF). Adobe, the American company responsible for introducing the file format into circulation, describes it as "allow[ing] the faithful, high-quality reproduction of printed matter in electronic form."[65] Text, when transmitted without formatting specifications, loses its shape to some extent. Think about writing an e-mail, for example. What appears to you as lines of a certain width may appear to the recipient in a completely different form. You may have written your e-mail on a large stationary monitor, for example, whereas your recipient reads on a small portable device. Because formatting is not fixed, e-mail programs are able to reflow the lines appropriately. You have in essence delegated the responsibility of formatting the text to the reader's device. Readers are then free to apprehend it in a manner most convenient for them, tailored to their specific needs, attention spans, geographies, and body types. The downside of having this freedom is that the sender cannot ensure excellence in formatting. The reader's software may render the text poorly or make it outright unreadable.

The PDF solves this problem by guaranteeing that its recipient receives the message exactly as written, without delegating the responsibility of rendering it to the reader. In essence, the format mimics the constraints of a printed page, which similarly preserves the shape of the message during transmission. When writing a letter by hand, you know that your recipient will see what you see, in the same shape and form. But to achieve the effect, the PDF must also limit the document's viewing possibilities. If the sender fixes the width of the page to the standard letter size, the reader would be pained to read such a document on a smaller portable device. The PDF converts digital formats into analog in the name of visual consistency. Strictly speaking, PDF documents do not contain text in the way that an e-mail does. Rather, they contain text like a photograph of a printed page does, as an image. Such constraint is useful for business communication, for example, when writing contracts. The party responsible for drafting a contract wants to know that it will be signed without alteration.

Yet for other purposes, such fixity of formatting is detrimental to communication. Whereas reading paper contracts sent by mail is free, the reading of PDF documents requires specialized software, which may cost money. PDF documents further hinder the copying and preservation of text, the formal prerequisites for digital media. The simple act of taking notes becomes a paid feature of the Adobe Acrobat software. What was gained in a minor (for scholarly communication) convenience of formatting is lost in a major concession to the privatization of public knowledge. We have in effect instituted a document format less flexible than paper. Because copying and preservation are key values for university libraries, the loss of unimpeded copying and preservation should outweigh any gains in purely ornamental stability of document format. This does not mean that we should not use Adobe Acrobat files, only that we must, in all cases, be intellectually invested in the compromises involved.

Technology does not determine literature. Loosely coupled to its material contexts, text continues its relentless drive from matter to idea and onto other matters so long as its passage is not hampered by regimes that prohibit further sharing, remixing, and transmediation. Under certain conditions, in the name of privacy, security, or property rights, it may become necessary to flatten out and to treat text as more of an analog, media-bound modality of communication, limited in its ability to move across minds and cultures. It is also in our broadly human, civic interest to keep such mechanisms of constraint visible to view, under continual scrutiny of critical, close, and closest possible reading.

Human Grounds for Computation

SPACE

The politics of inscription are not simply a matter for academic discussion. In the time that it took me to finish this book, a coalition of U.S. "data dissidents" won a temporary exemption from the Digital Millennium Copyright Act to allow them to modify their medical implants. This group included Hugo Campos, who wanted to access data collected by his Implantable Cardioverter Defibrillator, and Ben West and Jay Radcliffe, who fought for rights to modify their implanted insulin pumps. Marie Moe, of Norway, similarly struggled to rewrite her heart implant's software: "I want to know what code is running inside of my body. . . . Medical devices are black boxes. . . . You can't look into them, there's no transparency, we don't know how they work."[1]

Legal scholars from the Harvard Law School's Berkman Center for Internet and Society presented the coalition's concerns before the United States Copyright Office. They wrote:

> The purpose of a medical device company's source code is to enable the function of a medical device; researchers like the members of this Coalition use the code in order to publish criticism on how safe, secure, and effective these products actually are. The use therefore resembles that of a book critic quoting excerpts of a book in her critique, a paradigm case of fair use.[2]

In Pakistan the Skynet program, sponsored by the U.S. National Security Agency, has placed people on the U.S.-sanctioned "disposition matrix" or "kill list" based on predictive analytics: social network analysis, cellular machine learning, patterns of travel, and telephone use. Automated tools with names such as Smart Tracker, Smart Chart, and Cloud Travel Analytic select people for targeted strikes by unmanned aerial vehicles.[3] Our ability to interpret codes that kill on our behalf also stems from our capacity to access, read, understand, modify, and publish criticism on them.

Readers everywhere are engaged in a political struggle to control and deploy codified resources. The heart and the sky are sites at which the tactics of inscription are increasingly contested. They require a capacity to meet the machine and a poetics capable of new emendations.

A media archaeology of digital inscription recovers the stratified depths extant in all meaning-bearing literary devices. Files deep within an implant or on a military command-and-control server recapitulate the history of laminate semiotics. Even print, which seems to escape computational complexity, can fracture at the point of origin. Most contemporary texts still voyage from keyboard to screen and electromagnetic storage, where they diffuse, multiply, and resist comprehension. The screen subsequently simulates extinct interpretive affordances.

In its advanced form the simulation usurps the simulated. The avatar continues to mimic its object, even as the object passes from use. Scrolling text, for example, has no basis in our experience of handling scrolls. The page may go the same way. Readers who have never seen paper pages—recall the viral image of a child trying to "swipe" a magazine cover—will cease to identify it with a material unit of information. But like the scrolling of scrolls, word processors and e-books will continue to simulate paper. No longer connected to any recognized physics, reading will pass into the realm of dead metaphor. Consider the possibility of interpretation as we know it being a historical anomaly, connected to the contingencies of print.

The gap between input and output is what makes digital texts appear ephemeral. Temporary storage media, located between keyboard and screen, allow for rapid remediation. They keep ink in motion, across surfaces, unattached to sticky media like paper. Such spatial elongation comes at a cost: The inscription passes from view. The sign reappears again on-screen, already processed, that is, altered by the intervention of control units. Reading no longer identifies solitary, self-directed activity. Machine operators far removed from the site of interpretation intervene between readers, writers, and texts.

The consequences of their persistent intervention are immense. Supplemental control characters, originally used for formatting, fuse with programming languages capable of generalized Turing-complete control and computation. Technological and legal fictions rise to restore a measure of stickiness to ephemeral text. Digital rights management circuits are routinely embedded into video-streaming devices to artificially limit the duplication of broadcast material. Similarly, e-book sellers often prevent their readers from copying and pasting content. Such measures mimic the constraints associated with static paper-and-ink-bound media regimes.

I began this book by noticing the duplicity of digital text, which splits its energies between sites of storage and projection. The revealed complexity of that state belies our alienation. Not since premodern times have we been so removed from the material contexts of knowledge production. The average reader today is privy only to surface phenomena. To meet the machine, we must base our strategies of interpretation on newly emergent computational realities. Technologies that govern literacy cannot be allowed to develop apart from the humanities. Such detachment threatens the legacy of interpretive practice, enacted on page or pacemaker. Whatever their politics, literary scholars, philosophers, and historians must negotiate the tactics of reading alongside lawmakers and software engineers. The right to access embedded inscription—to share, repair, remix, modify—underlies the very possibility of interpretation.

TIME

I am tempted to believe, like others before me, that I have enacted here something akin to systems phenomenology: a glimpse into the assemblage of people, texts, and technologies. In such cases, astute readers often reach for Jakob von Uexküll's *Foray into the Worlds of Animals and Humans* to draw on his notion of perceptual worlds (*umwelten*).[4] In his forays Uexküll saw our world from the perspectives of sea urchins, pea weevils, and ichneumon wasps. Uexküll believed that the biologist's task is to imagine such alien life-forms.[5] Consequently, Uexküll insisted on the ultimate subjectivity of perceptual experience. A tick projects its own sense of time and space onto the world, which the biologist recovers in thick description of the animal's perceptual apparatus.

Uexküll was also a pioneer of systems theory, advancing an organism-based model of meaning making. An oak tree's canopy, he wrote, acts in unison with rain to capture and distribute liquid down to its roots. According to his model, capturing and distributing liquid to the roots established the meaning of the oak-rain circuit. "Meaning" in this sense is a property of the system, not the subject. It emerges from environmental interaction. A circuit of meaning is thereby created between the organism and its surroundings. Neither make sense in isolation. The subject and object are brought into harmony:

> If the flower were not bee-like
> If the bee were not flower-like
> The harmony would never succeed.[6]

Posthumanism privileges moments of such alien subjectivity because they destabilize an anthropocentric worldview. What gets lost in the shift of perspectives is the apparent contradiction at the core of what Dorion Sagan has called the Gaia sciences.[7] An idea ascendant in diverse fields from literary studies to information theory and free-market economics shifts the capacity for meaning making from subject to assemblage and from individual to complex system. Meaning in that model is always an aggregate: oak plus rain, bee plus flower. Consequently, it is never available to the subject alone: oak, bee, or biologist. The quest for alien semiotics leads to, in Uexküll's own words, "mute interaction" that is meaningful only from some vantage point outside the system.[8] The forest always understands more than the tree, the planet more than the forest, and so on to the universe. The quest to diminish human import paradoxically leads to the most grandiose point of view possible.

In his essay on the subjective experience of bats, the philosopher Thomas Nagel argued against such presumption. He wrote that there must be something about the experience of being a bat *for* a bat that remains inaccessible to human description.[9] To accept the complex systems worldview is therefore to acknowledge the limits of human imagination. An organ cannot speak for the organism. From the human perspective, to encounter bats (or dogs or trees or machines) for what they are is to retain a measure of the other's ineffable alienness.

There is a quiet humanism in Nagel's insistence on empirical phenomenology.[10] It would be wrong to confuse imagination for lived experience,
he argued: "Certainly it *appears* unlikely that we will get closer to the real
nature of human experience by leaving behind the particularity of our human
point of view and striving for a description in terms accessible to beings
that could not imagine what it was like to be us."[11] Nagel continued, "In
discovering sound to be, in reality, wave phenomenon in air or other media,
we leave behind one viewpoint to take up another."[12] This gets us no closer
to understanding the common reality of the external world.

A media history derived from Nagel's insight does not proceed in isolation
from the human condition. We know technology only through based habitation, tied to our culture and physiology. I therefore advance a descriptive
history from the only perspective available to me. As humanists struggle to
theorize digital modes of being, I find a need to reexamine the category of
the human. No other point of view can sustain analysis or critique. Posthuman humanities are an apparent contradiction. One can purport to speak for
neither things nor assemblages.

In refracting the technological other's gaze, we see only ourselves. In a
fragmentary contemplation of otherness, Bakhtin wrote:

Falsehood and deception unavoidably peering out of their own correlation.
The external image of thought, feeling, the external image of the soul. It is
not I who looks out from the inside, but I look at myself with the eyes of the
world, strange eyes; I am possessed by another. There is no integrity of
internal and external here. To glimpse my own preocular image. The naïve
confluence of self and the other in the mirror image. The surplus of the
other. There is no point of view outside of myself; I cannot access my own
internal image. From my eyes stare a stranger's eyes.[13]

An act of imagination accompanies analysis, but not in a way that exhausts
extrinsic perspective. The difficulty is one of retaining a "surplus of the other."
To encounter one's own "preocular" image is to inquire into the nature of
mediation.

I return, then, to the subject of time, continually in the background of
this book. The tick lies in wait for its next warm meal for decades (Uexküll
reports up to eighteen years). Species time advances only by such remark-

able events. Although it seemed objective and universal, we now see it as relative to the subject and its environment.[14] Popular reception of digital technology belies a deep sense of anxiety about the pace it sets for our existence. Throughout, one observes the delicate negotiation of synchronicity between human and machine. A complex chain of transfiguration (encoding and decoding) connects incongruent media (wetware and hardware). Homeostasis is found at some arbitrary point, incidentally attached to human biology in a state of technical augmentation. The resulting cyborg can either acquiesce to contingent timelines or project its own. The question of what constitutes a moment, when watching television or reading a book, can finally be better rephrased into what it *should* constitute.

Integrated crystal oscillators pace all forms of digital life: poetry, drone, and heart implant. Against this rhythm we advance a computational poetics, the study of temporal arrangements: prosody, meter, enjambment, dissonance, and syncopation.

GLOBAL PERSPECTIVES

A history of digital text undoubtedly reflects the legacy of European and, later, North American colonialism. Treaties that negotiated early character encodings initially did so in the dominant diplomatic languages, French and English.[15] Even though modern character encodings such as UTF-8 render many more international scripts, the overall camber of digital literacy still skews toward English. Speaking English is a requirement for software practice. The challenge and consequence of the book will be in exposing such technological bias.

It is easy to forget the blunt effectiveness of physical restraints to speech in the global northwest. Books that are burned or redacted cannot be read at all. Elsewhere, inequities of access to knowledge compel readers to print their own books and build their own libraries. Witness the so-called shadow libraries of Eastern Europe and Central Asia, the street book vendors of India and Pakistan, and the gray market presses of Nigeria arising from the country's "book famine."[16] More than mere piracy, such samizdat-like practices preserve the literary sphere.[17] Informal book exchange networks create reading publics that own the means of textual production and dissemination. Under duress, readers build homemade knowledge infrastructures; they duplicate, distribute, catalog, and archive.

By contrast, in wealthier economies, such infrastructures are commodified. Readers consequently receive the material contexts of their meaning making passively. The costs of knowledge production and barriers to its distribution disappear from view. For many readers, technologies that support reading, writing, and interpretation further pass from tools to fetishes. They are swaddled in protective vestments and given a prominent place in the home. They are imbued with animate spirits. We form emotional rather than intellectual bonds with them, on aesthetic rather than ethical grounds. Thus we exist in a state of profound alienation from mechanisms closest to our mental activity.

I look east and south, then, to see that whatever the technology, the choice to wield an epistemic thing—word processor or character set—is never neutral. Technology embodies power in nonobvious ways. One must insist on dragging it into a dialectic, by which ideals are shown to reify into specific technological commitments.

I want to ask in parting, How do we, as a society, escape the quietly smothering embrace of technology? A multitude of microscopic prosthetics in aggregate exert an enormous pressure on the mind's centers of pleasure and satiation. A quietude descends on the dwellings of our intellectual life. The digitally displaced hold on to the discomfort of the encounter with the machine. Estrangement, always at the heart of immigrant or queer poetics, reconciles without seeking wholeness or integration. I dedicate this book, then, to queers and immigrants, literal and figurative—spatial, literary, technological—to those being displaced unwillingly, to those exiled within and without, to those who understand the need for self-displacement, to those who transgress purposefully, and to those who continue to trespass.

NOTES

INTRODUCTION

1. Patricia MacCormack often uses the term *asemiosis* in a more evocative, Deleuzian sense. See, for example, MacCormack, "Cinema of Desire." I use it here in a direct, Peircean sense as an antonym to semiosis, the alignment of sign, object, and interpretant. See Peirce, "Pragmatism in Retrospect," 282.

2. Christian Bök writes: "I have been striving to write a short verse about language and genetics, whereupon I use a 'chemical alphabet' to translate this poem into a sequence of DNA for subsequent implantation into the genome of a bacterium (in this case, a microbe called *Deinococcus radiodurans*—an extremophile, capable of surviving, without mutation, in even the most hostile milieus, including the vacuum of outer space)" (Bök, "Xenotext Works," n.p.). See also Bök, *Xenotext*.

3. Unicode Consortium, *Unicode Standard*, 9, 10.

4. Cook, "Some Considerations," 91.

5. See Fry, "Circumventing Access Controls"; Ginsburg, "Legal Protection"; and Ku, "Critique."

6. The retailer has since introduced a program that allows for limited sharing of materials, restricted by time and geography.

7. Winner, *Autonomous Technology*, 335.

8. Scholars such as Alexander Galloway, David Golumbia, and Bernard Harcourt have advanced critiques along similar lines. See Galloway, *Protocol*; Golumbia, *Cultural Logic*; and Harcourt, *Exposed*.

9. Halstead, "Genesis and Speed," 456.

10. I borrow the term *microanalysis* from Boris Iarkho, a largely forgotten (in the West) Russian literary scholar and member of the Moscow Linguistic Circle. In his *Methodologies of Exact Literary Study* (circa 1935–1936) he wrote: "I understand

'atomism' as a sort of an ideal aspiration, an orientation toward the liminally small. But under no circumstances do I advocate working with hypothetical quantities, like molecules, atoms, positrons, and so on, which are located beyond the limits of perception. That this applied mythology gave us such splendid results in chemistry should not conceal its true nature. Tomorrow, all such explanations of visible through the invisible could give way to other hypotheses, as was the case with their no less fertile predecessors (elemental spirits, phlogiston, and light ether). But the cell, the nucleus, and the chromosome endure as lasting accomplishments of microanalysis. I suggest moving as far as a microscope can reach, and no further" (Iarkho, *Metodologia*, 363–64; translation mine).

11. Affordances, as Caroline Levine explains, "describe the potential uses or actions latent in materials and designs." For example, "glass affords transparency," whereas "steel affords strength" (C. Levine, *Forms*, 6). See also Hutchby, "Technologies," 447.

12. Leroi-Gourhan, *Gesture and Speech*, 83–84; Siegert, *Cultural Techniques*.

13. I am influenced in this regard by the philosophical poetics of Gaston Bachelard and Henri Lefebvre, extended into the realm of everyday computation. See Bachelard, *Poetics of Space*; and Lefebvre, *Production of Space*.

14. Works by Finn Brunton, Wendy Chun, Lisa Gitelman, Yuk Hui, Helen Nissenbaum, John Durham Peters, Mary Poovey, and Jonathan Sterne, among many others, left their mark on this text.

15. Flusser, *Freedom*, 13. See also Finger et al., *Vilém Flusser*, 132.

16. Flusser, *Freedom*, 13.

17. Flusser, *Freedom*, 81.

18. Flusser, *Freedom*, 82–83.

19. Shklovsky et al., *Sborniki*, 7.

20. Shklovsky et al., *Sborniki*, 7.

21. Shklovsky et al., "Isskustvo, kak priem," 104. Translations are mine unless source cited is explicitly in English.

22. For more on alienation, see the relevant discussion in Marx, *Economic and Philosophic Manuscripts*; and Marx, *Theories of Surplus-Value*.

23. For example: "Writers concerned with problems of technology-out-of-control have frequently echoed Hobbes in suggesting that such an artifact—the Leviathan of interconnected technical systems—has a soul of its own. . . . A ghost appears in the network. Unanticipated aspects of technological structure endow the creation with an unanticipated *telos*" (Winner, *Autonomous Technology*, 280).

24. Atzori, "Smart Objects"; Bohn et al., "Living"; Calverley, "Android Science"; Hildebrandt, "Ambient Intelligence"; and Ma et al., "Towards a Smart World."

25. Marx, *Capital* (1906), 82; Wigdor et al., "Designing User Interfaces."

26. Kittler, *Gramophone*, 263.

27. See, for example, C. N. Davidson, *Now You See It*; Negroponte, *Being Digital*; Obama, "2016 State of the Union Address"; and Postman, *Technopoly*.

28. Fry, "Circumventing Access Controls."

29. I am influenced here by the discussion of epistemic things in Rheinberger, *History of Epistemic Things*, 24–37.

30. Flusser, *Freedom*, 81.

31. Flusser, *Freedom*, 12.

32. Flusser, *Freedom*, 12.

33. Flusser, *Freedom*, 84.

34. Kirschenbaum, *Mechanisms*, 15. On the role of reverse engineering in media studies, see also Fuller and Goffey, *Evil Media*, 9.

35. Petroski, *Invention by Design*, 3–7. See also Conti et al., "Visual Reverse Engineering."

36. Drucker, "Digital Ontologies"; Hayles, "Print Is Flat"; McGann, *Radiant Textuality*.

37. On the Obscene Publication Acts, see McCalman, "Unrespectable Radicalism"; and Roberts, "Morals."

38. See discussion in Chun, "On Software," 27–28; Galloway, "Anti-Language"; and Manovich, *Language*, 48.

39. See Barthes, "Death of the Author"; Foucault, "What Is an Author?"; and Nesbit, "What Was an Author?"

40. See, for example, Martin Heidegger: "For the phenomenon most worthy of thought and questioning remains the mystery of language—wherein our entire reflection has to gather itself—above all when it dawns on us that language is not a work of human beings: language speaks" (Heidegger, *Pathmarks*, 57). See also Barthes, *Rustle of Language*, 5; Blanchot, *Work of Fire*, 41; Nuttall, *New Mimesis*, 6–25; and Varela et al., "Autopoiesis."

41. Bernard, *Introduction*, 3, 15. On Bernard, see Petit, "Claude Bernard"; McLuhan, *Gutenberg Galaxy*, 4, 206; and Sattar, "Aesthetics."

42. Kittler's *Gramophone, Film, Typewriter* ends as follows: "And while professors are still reluctantly trading in their typewriters for word processors, the NSA is preparing for the future: from nursery school mathematics, which continues to be fully sufficient for books, to charge-coupled devices, surface-wave filters, digital signal processors including the four basic forms of computation. Trenches, flashes of lightning, stars—storage, transmission, *the laying of cables*" (Kittler, *Gramophone*, 263).

43. Kittler, *Gramophone*, xxxix.

44. Horkheimer, *Critical Theory*, 143.

45. Horkheimer, *Critical Theory*, 233.

46. Fitzpatrick, *Planned Obsolescence*; Scholz, *Digital Labor*; Terranova, *Network Culture*.

47. See Brouillette, "Unesco"; Brouillette, "Wither Production?"; and English, *Economy of Prestige*.

48. See Freeman, *High Tech*; and Patel, *Working the Night Shift*.

49. Sartre would write "transcendence" and "facticity." See Sartre, *Being and Nothingness*, 86–119.

50. James, "Pragmatism's Conception," 233.

51. For a more thorough discussion on the topic, see Pihlström, *Structuring the World*; Putnam, "James's Theory"; and Seigfried, *James's Radical Reconstruction*.

52. James, "Pragmatism's Conception," 200.

53. Ramsey, *Foundations of Mathematics*, 155.

54. Wittgenstein, *Philosophical Investigations*, 67–77. For more on the connection between Wittgenstein and James, see R. B. Goodman, "James on the Nonconceptual."

55. Knobe and Nichols, *Experimental Philosophy*, 3.

56. P. H. Smith et al., *Ways of Making and Knowing*, 12.

57. Mumford, "Authoritarian and Democratic Technics"; Winner, "Do Artifacts Have Politics?"

58. Haugeland, "Analog."

CHAPTER 1: METAPHOR MACHINES

1. Baudrillard, "Symbolic Exchange," 139–40.

2. Baudrillard, "Symbolic Exchange," 139.

3. Baudrillard, "Symbolic Exchange," 140.

4. Jakobson, "Linguistics and Poetics," 355; see also Malinowski et al., "Problem of Meaning," 146.

5. Aaron and Leburton, "Flash Memory"; Bez et al., "Introduction to Flash Memory"; Pavan et al., "Flash Memory Cells."

6. Boyden et al., "Methods and Systems," 1.

7. Boyden et al., "Methods and Systems," 1.

8. Beard et al., "Data Processor," 1.

9. Pajak, "Electronic Library," 1.

10. Pajak, "Electronic Library," 1.

11. All quotes from Card et al., "Methods," 2.

12. Lakoff, "Contemporary Theory of Metaphor"; Lakoff and Johnson, *Metaphors We Live By*; Searle, "Metaphor"; M. Turner, *Death*.

13. Lakoff, "Contemporary Theory of Metaphor," 212. See also Lakoff and Johnson, "Metaphorical Structure."

14. It bears mentioning at the outset that in the language of cognitive metaphor theory, all figurative tropes of comparison—hyperbole, metonymy, synecdoche, or simile—fall under the category of metaphor.

15. Lakoff and Johnson, "Metaphorical Structure," 195–98.

16. Lakoff, "Contemporary Theory of Metaphor," 239.

17. Lakoff, "Contemporary Theory of Metaphor," 243.

18. Lakoff, "Contemporary Theory of Metaphor," 245.

19. Lakoff, "Contemporary Theory of Metaphor," 245. See also Lakoff, "Invariance Hypothesis"; Ruiz de Mendoza Ibáñez, "Nature of Blending"; and M. Turner and Fauconnier, "Conceptual Integration."

20. Lakoff and Johnson, *Metaphors We Live By*, 61; see also the discussion on pp. 61–68.

21. J. M. Carroll and Thomas, "Metaphor," 107–8.

22. Apple Inc., *Apple Human Interface Guidelines*, 4.

23. Apple Inc., *Apple Human Interface Guidelines*, 5.

24. Cox et al., "Method and System," n.p.

25. Moll-Carrillo et al., "Articulating a Metaphor," 572; emphasis mine.

26. Glaser and Leung, "Graphical User Interface," abstract.

27. Lakoff, "Contemporary Theory of Metaphor," 210–11.

28. Lakoff, "Contemporary Theory of Metaphor," 211.

29. Richards, *Philosophy of Rhetoric*, 95.

30. Richards, *Philosophy of Rhetoric*, 94.

31. Shelley, *Essays*, 5; quoted in Richards, *Philosophy of Rhetoric*, 90–91.

32. Billig and MacMillan, "Metaphor"; Mojtabai, "Delusion as Error."

33. In modern Greek *metaphor* is the ordinary word for "transportation," often inscribed on trucks and shipping containers.

34. For a book-length discussion of dead metaphors, see Müller, *Metaphors Dead and Alive*.

35. Shklovsky, *Voskreshenie Slova*, 3.

36. Flusser, *Freedom*, 13, 82.

37. Lakoff, "Death of Dead Metaphor."

38. Lakoff, "Death of Dead Metaphor"; Müller, *Metaphors Dead and Alive*.

39. L. Carroll, *Annotated Alice*, 55. For a range of possible answers, see Huxley, *The Raven*; and Susina, "Raven." Here is Carroll's own answer: "Because it can produce a few notes, though they are very flat; and it is nevar [*sic*] put with the wrong end in front" (L. Carroll, *Alice's Adventures*, xv; also Susina, "Raven," 16–17).

40. Lakoff, "Contemporary Theory of Metaphor," 215.

41. The notion of digital text is itself a metaphor. Files do not really hold texts. The idea of a text identifies a segment of stored memory coupled with control codes that govern layout and projection in specific material context. Together, these diverse signals and physical affordances create the illusion of a single text.

42. Richards, *Philosophy of Rhetoric*, 96–97.

43. Baudrillard, *Simulacra and Simulation*, 2.

44. *Oxford English Dictionary* (online), s.v. "Simulation," definition 1b. December 2016. www.oed.com/view/Entry/180009?redirectedFrom=simulation& (accessed December 14, 2016).

45. See J. M. Carroll and Thomas, "Metaphor"; J. M. Carroll et al., *Interface Metaphors*; and Spolsky, *User Interface Design*.

46. See Fry, "Circumventing Access Controls"; Ginsburg, "Legal Protection"; Ku, "Critique"; Perzanowski, "Rethinking Anticircumvention's Interoperability Policy"; and von Lohmann, *Unintended Consequences*.

47. Ricoeur says: "The most obvious change from speaking to writing concerns the relation between message and its medium or channel. At first glance, it concerns only this relation, but upon closer examination, the first alteration irradiates in every direction, affecting in a decisive manner all the factors and functions" (Ricoeur, *Interpretation Theory*, 26).

48. Gadamer, *Truth and Method*, 110.

49. Ricoeur, *Interpretation Theory*, 28. See Ricoeur's discussion at pp. 26–29.

50. See Bez et al., "Introduction to Flash Memory"; and Pavan et al., "Flash Memory Cells."

51. Kittler, "There Is No Software."

52. Laurel, "Interface as Mimesis," 67.

53. See Taussig, *Mimesis and Alterity*, 129–44.

54. Coleridge, *Collected Works*, 7: 6–7.

55. S. H. Cameron et al. "DIALOG"; Gaines, "Technology of Interaction"; Orr, *Conversational Computers*.

56. Beatty et al., "Interactive Documentation System"; Coltheart, "Iconic Memory"; Gaines and Shaw, "Timesharing"; Hutchins et al., "Direct Manipulation Interfaces."

57. Hotson et al., "Individual Finger Control"; Leuthardt et al., "Brain-Computer Interface"; S. P. Levine et al., "Direct Brain Interface"; Wolpaw et al., "Brain-Computer Interface Technology."

58. S. H. Cameron et al., "DIALOG"; Gaines and Shaw, "Timesharing"; J. Martin, *Design of Man-Computer Dialogues*; J. Martin and Norman, *Computerized Society*; J. C. Shaw, "JOSS."

59. Turing, "Computing Machinery," 446.

60. Gruenberger, "History of the JOHNNIAC."

61. Gruenberger, "History of the JOHNNIAC," 58.

62. J. C. Shaw, "JOSS," 456.

63. J. C. Shaw, "JOSS," 456.

64. Montfort, *Twisty Little Passages*.

65. Walther and O'Neil, "On-Line User-Computer Interface," 379. See also Gaines and Shaw, "Timesharing," 15.

66. Rick Adams maintains the source code for a number of the game's early versions at rickadams.org/adventure/e_downloads.html. I ran tr, uniq, and wc Unix utilities against the PDP-10 Fortran sources to calculate vocabulary. Later versions of the game contain a slightly enriched lexicon.

67. Shneiderman, "Future of Interactive Systems," 251. See also Hutchins et al., "Direct Manipulation Interfaces," 91.

68. Shneiderman, "Direct Manipulation," 57. See also Leibniz, *Der Briefwechsel*, 1: 375.

69. Shneiderman, "Direct Manipulation," 57. See also Leibniz, *Der Briefwechsel*, 1: 375.

70. Cajori, "History of Notations"; Grabiner, "Mathematical Truth"; Thurston, "Leibniz's Notation."

71. Shneiderman, "Direct Manipulation," 60.

72. Shneiderman, "Direct Manipulation," 65.

73. Jakobson, "A Few Remarks"; Norman and Draper, *User Centered System Design*, 110; Peirce, "Algebra of Logic."

74. Norman, "Cognitive Artifacts," 123.

75. I am using the traditional Peircean distinction between symbol, icon, and index. Peirce writes, "Icons are so completely substituted for their objects as hardly to be distinguished from them" (Peirce, "Algebra of Logic," 226).

76. Charles Sanders Peirce, a philosopher of language whose vocabulary I have been using here, suggests *simulacra* as a possible synonym for *icon*, citing also Plato's *Phaedrus* in relation to the Greek *omoiōma* or imitation. See Peirce, "Excerpts," 481; and Plato, "Phaedrus," 483–85, ll. 250a–b.

77. Laurel, "Interface as Mimesis," 76.

78. See Glaser and Leung, "Graphical User Interface"; and Pajak, "Electronic Library."

79. Laurel, "Interface as Mimesis," 67–86. See also Norman and Draper, *User Centered System Design*, 490–91.

80. Hutchins et al., "Direct Manipulation Interfaces," 98–99.

81. Hutchins et al., "Direct Manipulation Interfaces," 99.

82. Laurel, "Interface as Mimesis," 74.

83. Laurel, "Interface as Mimesis," 75.

84. Hutchins et al., "Direct Manipulation Interfaces," 110.

85. Laurel, "Interface as Mimesis," 75.

86. Laurel, "Interface as Mimesis," 75.

87. Laurel, "Interface as Mimesis," 85.

88. Laurel, "Interface as Mimesis," 75.

89. Hutchins et al., "Direct Manipulation Interfaces," 118.

90. Halstead, "Genesis and Speed," 451.

91. The American toy giant Mattel makes a game called *Mindflex*. The Frequently Asked Questions page includes the following prompt: "Have you ever dreamed of moving an object with the power of your mind? Mindflex Duel™ makes that dream a reality! Utilizing advanced Mindflex Duel™ technology, the wireless headset reads your brainwave activity. Concentrate . . . and the ball rises on a cushion of air! Relax . . . and the ball descends. It's literally mind over matter!" (Mindflex, "Mindflex," n.p.).

92. Leuthardt et al., "Brain-Computer Interface"; K. J. Miller et al., "Spectral Changes."

93. Collinger et al., "Collaborative Approach"; Prabhakar, "Future of War."

94. Heidegger says: "When something at hand is missing whose everyday presence was a matter of course that we never even paid attention to it, this constitutes a *breach* in the context of references discovered in our circumspection. Circumspection comes up with emptiness and now sees for the first time what the missing thing was at hand *for* and at hand *with*. Again the surrounding world makes itself known" (Heidegger, *Being and Time*, 70).

95. Heidegger, *Being and Time*, 65.

96. Heidegger, *Being and Time*, 69.

97. Heidegger, *Being and Time*, 65.

98. Heidegger, "Question Concerning Technology," 319.

99. Heidegger, "Question Concerning Technology," 323–24.

100. Heidegger, "Question Concerning Technology," 331–34.

CHAPTER 2: LAYING BARE THE DEVICE

1. Moreno, *Who Shall Survive*, 233.

2. Moreno is remembered today as a pioneer of group therapy and an early critic of Freud and socialism. Sociologists have also recently rediscovered his formative work on network analysis. His books contain beautiful diagrams, sprouting nodes and edges, with titles such as "Structure of a Cottage Family," "A Handicraft Group," and "The Civilian Social Atom." Moreno was also a humanist and a philosopher of technology and culture. In opposition to eugenics, a popular philosophy at the time, his answer to "who shall survive?" was "everyone." See Moreno, *Who Shall Survive*, 245.

3. Moreno, *Who Shall Survive*, 233.

4. Moreno, *Who Shall Survive*, 234.

5. Moreno, *Who Shall Survive*, 238–39.

6. Moreno, *Who Shall Survive*, 235, 239.

7. Moreno, *Who Shall Survive*, 236.

8. Plato, "Phaedrus," (250a).

9. Moreno, *Who Shall Survive*, 233–52.

10. Lapsed consent is a common theme in the works of Thomas Hobbes, John Locke, and John Stuart Mill. To paraphrase, they ask, What makes whatever voluntary compacts made by past generations still valid today?

11. Moreno, *Who Shall Survive*, 238.

12. Marx, *Capital* (1967 ed.), 72.

13. See Logicworks, "Government Cloud"; and Soyata et al., "COMBAT."

14. Merriam-Webster Online, s.v. "Device," 2015. https://www.merriam-webster.com/dictionary/device (accessed December 15, 2015).

15. I am influenced here, in part, by the discussion on epistemic things in Rheinberger, *History of Epistemic Things*, 11–37.

16. I rely on the Russian originals throughout but cite the English translations where possible as well. See Shklovsky, "Art as Technique"; Shklovsky, *Voskreshenie Slova*; and Shklovsky, "Isskustvo, kak priem."

17. Nabokov, "Guide to Berlin," 27; See also D. B. Johnson, "Guide," 354.

18. Kranzberg, "At the Start," 5, 6.

19. Winner, *Autonomous Technology*, 4.

20. *Technology* overtakes *technique* around 1979, judging by the relative frequency of occurrence in the Google Books n-gram corpus. Michel et al., "Quantitative Analysis of Culture."

21. See, for example, the essays by Osip Brik ("Against Creative Individualism," 76–79) and Viktor Shklovsky ("On Authorship and Production," 194–99) in Chuzhak, *Literatura Fakta*.

22. What can be said about literature here also applies to culture more generally.

23. Benjamin, "Author as Producer," 87.

24. Benjamin, "Author as Producer," 87.

25. Schopenhauer, *World as Will*, 1: 249, 1: 217–346.

26. Shklovsky, "Isskustvo, kak priem," 102.

27. Shklovsky, "Isskustvo, kak priem," 105.

28. Spencer, *Philosophy of Style*, 7.

29. Spencer, *Philosophy of Style*, 3.

30. Spencer, *Philosophy of Style*, 32.

31. Taylor, *Principles of Scientific Management*, 7.

32. Shklovsky, "Isskustvo, kak priem," 103–4.

33. Moréas, "Le symbolisme," 150.

34. Bakhtin, "K voprosam," 270–71.

35. Bakhtin, "K voprosam," 308.

36. Bakhtin, "K voprosam," 310.

37. Bakhtin, "K voprosam," 373, 374.

38. Bakhtin, "K voprosam," 249.

39. Bakhtin, "K voprosam," 275.

40. Nabokov, *Invitation to a Beheading*, 223.

41. Lubbock, *Craft of Fiction*, 1.

42. Lubbock, *Craft of Fiction*, 272.

43. Lubbock collapses the difference between painting and sculpture. See, by contrast, the extended discussion in Herder, *Sculpture*.

44. Lubbock, *Craft of Fiction*, 12, 28. See also Eichenbaum, "Gogol's Overcoat"; and Shklovsky, "Isskustvo, kak priem."

45. Lubbock, *Craft of Fiction*, 274.

46. Lubbock, *Craft of Fiction*, 273.

47. Lubbock, *Craft of Fiction*, 4.

48. Lubbock, *Craft of Fiction*, 6.

49. Lubbock, *Craft of Fiction*, 6.

50. Lubbock, *Craft of Fiction*, 273, 274.

51. Evidence suggests that Wittgenstein read Russian and that he visited the Soviet Union in the 1930s. Both he and Shklovsky fought in Galicia at the Eastern Front. Nothing in the sources suggests that they met or knew of one another's work. See Moran, "Wittgenstein and Russia."

52. Harcourt, *Exposed*; Pasquale, *Black Box Society*.

53. Church and Turing, "Computable Numbers."

54. Descartes, *Discourse*, 36.

55. Gillespie, "Primal Utterance," 32.

56. Searle, "Minds."

57. Searle, "Minds."

58. See Plato, *Plato in Twelve Volumes*. I translate the passage into literal English to preserve characteristics notable in the original. In particular, note the parallelism between *exōthen* and *endothen*, the ambiguity of *allotrion*, as a foreign other, and the subtle slide between *graphō* (letter, figure, writing) and *tupōn* (type,

impression, trace). I extend my gratitude to Stathis Gourgouris, Simos Zenios, and Guy Smoot for their help with Greek translations.

59. See, for example, Ceruzzi, *Computing.*

60. To give you a sense of the timeline, Turing entered King's College in 1931. See Hodges, *Alan Turing,* 78. Turing's paper on computable numbers appeared in print in 1936. It is likely that Turing and Wittgenstein met at the Moral Science Club, where by the 1930s Wittgenstein "monopolized the discussion," even in the presence of such prominent philosophers as George Edward Moore. See Duncan-Jones, "G. E. Moore," 25. Turing attended Wittgenstein's lectures on the foundations of mathematics in 1939.

61. Wittgenstein, *Blue and Brown Books,* 6–7.

62. Wittgenstein, *Blue and Brown Books,* 16.

63. Wittgenstein, *Blue and Brown Books,* 16. See also the related discussion in Dennett, "Can Machines Think," 297.

64. Wittgenstein, *Blue and Brown Books,* 16, 46–49.

65. Wittgenstein, *Blue and Brown Books,* 119.

66. Wittgenstein, *Blue and Brown Books,* 121–22.

67. Wittgenstein, *Blue and Brown Books,* 120.

68. Wittgenstein, *Blue and Brown Books,* 185.

69. Wittgenstein, *Blue and Brown Books,* 185.

70. Wittgenstein, *Philosophical Grammar,* 5.

71. Wittgenstein, *Philosophical Grammar,* 41.

72. Wittgenstein, *Philosophical Grammar,* 42; emphasis mine.

73. Wittgenstein, *Philosophical Grammar,* 45.

74. Wittgenstein, *Philosophical Grammar,* 10.

75. Wittgenstein, *Philosophical Grammar,* 69.

76. Wittgenstein, *Philosophical Grammar,* 69–70.

77. Wittgenstein, *Philosophical Grammar,* 70.

78. Wittgenstein, *Philosophical Grammar,* 190.

79. Wittgenstein, *Philosophical Grammar,* 187–88.

80. Wittgenstein, *Philosophical Grammar,* 190.

81. I am forgoing the distinction between interpreters and compilers for simplicity's sake. See Bashkow et al., "System Design"; Elbourn and Ware, "Evolution of Concepts," 1060; McCarthy, "LISP Interpreter System"; and Neuhold, "Formal Description," 95.

82. Wittgenstein, *Philosophical Grammar,* 194–96.

83. Wittgenstein, *Wittgenstein's Lectures,* 197.

84. Wittgenstein, *Wittgenstein's Lectures,* 282.

85. Wittgenstein, *Wittgenstein's Lectures,* 195.

86. Wittgenstein and Barrett, *Lectures and Conversations,* 13, 16.

87. Not much is written on the intellectual connections between Turing and Wittgenstein. See Copeland and Proudfoot, "What Turing Did"; and Wagner, "Wittgenstein."

88. Wittgenstein, *Wittgenstein's Lectures,* 67–68.

89. The intellectual history of the Turing machine follows works by Diophantus, René Descartes, Georg Cantor, David Hilbert, Gottlob Frege, Bertrand Russell, Kurt Gödel, and Ludwig Wittgenstein. See Grattan-Guinness, "Development of Logics"; Herken, *Universal Turing Machine*; and Petzold, *Annotated Turing*.

90. Turing's later work suggests that his use of cognitive language throughout "On Computable Numbers" was not accidental and that he meant it to define sentience more generally. See Turing, "Computing Machinery."

91. Turing, "Computing Machinery," 458.

92. Turing, "On Computable Numbers," 231.

93. Turing, "On Computable Numbers," 231.

94. Turing, "On Computable Numbers," 231.

95. Turing, "On Computable Numbers," 231.

96. Turing, "On Computable Numbers," 231.

97. Turing, "On Computable Numbers," 241.

98. "We may hope that machines will eventually compete with men in all purely intellectual fields" (Turing, "Computing Machinery," 460).

99. To what extent a personal computer is a Turing machine is matter of contention. The Turing machine is a *thought experiment* that imagines a machine. The PC is a machine simulating the thought experiment. See Chalmers, "Does a Rock Implement"; Petzold, *Code*; and Putnam, *Representation and Reality*, 121–25.

100. Haigh, "Actually," 241.

101. Haigh, "Actually," 241.

102. Church and Turing, "Computable Numbers," 42–43; also cited in Petzold, *Annotated Turing*, 63.

103. This is a topic of some contention in the literature. James Moor includes software immateriality as one of the "three myths" of computer science: "As a practical matter what we regard as computer instructions, and consequently what we regard as computer programs, is determined by the computers available" (Moor, "Three Myths," 215). Nurbay Irmak argues that software is instead a purely abstract artifact, akin to a musical work. See Irmak, "Software." See also Colburn, "Software"; and R. Turner, "Programming Languages."

104. A true universal Turing machine would require a tape that is infinitely long. See Turing, "Computable Numbers," 249.

105. Mike Davey built and displayed a similar instrument at Harvard University's Collection of Historical Scientific Instruments in 2012. He writes: "My goal in building this project was to create a machine that embodied the classic look and feel of the machine presented in Turing's paper. I wanted to build a machine that would be immediately recognizable as a Turing machine to someone familiar with Turing's work" (Davey, "Turing Machine Overview," n.p.).

106. Daugherty, "Numeral Adding"; Degener, "Combined Type-Writing and Adding Machine"; Ellis, "Combined Type-Writing and Adding Machine"; Wright, "Computing Attachment"; Wright, "Computing Mechanism."

107. Cuttriss, "Telegraphy."

108. Bumstead and Bumstead, "Telegraphy," 1.

109. Brown, "Automatic Program System"; Brown, "Selective Program System"; Bumstead and Bumstead, "Telegraphy"; Creed, "Printing Apparatus"; Hallden, "Printing-Telegraph System"; Murray, "Tape-Controlled Telegraphic Transmitting Apparatus"; Vriendt, "Program Distribution System"; Wheatstone, "Improvement."

110. Bumstead and Bumstead, "Telegraphy," 13–14.

111. Bumstead and Bumstead, "Telegraphy," 14.

112. Bumstead and Bumstead, "Telegraphy," 6.

113. Bumstead and Bumstead, "Telegraphy," 13.

114. Bumstead and Bumstead, "Telegraphy," 12.

115. Bumstead and Bumstead, "Telegraphy," 12.

116. Murray, "Setting Type," 556.

117. The institutional distinctions between software engineering and computer science often hinge on the extent to which the discipline pays heed to the physical limitations of computing. As usual, the situation on the ground is much more complicated, and the boundaries between software engineering and computer science are fast eroding. Still, North American students often have the choice to major in computer science or software engineering. It would not be unusual for the one faculty to be located in the School for Liberal Arts and Sciences and the other in the School of Engineering. Consider also the two major professional organizations: the Institute for Electrical and Electronics Engineers (IEEE) and the Association for Computing Machinery (ACM). See Glass, "Comparative Analysis"; Glass et al., "Analysis of Research"; Parnas, "Software Engineering Programs"; and Vessey et al., "Unified Classification System."

118. Deutsch, "Quantum Theory"; Lloyd, "Ultimate Physical Limits"; Piccinini, "Computational Modelling."

119. Kittler, "There Is No Software," opening paragraph.

120. There is a long-standing joke in Marxist literature that involves flipping Hegel, who prioritized the transcendent spiritual over the physical and material forms of life, "back to his feet." For example: "The form of wood, for instance, is altered, by making a table out of it. Yet, for all that, the table continues to be that common, every-day thing, wood. But, so soon as it steps forth as a commodity, it changes into something transcendent. It not only stands with its feet on the ground, but, in relation to all other commodities, it stands on its head, and evolves out of its wooden brain grotesque ideas, far more wonderful than 'table-turning' ever was" (Marx and Engels, *Marx-Engels Reader,* 320). Or this example: "Thereby the dialectic of the concept itself became merely the conscious reflex of the dialectical motion of the real world and the dialectic of Hegel was placed upon its head; or rather, turned off its head, on which it was standing before, and placed on its feet again" (Engels, *Ludwig Feuerbach,* 44).

121. Manovich, "There Is Only Software," 273.

122. Kay, "Computer Software," 59, quoted in Manovich, *Software Takes Command,* 105–6.

123. Manovich, *Software Takes Command,* 150–51.

CHAPTER 3: FORM, FORMULA, FORMAT

1. Andrews et al., "Survey and Critique"; Karim and Zhou, "X-TREPAN."
2. Baudrillard, *Simulacra and Simulation*, 139–40.
3. ISO, "Document Management," vii.
4. Sterne, *MP3*, 11.
5. C. Levine, *Forms*, 7.
6. The Unicode Consortium defines fancy text as "text representation consisting of plain text plus added information" (Unicode Consortium, *Unicode Standard*, 9–10).
7. Sterne wrote of the need for format theory that "demands greater specificity when we talk in general terms about *media*." See Sterne, *MP3*, 11.
8. Sterne, *MP3*, 11.
9. Stensola et al., "Entorhinal Grid Map."
10. See Wittgenstein, *Philosophical Grammar*, 45. On incommensurate languages, see also D. Davidson, *Essays*, 187–99.
11. Sontag, *Against Interpretation*, 14
12. For example, see the Introduction to C. Levine, *Forms*.
13. Gitelman, *Paper Knowledge*, 2.
14. Tanselle, "Concept of Format," 113.
15. Tanselle, "Concept of Format," 67.
16. Collingwood, "Form and Content," 335.
17. McKeown, *Text Generation*, 1 (emphasis mine).
18. Hayles, "Print Is Flat," 72.
19. Hoare, "Record Handling"; Nygaard and Dahl, "Development of the SIMULA Languages."
20. It is difficult to resist quoting from Descartes's *Meditations on First Philosophy* when discussing idealism. He wrote: "Let us take, for instance, this piece of wax. It has been taken quite recently from the honeycomb. . . . It retains some of the scent of the flowers from which it was collected. Its color, shape, and size are manifest. It is hard and cold; it is easy to touch. . . . But notice that, as I am speaking, I am bringing it close to the fire. The remaining traces of the honey flavor are disappearing; the scent is vanishing; the color is changing . . . it is becoming liquid and hot. . . . Does the same wax still remain? I must confess that it does" (Descartes, *Meditations*, 21 (30).
21. Gombrich, *Art and Illusion*, 60.
22. Gombrich, *Art and Illusion*, 62.
23. "What I have called the 'schema' refers to universals," Gombrich writes in reference to Plato. See the discussion in Gombrich, *Art and Illusion*, 123–25.
24. Plato, *Timaeus* (trans. Jowett), 469 (49d).
25. Plato, Timaeus (trans. Bury), 115 (49d).
26. Plato, *Dialogues*, 389a–b.
27. My reading of Plato would be impossible without help from the Perseus Digital Library Project, which allows the reader to explore the Greek originals side by side with translations, maps, dictionaries, and other parallel texts. Sources consulted on Plato's theory of forms include Dixsaut, "Ousia"; Hegel, "Philosophy of Plato";

Rist, "Plato's Earlier Theory"; and Woods, "Form." I would also like to thank Stathis Gourgouris for his generous comments on these passages.

28. Hegel, *Hegel's Aesthetics*, 70.

29. German words collected from the introduction to volume 13 of Hegel, *Werke*.

30. Hegel, *Hegel's Aesthetics*, 81.

31. Hegel, *Hegel's Aesthetics*, 89.

32. Hegel, *Hegel's Aesthetics*, 81.

33. Hegel, *Werke*, Introduction (*Einleitung*) to volume 13.

34. Hegel, "Philosophy of Plato," 249.

35. In an essay on Hegel's formalism, John Crowe Ransom likens the concrete universal to a "formula of a chemical reaction," a "recipe for a dish," and a "blueprint of a machine." Crucially, the Hegelian universal becomes concrete when the machine "has been materialized" and is "working" properly. Turing machines from the previous chapter are concrete universals to the extent that they embody an idealized algorithm and a specified device. See Ransom, "Concrete Universal," 387.

36. Wimsatt, "Structure of the Concrete Universal," 262.

37. Wimsatt, "Structure of the Concrete Universal," 280.

38. Shklovsky et al., *Sborniki*, 1: 25.

39. Khlebnikov, *Collected Works*, 179; Khlebnikov, *King of Time*, 151; LaBelle, *Lexicon of the Mouth*, 63.

40. Khlebnikov, *King of Time*, 152.

41. Shklovsky et al., *Poetika*, 13.

42. To this strain of formalism one could also adduce Vladimir Propp's well-known *Morphology of the Folktale*, a text that finds a limited number of universal principles of composition in the multiplicity of folktale traditions.

43. Veselovsky, "O metode i zadachah," 16–17; and Veselovsky, "Tri glavy," 227.

44. Veselovsky, "Psihologicheskii paralelism," 185; Veselovsky, "Tri glavy," 475.

45. Veselovsky, "Tri glavy," 475–76.

46. Jameson, *Marxism and Form*, 404.

47. Heidegger, *Being and Time*, 202 (220). For a defense of Heidegger's etymological methods, see King, "Heidegger's Etymological Method."

48. Best and Marcus, "Surface Reading," 9.

49. Best and Marcus, "Surface Reading," 12.

50. Sontag, *Against Interpretation*, 12.

51. Sontag, *Against Interpretation*, 12.

52. Sontag, *Against Interpretation*, 14.

53. Sontag, *Against Interpretation*, 9, 10.

54. Sontag, *Against Interpretation*, 3.

55. Sontag, *Against Interpretation*, 9.

56. Sontag, *Against Interpretation*, 10.

57. Best and Marcus, "Surface Reading," 10.

58. Martin Luther said, "Not only are we the freest of rulers, we are also priests forever, which is far more excellent than being kings, for as priests we are worthy to

appear before God to pray for others and to teach one another divine things" (Luther, "Freedom," 43).

59. Tanselle, "Concept of Format," 67.

60. See, for example, the discussion on the limits of the inductive method in bibliographic study in McKenzie et al., *Making Meaning*, 16–17. See also McGann, "Socialization of Text"; and Tanselle, "Textual Instability."

61. Phelps, "Edition as Art Form," 65.

62. Shillingsburg, "Being Textually Aware," 171.

63. McKay, *Harlem Shadows*.

64. Drucker and McGann, "Images as the Text," n.p.

65. Lubbock, *Craft of Fiction*, 1.

66. Drucker and McGann, "Images as the Text," n.p.

67. See Blair, "Note Taking"; Daston, "Taking Note(s)"; and Piper, "Of Note."

68. Adobe Systems Inc., "Plans and Pricing."

69. Adobe Systems Inc., "Adobe Acrobat Reader."

70. Adobe Systems Inc., "Plans and Pricing."

71. "Amazon Kindle: Welcome."

72. "Amazon Kindle: FAQ."

73. Google Inc., "Read Books."

74. Manovich, *Software Takes Command*, 71, 79–80. See also Nelson, "File Structure."

75. On epistemic disobedience, see Mignolo, "Epistemic Disobedience."

76. On the movie theater as the intersection of incommensurate media, see Galloway, *Gaming*, 39.

77. See Best and Marcus, "Surface Reading."

78. Kaiman, "Computer-Aided Publications Editor," 65–66.

79. Kaiman, "Computer-Aided Publications Editor," 66.

80. Kaiman, "Computer-Aided Publications Editor," 68.

81. Ritchie and Thompson, *QED Text Editor*.

82. Angluin and Deutsch, *Reference Manual*, 1–2.

83. Angluin and Deutsch, *Reference Manual*, 3-1.

84. Berns, "Format Program," 85; Berns, "Description of FORMAT," 141.

85. Berns, "Description of FORMAT," 141–42.

86. Berns, "Format Program," 91. See also Berns, "Description of FORMAT," 145.

87. Kernighan and Ossanna, "Troff User's Manual," 1.

88. Furuta et al., "Document Formatting Systems," 418.

89. Furuta et al., "Document Formatting Systems," 418.

90. Furuta et al., "Document Formatting Systems," 417–19; A. C. Shaw, "Model for Document Preparation Systems."

91. Furuta et al., "Document Formatting Systems," 421.

92. Furuta et al., "Document Formatting Systems," 419–22.

93. O'Gorman, "Document Spectrum," 1162–63. See also O'Gorman and Kasturi, *Document Image Analysis*, 82–99.

94. There are also genres of literature where the rivers do become meaningful, as in concrete poetry, for example.

95. A series of paper sizes are governed by the international standard ISO 216. In the Imperial System these equate to 33.1 in. x 46.8 in. for A1 paper and 8.27 in. x 11.7 in. for A4 paper. See ISO, "Writing Paper."

96. Furuta et al., "Document Formatting Systems," 419–20; Kimura and Shaw, "Structure of Abstract Document Objects."

97. See ISO 8879:1986.

98. Madnick and Moulton, "SCRIPT," 92, 97.

99. Berns, "Description of FORMAT," 141.

100. Kernighan and Ossanna, "Troff User's Manual," 1.

101. TROFF at least is actually Turing complete, according to Raymond, *Art of UNIX Programming*, 195.

102. Drafted in 1978 as ISO/TC97/Sc17/N46 and adopted by the International Organization for Standardization in 1984 as ISO 7498.

103. Quotes in this list are from L. J. Miller, "ISO Reference Model," 285–86. The full OSI protocol stack is composed of the following layers: Application, Presentation, Session, Transport, Network, Data Link, and Physical. See also Day, "(Un) Revised OSI Reference Model"; Day and Zimmermann, "OSI Reference Model"; and Piatkowski, "ISO-ANSI Open Systems Reference Model."

104. The DOM technically exists at the application layer of the OSI model.

105. Galloway, *Protocol*, 28–54.

106. The International Standards Organization (ISO) in the case of OSI, the Internet Engineering Task Force in the case of TCP/IP, and the World Wide Web Consortium (W3C) in the case of the DOM.

107. See U.S. Code, Title 17, §106.

108. Matthew Kirschenbaum writes: "Computers are unique in the history of writing technologies in that they present a premeditated material environment built and engineered to propagate an illusion of immateriality; the digital nature of computational representation is precisely what enables this illusion—or else call it a working model—of immaterial behavior" (Kirschenbaum, *Mechanisms*, 135).

109. For a more extended discussion about the impact of sharing technologies on the distribution of cultural goods, see Lessig, "Free(ing) Culture."

110. Clark, "Copyright Environment," 81.

111. Clark, "Copyright Environment," 84.

112. Clark, "Copyright Environment," 83–84. See also CITED Consortium, *CITED Final Report*.

113. Szabo, "Formalizing," abstract.

114. For examples, see Grundy, "Information Distribution System"; Robshaw, "Abuse-Resistant Object Distribution System"; and Takayuki and Naoya, "Licensee Notification System."

115. Benson and Urich, "Method and System," 1–2.

116. See Robshaw, "Abuse-Resistant Object Distribution System."

117. See U.S. Code, Title 17, §1201.

118. See U.S. Code, Title 17, §1201.a.1.A.

119. See U.S. Code, Title 17, §1201.a.3.A.

120. See U.S. Code, Title 17, §1201.a.3.B.

121. DMCA 1201 provides for a number of complicated exemptions that might, under some interpretations, sanction limited use for academic purposes. See Armstrong, "Digital Rights Management"; Herman and Gandy, "Catch 1201"; Ku, "Critique"; Liu, "DMCA"; and Stoltz, "Is It Illegal."

122. Von Lohmann, *Unintended Consequences*, 1.

123. Fry, "Circumventing Access Controls."

124. Ferullo, "Major Copyright Issues"; Mueller, "Reinventing Media Activism"; Postigo, "Information Communication Technologies."

125. *Agfa Monotype Corp. v. Adobe Systems, Inc.*, 404 F. Supp. 2d 1030 (N.D. Ill. 2005). See also; Lipton, "To (C) or Not to (C)?"; and von Lohmann, *Unintended Consequences.*

126. American Law Institute, *Restatement*, secs. 1–2.

127. Digital Millennium Copyright Act, 112 Stat. 2864-6, 2884 (web.archive.org/web/20161222002713/https://www.copyright.gov/legislation/pl105-304.pdf). See also Pike & Fischer Inc., *Digital Millennium Copyright Act*, 20–22, 34.

128. Seringhaus, "E-Book Transactions," 150.

129. Note that these effects are not necessarily limited to contemporary documents. Medieval texts often involved locking mechanisms, locks, and hidden compartments that would similarly alter the nature of the textual encounter, depending on the reader.

CHAPTER 4: RECONDITE SURFACES

1. Chun, "Enduring Ephemeral," 148.

2. Solid-state memory technology (e.g., flash memory) stores information in capacitor "circuit states," as opposed to electromagnetic storage, which works by modulating electrical charge over a magnetic surface. Solid-state capacitor storage was used in the earliest computers but was prohibitively expensive to manufacture until well into the twenty-first century, when solid-state drives began to replace electromagnetic storage in consumer electronics. See Kahng, "Semipermanent Memory," 1296. In an earlier paper Kahng and Sze explain: "A structure has been proposed and fabricated in which semipermanent charge storage is possible. A floating gate is placed a small distance from an electron source. When an appropriately high field is applied through an outer gate, the floating gate charges up. The charges are stored even after the removal of the charging field due to much lower back transport probability. . . . Such a device functions as a bistable memory with nondestructive read-out features. The memory holding time observed was longer than one hour" (Kahng and Sze, "Floating Gate," 1288). On floating-gate avalanche injection, see also Frohman-Bentchkowsky, "Fully Decoded"; and Horton, "Experimental Study."

3. Heim, *Electric Language*, 211; McCorduck, *Universal Machine*, 51.

4. McCorduck, *Universal Machine*, 51; also quoted in Heim, *Electric Language*, 192.

5. Kirschenbaum, *Mechanisms*, 51.

6. Drucker, "Performative Materiality," para. 2.

7. "Google's mission is to organize the world's information and make it universally accessible and useful" (Google Inc., "About Google"). See also Johanna Drucker's discussion on "the totalizing drive of the digital" in Drucker, "Digital Ontologies," 145.

8. See Hayles, "Print Is Flat."

9. These stages correspond roughly to the "three generations of electronic computing" outlined in Peter Denning's "theory of operating systems." See Denning, "Third Generation Computer Systems."

10. Programmable media more generally have multiple origins, worthy of their own extended history. The French textile worker Basile Bouchon used "drill paper" to automate industrial drawlooms. The invention of the loom could also be attributed to the Banū Mūsā brothers, ninth-century automata inventors from Baghdad; to Jacques de Vaucanson, who delighted the public with his lifelike mechanisms in the mid-eighteenth century; or to Joseph Charles Marie Jacquard, who improved on and popularized Bouchon's looms on an industrial scale around the same time. See Koetsier, "Prehistory of Programmable Machines," 593–95; Randell et al., "History of Digital Computers"; and Riskin, "Defecating Duck."

11. Adler and Albertman, "Knitting Machine"; Casper, "Remote Control Advertising"; Hough, "Wired Radio Program Apparatus."

12. Murray, "Setting Type," 36.

13. Murray, "Setting Type," 36.

14. Murray, "Setting Type," 86.

15. ITU, *Documents diplomatiques*.

16. Brackbill, "Some Telegraphers' Terms," 288.

17. Boyd, "Telegraph-Key"; H. G. Martin, "Telegraphic Transmitter."

18. Halstead, "Genesis and Speed"; McNicol, *American Telegraph Practice*, 207; U.S. Bureau of Labor Statistics, "Displacement of Morse Operators."

19. Brackbill, "Some Telegraphers' Terms," 288; U.S. Bureau of Labor Statistics, "Displacement of Morse Operators."

20. Brackbill, "Some Telegraphers' Terms," 288.

21. Brackbill, "Some Telegraphers' Terms," 289.

22. See Brackbill, "Some Telegraphers' Terms," 288–89. Operators at the time were all almost exclusively male.

23. Hughes, "Improvement in Telegraphs," 2.

24. Hughes, "Improvement in Telegraphs," 1. See also Hayles, "Print Is Flat," 145–47; and Noll, *Evolution of Media*, 20–21.

25. Hausmann, *Telegraph Engineering*; Rowland, "Multiplex Printing-Telegraph."

26. Technical literature makes a distinction between space- and frequency-division multiplexing. On some level, space-division multiplexing simply involves the splitting of a signal into multiple physical channels (wires). Frequency-division multiplexing better "fills" the space of a single channel.

27. Murray, "Setting Type."

28. Leibnitz, "Explication."

29. Bacon, *Advancement of Learning*, 265.

30. Bacon, *Advancement of Learning*, 266.

31. Jennings, "Annotated History."

32. The Australian Donald Murray improved on the Baudot system to minimize the amount of holes needing to be punched, allotting fewer perforations to common English letters. See Murray, "Setting Type," 567.

33. Twenty-eight measures indicate the numerical "figure space" and twenty-six indicate double quotes, which share the encoding length with the letter *z*.

34. Beauchamp, *History of Telegraphy*, 380–97; Murray, "Setting Type."

35. Murray, "Setting Type," 557.

36. According to the U.S. Bureau of Labor Statistics, women made up 24 percent of the Morse operators in 1915 (before the widespread advent of automated telegraphy). By 1931 women made up 64 percent of printer and Morse manual operators. U.S. Bureau of Labor Statistics, "Displacement of Morse Operators," 514.

37. Brackbill, "Some Telegraphers' Terms," 290.

38. ITU, *Telegraph Regulations*, 12.

39. ITU, *Telegraph Regulations*, 12.

40. ITU, *Telegraph Regulations*, 13.

41. ITU, *Telegraph Regulations*, 13.

42. Goldberg, "Controller," 3.

43. Goldberg, "Controller," 1.

44. Goldberg, "Controller," 1–4.

45. Goldberg, "Controller," 1.

46. Chun, *Programmed Visions*, 3.

47. Susan Hockey writes, "Father Busa has stories of truckloads of punched cards being transported from one center to another in Italy" (Hockey, "History of Humanities Computing," n.p.).

48. Lee and Worral, *Electronic Composition*, 48.

49. Daniel et al., *Magnetic Recording*; Engel, "1888–1988"; Poulsen, "Method of Recording"; O. Smith, "Some Possible Forms"; Thiele, "Magnetic Sound Recording"; Vasic and Kurtas, *Coding and Signal Processing*.

50. Camras, "Magnetic Recording Tapes," 505.

51. Dee, "Magnetic Tape," 1775.

52. Fankhauser, "Telegraphone," 37–38.

53. Fankhauser, "Telegraphone," 40.

54. Fankhauser, "Telegraphone," 39–40.

55. Fankhauser, "Telegraphone," 44.

56. Fankhauser, "Telegraphone," 45.

57. Fankhauser, "Telegraphone," 41.

58. The staff of the Computation Laboratory of Harvard University wrote: "Two means are available for preparing the functional tapes required for the operation of

the interpolators. First, when the tabular values of $f(x)$ have been previously published, they may be copied on the keys of the functional tape preparation unit . . . and the tape produced by the punches associated with this unit, under manual control. Second, as suitable control tape may be coded directing the calculator to compute the values of $f(x)$ and record them by means of one of the four output punches, mounted on the right wing of the machine" (Computation Laboratory, *Relay Calculator*, 33).

59. Computation Laboratory, *Relay Calculator*, 30.

60. Computation Laboratory, *Magnetic Drum Calculator*, 1.

61. Computation Laboratory, *Magnetic Drum Calculator*, 34–35.

62. Computation Laboratory, *Magnetic Drum Calculator*, 35, 143–88.

63. Epstein and Innes, "Electrographic Printer," 1.

64. Epstein and Innes, "Electrographic Printer," 2.

65. Eisenberg, "Word Processing."

66. American Bar Association, "$10,000 Typewriter," 416.

67. See Ohmori et al., "Memory Element"; and Stefanita, *Magnetism*, 1–69.

68. Recall Wittgenstein's broken reading machines, which exhibited a similarly recursive problem of verification. To check whether someone understood a message, one has to resort to another message, and so on.

69. Youngquist and Hanes, "Magnetic Reader," 1.

70. Youngquist and Hanes, "Magnetic Reader," 1.

71. Morgan and Norwood, "IBM Selectric Composer," 69.

72. Bishop et al., "Development," 387.

73. Clancy et al., "Data Reading," 1.

74. May, "IBM Word Processing Developments," 743.

75. May, "IBM Word Processing Developments," 743.

76. May, "IBM Word Processing Developments," 742.

77. Bishop et al., "Development," 382.

78. Bishop et al., "Development," 382. See also May, "IBM Word Processing Developments."

79. Frutiger, "IBM Selectric Composer," 10.

80. Rogers, "The Demo"; Tweney, "Mother of All Demos."

81. Engelbart, "Doug Engelbart 1968 Demo."

82. Engelbart, *Human Intellect Augmentation Techniques*, 1.

83. The source of the cryptic phrase is likely Charles Edward Weller: "We were then in the midst of an exciting political campaign, and it was then for the first time that the well known sentence was inaugurated—'Now is the time for all good men to come to the aid of the party'; also the opening sentence of the Declaration of Independence, . . . which sentences were repeated many times in order to test the speed of the machine" (Weller, *Early History of the Typewriter*, 21, 30).

84. Weller, *Early History of the Typewriter*, 1.

85. Engelbart, *Human Intellect Augmentation Techniques*, 48–49. I have reproduced the text verbatim, preserving the line breaks, because formatting is an important part of the reported experience.

86. Engelbart, *Human Intellect Augmentation Techniques*, 50.
87. Engelbart, *Human Intellect Augmentation Techniques*, 50–51.
88. Engelbart, *Human Intellect Augmentation Techniques*, 51.
89. Engelbart and English, "Research Center," 396.
90. Engelbart, *Human Intellect Augmentation Techniques*, 6.
91. Engelbart, *Human Intellect Augmentation Techniques*, 6.
92. Engelbart, *Human Intellect Augmentation Techniques*, 67.
93. Engelbart, *Human Intellect Augmentation Techniques*, 67.

CHAPTER 5: LITERATURE DOWN TO A PIXEL

1. Mauss, *Techniques*, 78.
2. One definition of *medium* in the *Oxford English Dictionary* is "any physical material (as tape, disk, paper, etc.) used for recording or reproducing data, images, or sound" (*OED Online*, s.v. "Medium," December 2016; www.oed.com/view/Entry/115772 [accessed December 26, 2016]).
3. J. Cameron, *The Terminator*; J. Cameron, *Terminator 2*.
4. The term *digital being* was made popular by Nicholas Negroponte in the 1990s. See Negroponte, *Being Digital.*
5. Golumbia, *Cultural Logic*, 19.
6. Golumbia, *Cultural Logic*, 11.
7. Golumbia, *Cultural Logic*, 22, 130–35.
8. Golumbia, *Cultural Logic*, 222.
9. Marche, "Literature Is not Data," n.p.
10. Fish, "Digital Humanities," n.p.
11. Fish, "Digital Humanities," n.p.
12. For a summary of digital physics and metaphysics, see Floridi, "Against Digital Ontology"; and Steinhart, "Digital Metaphysics."
13. I say "a priori" because one must already inhabit the category (of being human) to engage in its analysis.
14. Gregory Hickok, a prominent University of California, Irvine, cognitive scientist wrote: "The brain samples the world in rhythmic pulses, perhaps even discrete time chunks, much like the individual frames of a movie. From the brain's perspective, experience is not continuous but quantized. . . . This is not to say that the brain dances to its own beat, dragging perception along for the ride. In fact, it seems to work the other way around: Rhythms in the environment, such as those in music or speech, can draw neural oscillations into their tempo, effectively synchronizing the brain's rhythms with those of the world around us" (Hickok, "It's not a Stream," n.p.).
15. Also known as the "single current" or "single Morse" system. See Weik, "Neutral Direct-Current Telegraph System." The later International Telegraph Alphabet No. 2 (ITA2), a convention that preceded ASCII, could also be adapted to work with "double current" devices, in which case 0 represented "negative current" and 1 "positive current" (ITU, *Telegraph Regulations*, 36).

16. Crehore and Squier, "Practical Transmitter"; Hausmann, *Telegraph Engineering*, 374.

17. Siegert, "Cacography."

18. Siegert takes the Pollak-Virag telegraph as an "apocryphal" emblem of a "systemic . . . logic" in the "dominant cultural technique," representative of the "order of digital signals" (Siegert, "Cacography," 41). Although not concerned with the history or philosophy of digital media explicitly, Siegert suggests that the writing telegraph symbolizes the cleansing of "the noise of all graphic form" (32). His theory of cultural techniques instead creates "an awareness for the plenitude of a world of as yet undistinguished things, that, as an inexhaustible reservoir of possibilities, remain the basic point of reference for every type of culture" (35). The world of undistinguished things hints that his position is on the analog side of the continuous-discrete dichotomy of human experience.

19. Pollak and Virag, "Writing-Telegraph," 3.

20. Pollak and Virag, "Writing-Telegraph," 1.

21. Pollak and Virag, "Writing-Telegraph," 1.

22. Bergson, *Creative Evolution*, 36.

23. See Bergson, *Creative Evolution*, 36. On the rather complex topic of discrete versus continuous multiplicities in Bergsonian thought, see also Deleuze, *Bergsonism*; and James, *Pluralistic Universe*.

24. Bergson, *Creative Evolution*, 332.

25. Bergson, *Creative Evolution*, 167–82; Russell, *Philosophy of Bergson*, 4.

26. Bergson, *Creative Evolution*, 109.

27. Bergson, *Matter and Memory*, 19, 280.

28. Bergson, *Matter and Memory*, 123.

29. Russell, *Philosophy of Bergson*, 24.

30. Regarding the "gross error of those who assert the materiality of the soul, affirming it to be homogeneous, and continuous with the body; whereas it is heterogeneous, and discrete," see Swedenborg, *Treatise*, 24. It is otherwise in the "Angelic Idea of Creation": "The question was asked, 'Whence, then, is hell?' They [the angels] said, 'From man's freedom, without which a man would not be a man,' because man, from that freedom, broke the continuity in himself; and this being broken, separation took place; and the continuity, which was in him from creation, became like a chain, or a piece of linked work, which falls to pieces when the hooks above are broken or torn out, and then hangs down from small threads. Separation or rupture was brought about, and is brought about, by the denial of God" (Swedenborg, *Apocalypse*, 290).

31. Brittan, *Spiritual Telegraph*, 169.

32. Brittan, *Spiritual Telegraph*, 169.

33. Brittan, *Spiritual Telegraph*, 169.

34. Brittan, *Spiritual Telegraph*, 169.

35. Dole, *Philosophy of Creation*, 236–37.

36. Edwards, "Neglected Texts"; Shaked, *Dualism in Transformation*, 52–71.

37. Murray, "Setting Type," 559.

38. One could make more of Dervish orientalism here. Murray himself was an empire outsider, born in the small, remote town of Invercargill, New Zealand (a town that also happens to be one of the southernmost cities in world): "I am a child of the Southern Cross, and I have no preordained respect for geniuses born under the Northern constellations" (Murray, *Philosophy of Power*, 51).

39. See, for example, Dale Angell: "The telegraph is a digital device, sending only high and low pulses through the wire" (Angell, *Pro Tools*, 233). Thomas C. Jepsen says, "The telegraph was a digital device that used dots and dashes in a manner similar to the ones and zeroes of digital logic" (Jepsen, *My Sisters Telegraphic*, 195). And Douglas E. Comer writes, "The telegraph is a digital device because instead of sending a continuous signal that is an exact analog of the input, the telegraph clicks to send the individual characters" (Comer, *Internet Book*, 32).

40. On intermedia in concrete poetry, see Higgins, "Intermedia" and Wendt, "Sound Poetry."

41. For a detailed description of contemporary internet infrastructure, see Starosielski, *Undersea Network*.

42. See Mishima and Itoh, "Novel Frame Interpolation Method." See also Lehmann, *Flüssige Kristalle*; and Reinitzer, "Beiträge zur Kenntniss des Cholesterins."

43. Brannan, *Applications of Parallel Processing*; Coltheart, "Iconic Memory"; Efron, "Conservation."

44. Burr, "Temporal Summation"; Didyk et al., "Perceptually-Motivated Real-Time Temporal Upsampling."

45. Didyk et al., "Perceptually-Motivated Real-Time Temporal Upsampling"; Purves et al., "Types of Eye Movements"; Rottach et al., "Comparison."

46. Har-Noy and Nguyen, "LCD Motion Blur Reduction"; Klompenhouwer and Velthoven, "Motion Blur Reduction."

47. Kurita, "35.1"; Pan et al., "LCD Motion Blur Modeling."

48. Edgerton, *History of American Television*.

49. It would be interesting to create the reverse effect by reducing the fidelity of a "cheap" soap opera video feed to the more "expensive" look of film shot at 24 frames per second.

50. For a primer on both sides of social constructivism, see Boghossian, *Fear of Knowledge*; and Hacking, *Social Construction of What*.

51. Yet other techniques of apprehension are socially constructed. Thus although all opera is in the human audible frequency range, acculturation to opera listening helps greatly in its enjoyment. Some aspects of opera appreciation are learned (such as knowing the plot), whereas others are physiologically determined (such as the ability to hear sounds).

52. Corey J. Maley writes, "The received view is that analog representations vary smoothly, while digital representations vary in stepwise manner. In other words, 'digital' is synonymous with 'discrete,' while 'analog' is synonymous with 'continuous'" (Maley, "Analog and Digital," 117). Friedrich A. Kittler writes, "Confronted as they are

with a continuous environment of weather, waves, and wars, digital computers can cope with this real number-avalanche only by adding element to element" (Kittler, "There Is No Software," n.p.).

53. Kernighan, *D Is for Digital*, 21.

54. Kernighan, *D Is for Digital*, 22.

55. N. Goodman, *Languages of Art*, 161.

56. Goodman differentiates between "syntactic" and "semantic" density. Some notational systems such as writing and the decimal system are, according to Goodman, "syntactically differentiated but semantically dense." The key distinction for him seems to be a "limit on the length of message," by which I think he means something related to infinite divisibility. The decimal system as a whole can continue to approach a quantity indefinitely, reaching an arbitrary point of precision. The computer limits decimal precision to some arbitrary depth of approximation, making it semantically discrete. I find this part of the argument unconvincing. See N. Goodman, *Languages of Art*, 161–64.

57. Haugeland, "Analog," 213.

58. Haugeland, "Analog," 214.

59. Wu-Tang Clan, *Once Upon a Time in Shaolin*. See Budnik, "Copyright"; Cohen, "For What It's Worth"; and Morris, *Selling Digital Music*.

60. Katz, "Analog and Digital Representation."

61. Drucker and McGann, "Images as the Text," n.p.

62. Winner, "Do Artifacts Have Politics," 135.

63. Winner, "Do Artifacts Have Politics," 135.

64. Winner, "Do Artifacts Have Politics."

65. Shore, "Acrobat 2.0," 379.

CONCLUSION:

1. McGowan, "I Want to Know," n.p. See also Sellars, "Petition."

2. Sellars, "Petition," 4. See also U.S. Copyright Office, "Exemption."

3. McNeal, "Targeted Killing"; Weber, "Keep Adding."

4. See, for example, Agamben, *The Open*, 39–49; and Hayles, "Print Is Flat," 16–17.

5. Uexküll, *Foray*, 44–53.

6. Uexküll, *Foray*, 198.

7. Uexküll, *Foray*, 12.

8. Uexküll, *Foray*, 148.

9. Nagel, "What Is It Like," 439.

10. Nagel, "What Is It Like," 449.

11. Nagel, "What Is It Like," 444.

12. Nagel, "What Is It Like," 445–46.

13. Bakhtin, "Man at the Mirror," 71; translation mine.

14. Uexküll, *Foray*, 52.

15. ITU, *Documents diplomatiques*.

16. Bodó, "Russian Digital Shadow Libraries"; *Elsevier Inc. et al. v. Sci-Hub et al.*, New York Southern District Court, Case 1:15-cv-04282-RWS; Liang, "Piracy"; Mahmood and Ilyas, "Copyright"; Nkiko, "Book Piracy in Nigeria"; Okiy, "Photocopying."

17. Tenen and Foxman, "Book Piracy."

BIBLIOGRAPHY

Aaron, V. Y., and J. Leburton. "Flash Memory: Towards Single-Electronics." *IEEE Potentials* 21, no. 4 (October 2002): 35–41.

Adler, Alfred, and Harry Albertman. "Knitting Machine." Patent US1927016 A, filed August 1, 1922, issued September 1933.

Adobe Systems Inc. "Adobe Acrobat Reader DC Install for All Versions." 2016. web. archive.org/web/20160308071105/https://get.adobe.com/reader/otherversions/ (accessed March 8, 2016).

———. "Plans and Pricing: Compare Plans Adobe Acrobat Dc." 2016. web.archive.org/ web/20160308075809/https://acrobat.adobe.com/us/en/pricing/pricing-compare -plans.html (accessed March 8, 2016).

Agamben, Giorgio. *The Open: Man and Animal*, trans. Kevin Attell. Stanford, CA: Stanford University Press, 2003.

"Amazon Kindle: FAQ." Amazon.com, 2016. web.archive.org/web/20160304133525/ https://kindle.amazon.com/faq#PublicNotes0 (accessed March 4, 2016).

"Amazon Kindle: Welcome." Amazon.com, 2015. web.archive.org/web/20160305181603 /https://kindle.amazon.com/ (accessed March 5, 2016).

American Bar Association. "The $10,000 Typewriter." *ABA Journal* 55, no. 5 (May 1966): 416.

American Law Institute. *Restatement of the Law Second: Contracts*. St. Paul, MN: American Law Institute Publishers, 1973.

Andrews, R., J. Diederich, and A. B. Tickle. "Survey and Critique of Techniques for Extracting Rules from Trained Artificial Neural Networks." *Knowledge-Based Systems* 8, no. 6 (December 1995): 373–89.

Angell, Dale. *Pro Tools for Film and Video*. Boston: Focal Press, 2009.

Angluin, D. C., and L. P. Deutsch. *Reference Manual: Q.E.D Time-Sharing Editor*. Washington, DC: Office of the Secretary of Defense, March 1968.

Apple Inc. *Apple Human Interface Guidelines: The Apple Desktop Interface.* Reading, MA: Addison-Wesley, 1987.

Armstrong, Timothy K. "Digital Rights Management and the Process of Fair Use." *Harvard Journal of Law and Technology* 20, no. 1 (fall 2006): 50–121.

Atzori, L., A. Iera, and G. Morabito. "From 'Smart Objects' to 'Social Objects': The Next Evolutionary Step of the Internet of Things." *IEEE Communications Magazine* 52, no. 1 (January 2014): 97–105.

Bachelard, Gaston. *The Poetics of Space,* trans. Maria Jolas, reprint ed. Boston: Beacon Press, 1994.

Bacon, Francis. *Of the Advancement and Proficience of Learning; Or, The Partitions of Sciences, IX Bookes. Written in Latin by the Most Eminent, Illustrious Lord Francis Bacon,* interpreted by Gilbert Wats. Oxford: L. Lichfield for R. Young & E. Forrest, 1640.

———. *The Oxford Francis Bacon,* vol. 4, *The Advancement of Learning,* ed. Michael Kiernan. Oxford: Oxford University Press, 2000.

Bakhtin, Michail. "K voprosam metodologii estetiki slovesnogo tvorchestva" [On the Questions of Methodology of the Language Arts]. In Michail Bakhtin, *Sobranie Sochineniy: Filosofskaia Estetika 20-h Godov* [Collected Works: Aesthetic Philosophy of the 1920s], ed. S. G. Bocharov and N. I. Nikolaev, 1: 265–325. Moscow: Russkie Slovari, 2003.

———. "Man at the Mirror" [Chelovek u Zerkala]. In *M. M. Bakhtin Sobranie Sochinenii v Semi Tomakh,* vol. 5, *Raboty 40-X: Nachala 60-X Godov,* 71. Moscow: IMLIRAN, Iazyki Slovianskikh Kultur, 1997.

Barthes, Roland. "The Death of the Author." In Roland Barthes, *Image, Music, Text,* trans. Stephen Heath, 142–49. New York: Hill & Wang, 1977.

———. *The Rustle of Language,* trans. Richard Howard. Berkeley: University of California Press, 1989.

Bashkow, T. R., A. Sasson, and A. Kronfeld. "System Design of a FORTRAN Machine." *IEEE Transactions on Electronic Computers* 16, no. 4 (August 1967): 485–99.

Baudrillard, Jean. *Simulacra and Simulation.* Ann Arbor: University of Michigan Press, 1994.

———. "Symbolic Exchange and Death." In Jean Baudrillard, *Selected Writings,* trans. Mark Poster, 119–47. Stanford, CA: Stanford University Press, 1988.

Beard, Marian H., Perry A. Caro, Jennifer B. Hsiao, Kevin J. Mackey, James G. Sandman Jr., Gary R. Steinbach, and Donald R. Woods. "Data Processor Having a User Interface Display with Metaphoric Objects." Patent US4899136 A, filed April 28, 1986, issued February 1990.

Beatty, John C., Janet S. Chin, and Henry F. Moll. "An Interactive Documentation System." In *SIGGRAPH '79: Proceedings of the 6th Annual Conference on Computer Graphics and Interactive Techniques,* 71–82. New York: Association for Computing Machinery (ACM), 1979.

Beauchamp, K. G. *History of Telegraphy.* London: Institution of Engineering and Technology, 2001.

Benjamin, Walter. "The Author as Producer." In Walter Benjamin, *Understanding Brecht*, trans. Anna Bostock, 105–22. London: Verso, 1983.

Benson, Greg, and Gregory H. Urich. "Method and System for Managing a Data Object so as to Comply with Predetermined Conditions for Usage." Patent US5845281 A, filed January 31, 1996, issued December 1998.

Benson, Greg, Gregory H. Urich, and Christopher L. Knauft. "Method and System for Managing a Data Object so as to Comply with Predetermined Conditions for Usage." Patent US8479305 B1, filed October 1, 1998, issued July 2, 2013.

Bergson, Henri. *Creative Evolution*, trans. Arthur Mitchell. New York: Modern Library, 1944.

———. *Matter and Memory*, trans. Nancy Margaret Paul and William Scott Palmer. London: G. Allen; and New York: Macmillan, 1929.

Bernard, Claude. *An Introduction to the Study of Experimental Medicine*. New York: Dover, 1957.

Berns, Gerald M. "Description of FORMAT, a Text-Processing Program." *Communications of the ACM* 12, no. 3 (March 1969): 141–46.

———. "The Format Program." *IEEE Transactions on Engineering Writing and Speech* 11, no. 2 (August 1968): 85–91.

Best, Stephen, and Sharon Marcus. "Surface Reading: An Introduction." *Representations* 108, no. 1 (November 2009): 1–21.

Bez, R., E. Camerlenghi, A. Modelli, and A. Visconti. "Introduction to Flash Memory." *Proceedings of the IEEE* 91, no. 4 (April 2003): 489–502.

Billig, Michael, and Katie MacMillan. "Metaphor, Idiom, and Ideology: The Search for 'No Smoking Guns' Across Time." *Discourse and Society* 16, no. 4 (July 2005): 459–80.

Bishop, D. A., R. S. Heard, R. E. Hunt, J. E. Jones, and R. A. Rahenkamp. "Development of the IBM Magnetic Tape Selectric Composer." *IBM Journal of Research and Development* 12, no. 5 (September 1968): 380–98.

Blair, Ann. "Note Taking as an Art of Transmission." *Critical Inquiry* 31, no. 1 (2004): 85–107.

Blanchot, Maurice. *The Work of Fire*. Stanford, CA: Stanford University Press, 1995.

Bodó, Balázs. "A Short History of the Russian Digital Shadow Libraries." November 4, 2014. dx.doi.org/10.2139/ssrn.2616631 (accessed December 26, 2016).

Boghossian, Paul. *Fear of Knowledge: Against Relativism and Constructivism*, 1st ed. Oxford: Clarendon Press, 2007.

Bohn, Jürgen, Vlad Coroamă, Marc Langheinrich, Friedemann Mattern, and Michael Rohs. "Living in a World of Smart Everyday Objects: Social, Economic, and Ethical Implications." *Human and Ecological Risk Assessment: An International Journal* 10, no. 5 (October 2004): 763–85.

Bök, Christian. "The Xenotext Works." *Harriet: The Blog*, 2011. web.archive.org/save /_embed/https://www.poetryfoundation.org/harriet/2011/04/the-xenotext-works/ (accessed December 26, 2016).

———. *The Xenotext: Book I*. Toronto: Coach House, 2015.

Boyd, Walter Anderson. "Telegraph-Key." Patent US1192270 A, filed July 29, 1914, issued July 25, 1916.

Boyden, James H., Daniel E. Cummings, Jesse L. Dorogusker, Thomas J. Dougherty, S. Joy Mountford, Brygg A. Ullmer, and Allen Philip A. Van. "Methods and Systems for Providing Human/Computer Interfaces." Patent WO1999019823 A3, filed October 8, 1988, issued August 19, 1999.

Boyle, W., and G. Smith. "Information Storage Devices." Patent US3858232 A, filed November 9, 1971, issued December 31, 1974.

Brackbill, Hervey. "Some Telegraphers' Terms." *American Speech* 4, no. 4 (April 1929): 287–90.

Brannan, J. R., ed. *Applications of Parallel Processing in Vision.* Amsterdam: Elsevier, 1992.

Brittan, Samuel Byron. *The Spiritual Telegraph.* New York: Partridge & Brittan, 1854.

Brouillette, Sarah. "Unesco and the World-Literary System in Crisis." *Amodern,* 2015. web.archive.org/web/20161226230728/http://amodern.net/article/unesco-brouil lette/ (accessed December 26, 2016).

———. "Wither Production?" *Historical Materialism* 23, no. 4 (November 2015): 197–209.

Brown, Scheibell Gordon. "Automatic Program System." Patent US2031074 A, filed March 12, 1931, issued February 18, 1936.

———. "Selective Program System." Patent US2031075 A, filed March 12, 1931, issued February 18, 1936.

Budnik, Ruslan. "Copyright and the Value of Attention." *Journal of Intellectual Property Law and Practice* 11, no. 5 (2016): 355–59.

Bumstead, Albert H., and Ralph W. Bumstead. "Telegraphy." Patent US1187035 A, filed May 1, 1911, issued June 13, 1916.

Burr, D. C. "Temporal Summation of Moving Images by the Human Visual System." *Proceedings of the Royal Society of London B: Biological Sciences* 211, no. 1184 (March 1981): 321–39.

Bush, Vannevar. "As We May Think." *The Atlantic* (July 1945): 101–8.

Cajori, Florian. "The History of Notations of the Calculus." *Annals of Mathematics* 25, no. 1 (1923): 1–46.

Calverley, David J. "Android Science and Animal Rights: Does an Analogy Exist?" *Connection Science* 18, no. 4 (December 2006): 403–17.

Cameron, James, dir. *The Terminator.* Santa Monica, CA: MGM Home Entertainment, 2001.

———, dir. *Terminator 2: Judgment Day.* Santa Monica, CA: Artisan Home Entertainment, 2003.

Cameron, Scott H., Duncan Ewing, and Michael Liveright. "DIALOG: A Conversational Programming System with a Graphical Orientation." *Communications of the ACM* 10, no. 6 (June 1967): 349–57.

Camras, Marvin. "Magnetic Recording Tapes." *Transactions of the American Institute of Electrical Engineers* 67, no. 1 (January 1948): 503–6.

Card, Stuart Kent, Richard Carl Gossweiler III, Allison Gyle Woodruff, and Jock Douglas MacKinlay. "Methods, Systems, and Computer Program Products for the Display and Operation of Virtual Three-Dimensional Books." Patent US7015910 B2, filed December 21, 2000, issued March 21, 2006.

Carroll, J. M, R. L. Mack, and W. A Kellogg. *Interface Metaphors and User Interface Design*. San Jose: IBM Thomas J. Watson Research Division, 1987.

Carroll, J. M., and John C. Thomas. "Metaphor and the Cognitive Representation of Computing Systems." *IEEE Transactions on Systems, Man, and Cybernetics* 12, no. 2 (March 1982): 107–16.

Carroll, Lewis. *Alice's Adventures in Wonderland: And, Through the Looking-Glass and What Alice Found There*, ed. Roger Lancelyn Green. London: Oxford University Press, 1971.

———. *The Annotated Alice: Alice's Adventures in Wonderland and Through the Looking Glass*, ed. Martin Gardner. New York: C. N. Potter, 1960.

Casper, Louis. "Remote Control Advertising and Electric Signalin[g] System." Patent US1953072 A, filed September 9, 1930, issued April 3, 1934.

Ceruzzi, Paul. *Computing: A Concise History*. Cambridge, MA: MIT Press, 2012.

Chalmers, David J. "Does a Rock Implement Every Finite-State Automaton?" *Synthese* 108, no. 3 (September 1996): 309–33.

Chun, Wendy Hui Kyong. "The Enduring Ephemeral, or the Future Is a Memory." *Critical Inquiry* 35, no. 1 (September 2008): 148–71.

———. "On Software, or the Persistence of Visual Knowledge." *Grey Room* 18 (2004): 26–51.

———. *Programmed Visions: Software and Memory*. Cambridge, MA: MIT Press, 2011.

Church, Alonzo, and A. M. Turing. "On Computable Numbers, with an Application to the Entscheidungsproblem." *Journal of Symbolic Logic* 2, no. 1 (March 1937): 42–43.

Chuzhak, N. F., ed. *Literatura Fakta: Pervyi Sbornik Materialov Rabotnikov Lefa*. Moscow: Zakharov, 2000.

CITED Consortium. *CITED Final Report: Copyright in Transmitted Electronic Documents*. Boston Spa, UK: British Library Publishing Division, 1994.

Clancy, Douglas, George Hobgood, and Frederick May. "Data Reading, Recording, and Positioning System." Patent US3530448 A, filed January 15, 1968, issued September 22, 1970.

Clark, Charles. "The Copyright Environment for the Publisher in the Digital World." Paper presented at the Joint ICSU Press/UNESCO Expert Conference on Electronic Publishing in Science, UNESCO, Paris, February 19–23, 1996. web.archive.org /web/20161226231600/http://www.library.illinois.edu/icsu/clark.htm (accessed December 26, 2016).

Cohen, Dan. "For What It's Worth: A Review of the Wu-Tang Clan's 'Once Upon a Time in Shaolin.'" Blog post, January 4, 2016. web.archive.org/web/20161019050405/ http://www.dancohen.org/2016/01/04/for-what-its-worth-a-review-of-the-wu-tang -clans-once-upon-a-time-in-shaolin/ (accessed October 19, 2016).

Colburn, Timothy R. "Software, Abstraction, and Ontology." *The Monist* 82, no. 1 (January 1999): 3–19.

Coleman, Clyde. "Electrically-Operated Musical Instrument." Patent US1107495 A, filed August 22, 1898, issued August 18, 1914.

Coleridge, Samuel Taylor. *The Collected Works of Samuel Taylor Coleridge*, vol. 7, *Biographia Literaria or Biographical Sketches of My Literary Life and Opinions*, ed. James Engell and Walter Jackson Bate. Princeton, NJ: Princeton University Press, 1983 [1917].

Collinger, Jennifer L., Michael A. Kryger, Richard Barbara, Timothy Betler, Kristen Bowsher, Elke H. P. Brown, Samuel T. Clanton et al. "Collaborative Approach in the Development of High-Performance Brain-Computer Interfaces for a Neuro-prosthetic Arm: Translation from Animal Models to Human Control." *Clinical and Translational Science* 7, no. 1 (February 2014): 52–59.

Collingwood, R. G. "Form and Content in Art." *Journal of Philosophical Studies* 4, no. 15 (July 1929): 332–45.

Coltheart, Max. "Iconic Memory and Visible Persistence." *Perception and Psychophysics* 27, no. 3 (May 1980): 183–228.

Comer, Douglas E. *The Internet Book: Everything You Need to Know About Computer Networking and How the Internet Works*. Upper Saddle River, NJ: Addison-Wesley, 2006.

Computation Laboratory, Harvard University. *Description of a Magnetic Drum Calculator*. Annals of the Computation Laboratory of Harvard University, vol. 25. Cambridge, MA: Harvard University Press, 1952.

———. *Description of a Relay Calculator*. Annals of the Computation Laboratory of Harvard University, vol. 24. Cambridge, MA: Harvard University Press, 1949.

Conti, Gregory, Erik Dean, Matthew Sinda, and Benjamin Sangster. "Visual Reverse Engineering of Binary and Data Files." In *Visualization for Computer Security*, ed. John R. Goodall, Gregory Conti, and Kwan-Liu Ma, 1–17. Berlin: Springer, 2008.

Cook, Don L. "Some Considerations in the Concept of Pre-Copy-Text." *Text* 4 (1988): 79–91.

Copeland, B. Jack, and Diane Proudfoot. "What Turing Did After He Invented the Universal Turing Machine." *Journal of Logic, Language, and Information* 9, no. 4 (October 2000): 491–509.

Cox, Paula J., Dana L. Gillihan, Donald Ray Hyatt, Paul T. Leone, Kenneth M. Nordby, Victor Edward Pullizzi, Thyra Lynne Rauch, and Robert W. Rinda. "Method and System for Organizing On-Line Books Using Bookcases." Patent US5907845 A, filed July 26, 1996, issued May 25, 1999.

Creed, Frederick George. "Printing Apparatus Controlled by Perforated Tape." Patent US985402 A, filed April 6, 1908, issued February 28, 1911.

Crehore, Albert C., and George O. Squier. "A Practical Transmitter Using the Sine Wave for Cable Telegraphy; and Measurements with Alternating Currents Upon an Atlantic Cable." *Transactions of the American Institute of Electrical Engineers* 17 (January 1900): 385–444.

Cuttriss, Charles. "Telegraphy." Patent US500226 A, filed February 21, 1893, issued June 27, 1893.

Daniel, Eric D., C. Denis Mee, and Mark H. Clark, eds. *Magnetic Recording: The First 100 Years*. New York: Wiley-IEEE Press, 1998.

Daston, Lorraine. "Taking Note(s)." *Isis* 95, no. 3 (2004): 443–48.

Daugherty, Denny. "Numeral Adding or Subtracting Attachment for Type-Writing Machines." Patent US517735 A, filed July 5, 1893, issued April 3, 1894.

Davey, Mike. "A Turing Machine Overview." web.archive.org/web/20161215072157/http://www.aturingmachine.com/ (accessed December 15, 2016).

Davidson, Cathy N. *Now You See It: How the Brain Science of Attention Will Transform the Way We Live, Work, and Learn*. New York: Viking, 2011.

Davidson, Donald. *Essays on Actions and Events*. Oxford: Clarendon Press and Oxford University Press, 1980.

Day, John. "The (Un)Revised OSI Reference Model." *SIGCOMM Computer Communication Review* 25, no. 5 (October 1995): 39–55.

Day, J. D., and H. Zimmermann. "The OSI Reference Model." *Proceedings of the IEEE* 71, no. 12 (December 1983): 1334–40.

Dee, R. H. "Magnetic Tape for Data Storage: An Enduring Technology." *Proceedings of the IEEE* 96, no. 11 (November 2008): 1775–85.

Degener, Gustave O. "Combined Type-Writing and Adding Machine." Patent US990238 A, filed October 20, 1909, issued April 25, 1911.

Deleuze, Gilles. *Bergsonism*, trans. Hugh Tomlinson and Barbara Habberjam, reissue ed. New York: Zone Books, 1990.

Dennett, Daniel. "Can Machines Think?" In *The Turing Test: Verbal Behavior as the Hallmark of Intelligence*, ed. Stuart M Shieber. Cambridge, MA: MIT Press, 2004.

Denning, Peter J. "Third Generation Computer Systems." *ACM Computing Surveys* 3, no. 4 (December 1971): 175–216.

Descartes, René. *Discourse on the Method and Meditations on First Philosophy*, ed. David Weissman. New Haven, CT: Yale University Press, 1996.

———. *Meditations on First Philosophy*, trans. Donald A. Cress, 3rd ed. Indianapolis: Hackett, 1993.

Deutsch, D. "Quantum Theory, the Church-Turing Principle, and the Universal Quantum Computer." *Proceedings of the Royal Society of London A: Mathematical, Physical, and Engineering Sciences* 400, no. 1818 (July 1985): 97–117.

Didyk, Piotr, Elmar Eisemann, Tobias Ritschel, Karol Myszkowski, and Hans-Peter Seidel. "Perceptually-Motivated Real-Time Temporal Upsampling of 3D Content for High-Refresh Rate Displays." *Computer Graphics Forum* 29, no. 2 (2010): 713–22.

Dixsaut, Monique. "'Ousia,' 'Eidos' et 'Idea' dans le 'Phédon.'" *Revue Philosophique de la France et de l'Étranger* 181, no. 4 (October 1991): 479–500.

Dole, George Henry. *The Philosophy of Creation: The System of Philosophy from the Standpoint of the Christian and of the Word*. New York: New-Church Board of Publication, 1906.

Drucker, Johanna. "Digital Ontologies: The Ideality of Form in/and Code Storage:

Or, Can Graphesis Challenge Mathesis?" *Leonardo* 34, no. 2 (January 2001): 141–45.

———. "Performative Materiality and Theoretical Approaches to Interface." *Digital Humanities Quarterly* 7, no. 1 (2013).

Drucker, Johanna, and Jerome McGann. "Images as the Text: Pictographs and Pictographic Logic." 2010. web.archive.org/web/20161220221532/http://www2.iath.virginia.edu/jjm2f/old/pictograph.html (accessed December 20, 2016). Originally published in *Information Design Journal* 10, no. 2 (2000): 95–106.

Duncan-Jones, Austin. "G. E. Moore: Some Impressions." *Analysis* 19, no. 2 (December 1958): 25–26.

Edgerton, Gary R. *The Columbia History of American Television.* New York: Columbia University Press, 2009.

Edwards, M. J. "Neglected Texts in the Study of Gnosticism." *Journal of Theological Studies*, n.s., 41, no. 1 (April 1990): 26–50.

Efron, Robert. "Conservation of Temporal Information by Perceptual Systems." *Perception and Psychophysics* 14, no. 3 (October 1973): 518–30.

Eichenbaum, Boris. "How Gogol's 'Overcoat' Is Made." In *Gogol from the Twentieth Century: Eleven Essays*, ed. Robert A. Maguire, 267–92. Princeton, NJ: Princeton University Press, 1995.

Eisenberg, Daniel. "Word Processing, History of." In *Encyclopedia of Library and Information Science*, ed. Allen Kent, 49: 268–78. New York: Dekker, 1992.

Elbourn, R. D., and W. H. Ware. "The Evolution of Concepts and Languages of Computing." *Proceedings of the IRE* 50, no. 5 (May 1962): 1059–66.

Ellis, Albert H. "Combined Type-Writing and Adding Machine." Patent US1091820 A, filed August 8, 1905, issued March 31, 1914.

Engel, Friedrich K. "1888–1988: A Hundred Years of Magnetic Sound Recording." *Journal of the Audio Engineering Society* 36, no. 3 (March 1988): 170–78.

Engelbart, Douglas. "Doug Engelbart 1968 Demo." December 1968. web.archive.org/web/20161226233225/http://web.stanford.edu/dept/SUL/library/extra4/sloan/mousesite/1968Demo.html (accessed December 26, 2016).

———. *Human Intellect Augmentation Techniques.* NASA Contractor Report, NASA CR-1270. Washington, DC: NASA, January 1969.

———. "X-Y Position Indicator for a Display System." Patent US3541541 A, filed June 21, 1967, issued November 17, 1970.

Engelbart, Douglas C., and William K. English. "A Research Center for Augmenting Human Intellect." In *AFIPS '68: Proceedings of the December 9–11, 1968, Fall Joint Computer Conference, Part I*, 395–410. New York: ACM, 1968.

Engels, Friedrich. *Ludwig Feuerbach and the Outcome of Classical German Philosophy*, ed. C. P. Dutt. New York: International Publishers, 1941.

English, James F. *The Economy of Prestige: Prizes, Awards, and the Circulation of Cultural Value.* Cambridge, MA: Harvard University Press, 2008.

Epstein, Herman, and Frank Innes. "Electrographic Printer." Patent US3012839 A, filed July 15, 1954, issued December 12, 1961.

Eyal, Nir. *Hooked: How to Build Habit-Forming Products*, ed. Ryan Hoover. New York: Portfolio, 2014.

Fankhauser, Charles. "The Telegraphone." *Journal of the Franklin Institute* 167 (January 1909): 37–70.

Ferullo, Donna L. "Major Copyright Issues in Academic Libraries." *Journal of Library Administration* 40, nos. 1–2 (May 2004): 23–40.

Finger, Anke, Rainer Guldin, and Gustavo Bernardo. *Vilém Flusser: An Introduction.* Minneapolis: University of Minnesota Press, 2011.

Fish, Stanley. "The Digital Humanities and the Transcending of Mortality." *Opinionator*, January 9, 2012. web.archive.org/web/20161119093440/http://opinionator.blog.ny times.com/2012/01/09/the-digital-humanities-and-the-transcending-of-mortality/ (accessed November 19, 2016).

Fitzpatrick, Kathleen. *Planned Obsolescence: Publishing, Technology, and the Future of the Academy.* New York: NYU Press, 2011.

Floridi, Luciano. "Against Digital Ontology." *Synthese* 168, no. 1 (May 2009): 151–78.

Flusser, Vilém. *The Freedom of the Migrant: Objections to Nationalism*, ed. Anke K. Finger; trans. Kenneth Kronenberg. Urbana: University of Illinois Press, 2003.

Foucault, Michel. "What Is an Author?" In Michel Foucault, *Language, Counter-Memory, Practice: Selected Essays and Interviews*, 113–38. Ithaca, NY: Cornell University Press, 1980.

Freeman, Carla. *High Tech and High Heels in the Global Economy: Women, Work, and Pink-Collar Identities in the Caribbean.* Durham, NC: Duke University Press, 2000.

Frohman-Bentchkowsky, D. "A Fully Decoded 2048-Bit Electrically Programmable Famos Read-Only Memory." *IEEE Journal of Solid-State Circuits* 6, no. 5 (October 1971): 301–6.

Frutiger, A. "The IBM Selectric Composer: The Evolution of Composition Technology." *IBM Journal of Research and Development* 12, no. 1 (January 1968): 9–14.

Fry, David. "Circumventing Access Controls Under the Digital Millennium Copyright Act: Analyzing the Securom Debate." *Duke Law and Technology Review* 8 (2009): 1–25. web.archive.org/web/20161226234530/http://scholarship.law.duke.edu/dltr /vol8/iss1/4/ (accessed December 26, 2016).

Fuller, Matthew, and Andrew Goffey. *Evil Media.* Cambridge, MA: MIT Press, 2012.

Furuta, Richard, Jeffrey Scofield, and Alan Shaw. "Document Formatting Systems: Survey, Concepts, and Issues." *ACM Computing Surveys* 14, no. 3 (September 1982): 417–72.

Gadamer, Hans-Georg. *Truth and Method.* New York: Seabury Press, 1975.

Gaines, Brian R. "The Technology of Interaction: Dialogue Programming Rules." *International Journal of Man–Machine Studies* 14, no. 1 (January 1981): 133–50.

Gaines, Brian R., and Mildred L. G. Shaw. "From Timesharing to the Sixth Generation: The Development of Human–Computer Interaction. Part I." *International Journal of Man–Machine Studies* 24, no. 1 (January 1986): 1–27.

Galloway, Alexander R. "The Anti-Language of New Media." *Discourse* 32, no. 3 (2010): 276–84.

——. *Gaming: Essays on Algorithmic Culture.* Minneapolis: University of Minnesota Press, 2006.

——. *Protocol: How Control Exists After Decentralization.* Cambridge, MA: MIT Press, 2006.

Gillespie, Gerald. "Primal Utterance: Observations on Kuhlmann's Correspondence with Kircher." In *Wolfgang Fleischhauer: Wege der Worte—Festschrift für Wolfgang Fleischhauer,* ed. Donald Riechel, 27–46. Cologne: Böhlau, 1978.

Ginsburg, Jane C. "Legal Protection of Technological Measures Protecting Works of Authorship: International Obligations and the U.S. Experience." Columbia Public Law and Legal Theory, Working Paper 05-93. Rochester, NY: Social Science Research Network, August 2005. web.archive.org/save/https://papers.ssrn.com/sol3/papers.cfm?abstract_id=785945 (accessed December 26, 2016).

Gitelman, Lisa. *Paper Knowledge: Toward a Media History of Documents.* Durham, NC: Duke University Press, 2014.

Glaser, Howard Justin, and Tony Kai-Chi Leung. "Graphical User Interface for Binder Notebook Control." Patent EP0657799 A1, filed October 10, 1994, issued June 14, 1995.

Glass, Robert L. "A Comparative Analysis of the Topic Areas of Computer Science, Software Engineering, and Information Systems." *Journal of Systems and Software* 19, no. 3 (November 1992): 277–89.

Glass, Robert L., V. Ramesh, and Iris Vessey. "An Analysis of Research in Computing Disciplines." *Communications of the ACM* 47, no. 6 (June 2004): 89–94.

Goldberg, Hyman Eli. "Controller." Patent US1165663 A, filed January 10, 1911, issued December 28, 1915.

Golumbia, David. *The Cultural Logic of Computation.* Cambridge, MA: Harvard University Press, 2009.

Gombrich, Ernst. *Art and Illusion: A Study in the Psychology of Pictorial Representation.* London: Phaidon Press, 1960.

Goodman, Nelson. *Languages of Art: An Approach to a Theory of Symbols.* Indianapolis: Hackett, 1968.

Goodman, Russell B. "James on the Nonconceptual." *Midwest Studies in Philosophy* 28, no. 1 (September 2004): 137–48.

Google Inc. "About Google." Google.com, August 2015. web.archive.org/web/20150827155059/http://www.google.com/about/ (accessed August 27, 2015).

——. "Read Books on Google Play: Computer—Google Play Help." Google Play, 2016. web.archive.org/web/20160308195659/https://support.google.com/googleplay/answer/185545 (accessed March 8, 2016).

Grabiner, Judith V. "Is Mathematical Truth Time-Dependent?" *American Mathematical Monthly* 81, no. 4 (1974): 354–65.

Grattan-Guinness, I. "On the Development of Logics Between the Two World Wars." *American Mathematical Monthly* 88, no. 7 (August 1981): 495–509.

Gruenberger, F. J. "The History of the JOHNNIAC." *Annals of the History of Computing* 1, no. 1 (January 1979): 49–64.

Grundy, Gregory. "Information Distribution System." Patent US5375240 A, filed April 7, 1992, issued December 20, 1994.

Hacking, Ian. *The Social Construction of What?* Cambridge, MA: Harvard University Press, 1999.

Haigh, Thomas. "Actually, Turing Did not Invent the Computer." *Communications of the ACM* 57, no. 1 (January 2014): 36–41.

Hallden, Frederick G. "Printing-Telegraph System." Patent US1721952 A, filed January 21, 1928, issued July 23, 1929.

Halstead, Frank G. "The Genesis and Speed of the Telegraph Codes." *Proceedings of the American Philosophical Society* 93, no. 5 (November 1949): 448–58.

Harcourt, Bernard E. *Exposed: Desire and Disobedience in the Digital Age.* Cambridge, MA: Harvard University Press, 2015.

Har-Noy, Shay, and T. Q. Nguyen. "LCD Motion Blur Reduction: A Signal Processing Approach." *IEEE Transactions on Image Processing* 17, no. 2 (February 2008): 117–25.

Haugeland, John. "Analog and Analog." *Philosophical Topics* 12, no. 1 (1981): 213–25.

Hausmann, Erich. *Telegraph Engineering: A Manual for Practicing Telegraph Engineers and Engineering Students.* New York: Van Nostrand, 1915.

Hayles, N. Katherine. "Print Is Flat, Code Is Deep: The Importance of Media-Specific Analysis." *Poetics Today* 25, no. 1 (March 2004): 67–90.

Hegel, G. W. F. *Hegel's Aesthetics: Lectures on Fine Art, Volume I,* trans. T. M. Knox. Oxford: Oxford University Press, 1998.

———. "The Philosophy of Plato." *Journal of Speculative Philosophy* 4, no. 3 (January 1870): 225–68.

———. *Werke in 20 Bänden und Registerband,* ed. Eva Moldenhauer, Vol. 13, *Vorlesungen über die Ästhetik I.* Frankfurt am Main: Suhrkamp, 1986.

Heidegger, Martin. *Being and Time,* trans. Joan Stambaugh. Albany: State University of New York Press, 1996.

———. *Pathmarks.* Cambridge, UK: Cambridge University Press, 1998.

———. "The Question Concerning Technology." In Martin Heidegger, *Basic Writings: From Being and Time (1927) to The Task of Thinking (1964),* ed. David Farrell Krell, 307–42. New York: Harper & Row, 1977.

———. *Sein und Zeit.* Tübingen: M. Niemeyer, 1967.

Heim, Michael. *Electric Language: A Philosophical Study of Word Processing.* New Haven, CT: Yale University Press, 1987.

Herder, Johann Gottfried. *Sculpture: Some Observations on Shape and Form from Pygmalion's Creative Dream,* trans. Jason Gaiger. Chicago: University of Chicago Press, 2002.

Herken, Rolf, ed. *The Universal Turing Machine: A Half-Century Survey.* Oxford: Oxford University Press, 1988.

Herman, Bill D., and Oscar Gandy. "Catch 1201: A Legislative History and Content Analysis of the DMCA Exemption Proceedings." *Cardozo Arts and Entertainment Law Journal* 24 (2006): 121–90.

Hickok, Gregory. "It's not a 'Stream' of Consciousness." *New York Times*, May 8, 2015. web.archive.org/web/20161225153038/http://www.nytimes.com/2015/05/10/opinion/sunday/its-not-a-stream-of-consciousness.html (accessed December 25, 2016).

Higgins, Dick. "Intermedia." *Leonardo* 34, no. 1 (2001): 49–54.

Hildebrandt, Mireille. "Ambient Intelligence, Criminal Liability, and Democracy." *Criminal Law and Philosophy* 2, no. 2 (October 2007): 163–80.

Hoare, C. A. R. "Record Handling." *ALGOL Bulletin* 21 (November 1965): 39–69.

Hodges, Andrew. *Alan Turing: The Enigma.* New York: Simon & Schuster, 1983.

Horkheimer, Max. *Critical Theory: Selected Essays.* New York: Continuum, 1982.

Horton, J. W. "Experimental Study of Electron-Beam Driven Semiconductor Devices for Use in a Digital Memory." *IBM Journal of Research and Development* 6, no. 4 (October 1962): 437–48.

Hotson, Guy, David P. McMullen, Matthew S. Fifer, Matthew S. Johannes, Kapil D. Katyal, Matthew P. Para, Robert Armiger et al. "Individual Finger Control of a Modular Prosthetic Limb Using High-Density Electrocorticography in a Human Subject." *Journal of Neural Engineering* 13, no. 2 (2016): 026017.

Hough, Clinton. "Wired Radio Program Apparatus." Patent US1805665 A, filed April 27, 1927, issued May 19, 1931.

Hughes, H. B. "Improvement in Telegraphs." Patent US14917 A, issued May 20, 1856.

Hutchby, Ian. "Technologies, Texts, and Affordances." *Sociology* 35, no. 2 (2001): 441–56.

Hutchins, Edwin, James Hollan, and Donald Norman. "Direct Manipulation Interfaces." In *User Centered System Design: New Perspectives on Human–Computer Interaction*, ed. Stephen W. Draper and Donald A. Norman. Hillsdale, NJ: Erlbaum Associates, 1986.

Huxley, Francis. *The Raven and the Writing Desk.* New York: Harper & Row, 1976.

Iarkho, Boris. *Metodologia tochnogo literaturovedenia* [Methodologies of Exact Literary Study]. Moscow: Philologica, 2006.

Irmak, Nurbay. "Software Is an Abstract Artefact." *Grazer Philosophische Studien* 86 (January 2013): 55–72.

ISO (International Organization for Standardization). "Document Management: Portable Document Format, Part 1, PDF 1.7." ISO 32000-1:2008. Geneva: International Organization for Standardization, July 1, 2008.

———. "Information Processing: Text and Office Systems—Standard Generalized Markup Language (SGML)" ISO 8879:1986. Geneva: International Organization for Standardization, July 29, 2008.

———. "Writing Paper and Certain Classes of Printed Matter: Trimmed Sizes, A and B Series." ISO 216:1975. Geneva: International Organization for Standardization, May 1, 1975.

ITU (International Telegraph Union). *Documents diplomatiques de la Conférence Télégraphique Internationale de Paris.* Paris: Imprimerie impériale, 1865.

———. *Telegraph Regulations and Final Protocol.* Madrid: International Telegraph Union, 1932.

Jakobson, Roman. "A Few Remarks on Peirce, Pathfinder in the Science of Language." *MLN* 92, no. 5 (1977): 1026–32.

———. "Linguistics and Poetics." In *Style in Language*, ed. Thomas A Sebeok, 350–77. Cambridge, MA: MIT Press, 1960.

James, William. *A Pluralistic Universe: Hibbert Lectures at Manchester College on the Present Situation in Philosophy*. New York: Longmans, Green, 1909.

———. "Pragmatism's Conception of Truth." In William James, *Pragmatism, a New Name for Some Old Ways of Thinking: Popular Lectures on Philosophy*, 197–238. New York: Longmans, Green, 1907.

Jameson, Fredric. *Marxism and Form: Twentieth-Century Dialectical Theories of Literature*. Princeton, NJ: Princeton University Press, 1972.

Jennings, Tom. "An Annotated History of Some Character Codes, or ASCII: American Standard Code for Information Infiltration." October 2004. web.archive.org/web/20120113050309/http://wps.com/projects/codes/index.html (accessed March 14, 2015).

Jepsen, Thomas C. *My Sisters Telegraphic: Women In Telegraph Office 1846–1950*. Athens: Ohio University Press, 2001.

Johnson, D. Barton. "A Guide to Nabokov's 'A Guide to Berlin.'" *Slavic and East European Journal* 23, no. 3 (October 1979): 353–61.

Johnson, J., T. L. Roberts, W. Verplank, D. C. Smith, C. H. Irby, M. Beard, and K. Mackey. "The Xerox Star: A Retrospective." *Computer* 22, no. 9 (September 1989): 11–26.

Kahng, D. "Semipermanent Memory Using Capacitor Charge Storage and Igfet Read-Out." *Bell Labs Technical Journal* 46, no. 6 (July 1967): 1296–1300.

Kahng, D., and S. M. Sze. "A Floating Gate and Its Application to Memory Devices." *Bell Labs Technical Journal* 46, no. 6 (July 1967): 1288–95.

Kaiman, Arthur. "Computer-Aided Publications Editor." *IEEE Transactions on Engineering Writing and Speech* 11, no. 2 (August 1968): 65–75.

Karim, Awudu, and Shangbo Zhou. "X-TREPAN: A Multi Class Regression and Adapted Extraction of Comprehensible Decision Tree in Artificial Neural Networks." ArXiv:1508.07551 [Cs], August 30, 2015. arxiv.org/abs/1508.07551 (accessed March 16, 2016).

Katz, Matthew. "Analog and Digital Representation." *Minds and Machines* 18, no. 3 (September 2008): 403–8.

Kay, Alan. "Computer Software." *Scientific American* 251, no. 3 (September 1984): 53–59.

Kernighan, Brian W. *D Is for Digital: What a Well-Informed Person Should Know About Computers and Communications*. Mountain View, CA: DisforDigital.net, 2011.

Kernighan, Brian, and Joseph Ossanna. "Troff User's Manual." Computer Science Technical Report 54. Murray Hill, NJ: AT&T Bell Laboratories, 1992.

Khlebnikov, Velimir. *Collected Works of Velimir Khlebnikov: Letters and Theoretical Writings*, ed. Ronald Vroon. Cambridge, MA: Harvard University Press, 1987.

———. *The King of Time: Selected Writings of the Russian Futurian*, ed. Charlotte Douglas; trans. Paul Schmidt. Cambridge, MA: Harvard University Press, 1990.

Kimura, Gary D., and Alan C. Shaw. "The Structure of Abstract Document Objects." In *COCS '84: Proceedings of the Second ACM-SIGOA Conference on Office Information Systems*, 161–69. New York: ACM, 1984.

King, Matthew. "Heidegger's Etymological Method: Discovering Being by Recovering the Richness of the Word." *Philosophy Today* 51, no. 3 (2007): 278–89.

Kirschenbaum, Matthew G. *Mechanisms: New Media and the Forensic Imagination.* Cambridge, MA: MIT Press, 2008.

Kittler, Friedrich A. *Gramophone, Film, Typewriter*, trans. Geoffrey Winthrop-Young and Michael Wutz. Stanford, CA: Stanford University Press, 1999.

———. "There Is No Software." Ctheory.net, a032 (October 18, 1995). web.archive.org /web/20161227002554/http://www.ctheory.net/articles.aspx?id=74 (accessed December 26, 2016).

Klompenhouwer, Michiel A., and Leo Jan Velthoven. "Motion Blur Reduction for Liquid Crystal Displays: Motion-Compensated Inverse Filtering." *Proceedings of SPIE: The International Society for Optical Engineering* 5308 (January 2004): 690–99.

Knobe, Joshua Michael, and Shaun Nichols. *Experimental Philosophy.* Oxford: Oxford University Press, 2008.

Koetsier, Teun. "On the Prehistory of Programmable Machines: Musical Automata, Looms, Calculators." *Mechanism and Machine Theory* 36 (2001): 589–603.

Kranzberg, Melvin. "At the Start." *Technology and Culture* 1, no. 1 (1959): 1–10.

Krishna, Golden. *The Best Interface Is No Interface: The Simple Path to Brilliant Technology.* San Francisco: New Riders, 2015.

Krug, Steve. *Don't Make Me Think, Revisited: A Common Sense Approach to Web Usability*, 3rd ed. Berkeley, CA: New Riders, 2014.

Ku, Vicky. "Critique of the Digital Millennium Copyright Act's Exception on Encryption Research: Is the Exemption Too Narrow?" *Yale Journal of Law and Technology* 2 (2004): 465–90.

Kurita, Taiichiro. "35.1: Moving Picture Quality Improvement for Hold-Type AM-LCDs." *SID Symposium Digest of Technical Papers* 32, no. 1 (2001): 986–89.

LaBelle, Brandon. *Lexicon of the Mouth: Poetics and Politics of Voice and the Oral Imaginary.* New York: Bloomsbury Academic, 2014.

Lakoff, George. "The Contemporary Theory of Metaphor." In *Metaphor and Thought*, ed. Andrew Ortony, 201–52. Cambridge, UK: Cambridge University Press, 1998.

———. "The Death of Dead Metaphor." *Metaphor and Symbolic Activity* 2, no. 2 (June 1987): 143–47.

———. "The Invariance Hypothesis: Is Abstract Reason Based on Image-Schemas?" *Cognitive Linguistics* 1, no. 1 (2009): 39–74.

Lakoff, George, and Mark Johnson. "The Metaphorical Structure of the Human Conceptual System." *Cognitive Science* 4, no. 2 (April 1980): 195–208.

———. *Metaphors We Live By.* Chicago: University of Chicago Press, 1980.

Land, Edwin. "Light Valve." Patent US1963496 A, filed January 16, 1933, issued June 19, 1934.

Laurel, Brenda. "Interface as Mimesis." In *User Centered System Design: New Perspec-*

tives on Human–Computer Interaction, ed. Donald A. Norman and Stephen W. Draper, 67–85. Hillsdale, NJ: Erlbaum Associates, 1986.

Lee, Richard W., and Roy W. Worral, eds. *Electronic Composition in Printing: Proceedings of a Symposium, National Bureau of Standards, June 15–16, 1967.* National Bureau of Standards Special Publication 295. Washington, DC: U.S. Government Printing Office, February 1968.

Lefebvre, Henri. *The Production of Space.* Oxford: Blackwell, 1991.

Lehmann, Otto. *Flüssige Kristalle und die Theorien des Lebens.* Leipzig: Johann Ambrosius Barth, 1906.

Leibnitz, Godefroy-Guillaume. "Explication de l'arithmétique binaire, qui se sert des seuls caractères o et i avec des remarques sur son utilité et sur ce qu'elle donne le sens des anciennes figures chinoises de Fohy." *Mémoires de Mathématique et de Physique de l'Académie Royale des Sciences* (1703).

Leibniz, Gottfried Wilhelm. *Der Briefwechsel von Gottfried Wilhelm Leibniz mit Mathematikern, Bd. 1,* ed. Carl Immanuel Gerhardt. Berlin: Mayer & Müller, 1899.

Leroi-Gourhan, André. *Gesture and Speech.* Cambridge, MA: MIT Press, 1993.

Lessig, Lawrence. "Free(ing) Culture for Remix." *Utah Law Review* 2004 (2004): 961–76.

Leuthardt, Eric C., Gerwin Schalk, Jonathan R. Wolpaw, Jeffrey G. Ojemann, and Daniel W. Moran. "A Brain-Computer Interface Using Electrocorticographic Signals in Humans." *Journal of Neural Engineering* 1, no. 2 (June 2004): 63–71.

Levine, Caroline. *Forms: Whole, Rhythm, Hierarchy, Network.* Princeton, NJ: Princeton University Press, 2015.

Levine, S. P., J. E. Huggins, S. L. BeMent, R. K. Kushwaha, L. A. Schuh, M. M. Rohde, E. A. Passaro, D. A. Ross, K. V. Elisevich, and B. J. Smith. "A Direct Brain Interface Based on Event-Related Potentials." *IEEE Transactions on Rehabilitation Engineering* 8, no. 2 (2000): 180–85.

Liang, Lawrence. "Piracy, Creativity, and Infrastructure: Rethinking Access to Culture." July 20, 2009. ssrn.com/abstract=1436229 (accessed August 17, 2015).

Lipton, Jacqueline D. "To (C) or Not to (C)? Copyright and Innovation in the Digital Typeface Industry." *UC Davis Law Review* 43, no. 1 (2009): 143–92. ssrn.com/abstract=1311402 (accessed May 4, 2015).

Liu, Joseph P. "The DMCA and the Regulation of Scientific Research." *Berkeley Technology Law Journal* 18 (2003): 501–37.

Lloyd, Seth. "Ultimate Physical Limits to Computation." *Nature* 406, no. 6799 (August 2000): 1047–54.

Logicworks. "Government Cloud on the Rise: NSA and DOJ Move to Amazon Web Services." *Cloud Tech News* (July 2015). web.archive.org/web/2015 0911050911/http://www.cloudcomputing-news.net/news/2015/jul/01/government-cloud-on-the-rise-nsa-doj-move-to-amazon-web-services/ (accessed September 11, 2015).

Lubbock, Percy. *The Craft of Fiction.* New York: Scribner's Sons, 1921.

Luther, Martin. "The Freedom of a Christian." In *The Protestant Reformation*, ed. Hans J. Hillerbrand, 31–58. New York: Harper, 2009.

Ma, Jianhua, Laurence T. Yang, Bernady O. Apduhan, Runhe Huang, Leonard Barolli, and Mokoto Takizawa. "Towards a Smart World and Ubiquitous Intelligence: A Walkthrough from Smart Things to Smart Hyperspaces and Ubickids." *International Journal of Pervasive Computing and Communications* 1, no. 1 (February 2005): 53–68.

MacCormack, Patricia. "A Cinema of Desire: Cinesexuality and Asemiosis." In Patricia MacCormack, *Cinesexuality*, 23–38. Farnham, UK: Ashgate, 2012.

Madnick, S. E., and Allen Moulton. "SCRIPT, an On-Line Manuscript Processing System." *IEEE Transactions on Engineering Writing and Speech* 11, no. 2 (August 1968): 92–100.

Mahmood, Khalid, and Muhammad Ilyas. "Copyright and Book Piracy in Pakistan." *IFLA Journal* 31, no. 4 (December 2005): 324–32.

Maley, Corey J. "Analog and Digital, Continuous and Discrete." *Philosophical Studies: An International Journal for Philosophy in the Analytic Tradition* 155, no. 1 (August 2011): 117–31.

Malinowski, Bronislaw, I. A. Richards, F. G. Crookshank, and J. P. Postgate. "The Problem of Meaning in Primitive Languages." In *The Meaning of Meaning: A Study of the Influence of Language upon Thought and of the Science of Symbolism*, ed. C. K. Ogden, 146–52. London: K. Paul, Trench, Trubner, 1923.

Manovich, Lev. *The Language of New Media*, rev. ed. Cambridge, MA: MIT Press, 2002.

———. *Software Takes Command*. New York: Bloomsbury Academic, 2013.

———. "There Is Only Software." In *FILE: Electronic Language International Festival* (2011): 272–74. web.archive.org/web/20150402014145/http://manovich.net/index.php/projects/there-is-only-software (accessed April 2, 2015).

Marche, Stephen. "Literature Is not Data: Against Digital Humanities." *Los Angeles Review of Books*, October 28, 2012. web.archive.org/web/20161122111616/https://lareviewofbooks.org/article/literature-is-not-data-against-digital-humanities/ (accessed November 22, 2016).

Martin, Horace G. "Telegraphic Transmitter." Patent US767303 A, filed May 7, 1904, issued August 9, 1904.

Martin, James. *Design of Man-Computer Dialogues*. Englewood Cliffs, NJ: Prentice-Hall, 1973.

Martin, James, and Adrian R. D. Norman. *The Computerized Society: An Appraisal of the Impact of Computers on Society over the Next Fifteen Years*. Englewood Cliffs, NJ: Prentice-Hall, 1970.

Marx, Karl. *Capital: A Critique of Political Economy*. New York: Modern Library, 1906.

———. *Capital, a Critique of Political Economy*, ed. Friedrich Engels. New York: International Publishers, 1967.

———. *Economic and Philosophic Manuscripts of 1844*. New York: International Publishers, 1964.

———. *Theories of Surplus-Value*. Moscow: Progress, 1963.

Marx, Karl, and Friedrich Engels. *The Marx-Engels Reader*, ed. Robert C. Tucker, 2nd rev. and enlarged ed. New York: W. W. Norton, 1978.

Mauss, Marcel. *Techniques, Technology, and Civilization*, ed. Nathan Schlanger. New York: Berghahn, 2006.

May, F. T. "IBM Word Processing Developments." *IBM Journal of Research and Development* 25, no. 5 (September 1981): 741–54.

McCalman, Iain. "Unrespectable Radicalism: Infidels and Pornography in Early Nineteenth-Century London." *Past and Present* 104 (1984): 74–110.

McCarthy, John. "The LISP Interpreter System." In *LISP 1.5 Programmer's Manual*, by John McCarthy, Paul W. Abrahams, Daniel J. Edwards, Timothy P. Hart, and Michael I. Levin, 15–19. Cambridge, MA: MIT Press, 1962.

McCorduck, Pamela. *The Universal Machine: Confessions of a Technological Optimist*. New York: McGraw-Hill, 1985.

McGann, Jerome. *Radiant Textuality: Literature After the World Wide Web*. New York: Palgrave Macmillan, 2001.

———. "Socialization of Text." In Jerome J. McGann, *The Textual Condition*, 69–87. Princeton, NJ: Princeton University Press, 1991.

McGowan, Kat. "'I Want to Know What Code Is Running Inside My Body.'" *Backchannel*, February 11, 2016. backchannel.com/i-want-to-know-what-code-is-running-inside-my-body-ff9a159da34b#.35rpokuaz (accessed February 16, 2016).

McKay, Claude. *Harlem Shadows: An Electronic Edition*, ed. Chris Forster and Roopika Risam. December 2015. web.archive.org/web/20161002143046/http://harlemshadows.org/ (accessed October 2, 2016).

McKenzie, Donald Francis, Peter D. McDonald, and Michael Felix Suarez. *Making Meaning: "Printers of the Mind" and Other Essays*. Amherst: University of Massachusetts Press, 2002.

McKeown, Kathleen. *Text Generation*. Cambridge, UK: Cambridge University Press, 1992.

McLuhan, Marshall. *The Gutenberg Galaxy: The Making of Typographic Man*. Toronto: University of Toronto Press, 1962.

McNeal, Gregory S. "Targeted Killing and Accountability." *Georgetown Law Journal* 102 (2014): 681–794.

McNicol, Donald Monroe. *American Telegraph Practice: A Complete Technical Course in Modern Telegraphy*. New York: McGraw-Hill, 1913.

Michel, Jean-Baptiste, Yuan Kui Shen, Aviva Presser Aiden, Adrian Veres, Matthew K. Gray, The Google Books Team, Joseph P. Pickett et al. "Quantitative Analysis of Culture Using Millions of Digitized Books." *Science* 331, no. 6014 (January 2011): 176–82.

Mignolo, Walter D. "Epistemic Disobedience, Independent Thought, and Decolonial Freedom." *Theory, Culture, and Society* 26, nos. 7–8 (December 2009): 159–81.

Miller, K. J., E. C. Leuthardt, G. Schalk, R. P. N. Rao, N. R. Anderson, D. W. Moran, J. W. Miller, and J. G. Ojemann. "Spectral Changes in Cortical Surface Potentials During Motor Movement." *Journal of Neuroscience* 27, no. 9 (February 2007): 2424–32.

Miller, Leslie Jill. "The ISO Reference Model of Open Systems Interconnection: A First Tutorial." In *ACM '81: Proceedings of the ACM '81 Conference*, 283–88. New York: ACM, 1981.

Mindflex. "Mindflex: Frequently Asked Questions." March 2015. web.archive.org/web/20150310195631/http://mindflexgames.com/faq.php (accessed March 10, 2015).

Mishima, N., and G. Itoh. "Novel Frame Interpolation Method for Hold-Type Displays." In *ICIP '04: 2004 International Conference on Image Processing* 3: 1473–76. New York: IEEE, 2004.

Mojtabai, Ramin. "Delusion as Error: The History of a Metaphor." *History of Psychiatry* 11, no. 41 (January 2000): 3–14.

Moll-Carrillo, Hector J., Gitta Salomon, Matthew Marsh, Jane Fulton Suri, and Peter Spreenberg. "Articulating a Metaphor Through User-Centered Design." In *CHI '95: Proceedings of the SIGCHI Conference on Human Factors in Computing Systems*, 566–72. New York: ACM Press/Addison-Wesley, 1995.

Montfort, Nick. *Twisty Little Passages: An Approach to Interactive Fiction.* Cambridge, MA: MIT Press, 2003.

Moor, James H. "Three Myths of Computer Science." *British Journal for the Philosophy of Science* 29, no. 3 (1978): 213–22.

Moran, John. "Wittgenstein and Russia." *New Left Review* 1, no. 73 (June 1972): 85–96.

Moréas, Jean. "Le symbolisme." *Le Figaro*, Supplément Littéraire (September 1886): 150–51.

Moreno, J. L. *Who Shall Survive? Foundations of Sociometry, Group Psychotherapy, and Sociodrama.* Beacon, NY: Beacon House, 1953.

Morgan, J. S., and J. R. Norwood. "The IBM Selectric Composer: Justification Mechanism." *IBM Journal of Research and Development* 12, no. 1 (January 1968): 68–75.

Morris, Jeremy Wade. *Selling Digital Music, Formatting Culture.* Oakland, CA: University of California Press, 2015.

Mueller, Milton. "Reinventing Media Activism: Public Interest Advocacy in the Making of U.S. Communication-Information Policy, 1960–2002." *Information Society* 20, no. 3 (July–August 2004): 169–87.

Müller, Cornelia. *Metaphors Dead and Alive, Sleeping and Waking: A Dynamic View.* Chicago: University of Chicago Press, 2008.

Mumford, Lewis. "Authoritarian and Democratic Technics." *Technology and Culture* 5, no. 1 (1964): 1–8.

Murray, Donald. *The Philosophy of Power.* London: Williams, 1939.

———. "Setting Type by Telegraph." *Journal of the Institution of Electrical Engineers* 34, no. 172 (May 1905): 555–97.

———. "Tape-Controlled Telegraphic Transmitting Apparatus." Patent US794242 A, filed January 5, 1905, issued July 11, 1905.

Nabokov, Vladimir. "A Guide to Berlin," trans. Dmitri Nabokov. *The New Yorker* (March 1976): 27–28.

———. *Invitation to a Beheading*. New York: Putnam's Sons, 1959.

Nagel, Thomas. "What Is It Like to Be a Bat?" *Philosophical Review* 83, no. 4 (October 1974): 435–50.

NCS (National Communications System). "Open Systems Interconnection (OSI) Reference Model (August 1981): ISO Second Draft Proposal (DP) 7498." Washington, DC: National Communications System, September 1981.

Negroponte, Nicholas. *Being Digital*. New York: Knopf, 1995.

Nelson, Theodore H. "A File Structure for the Complex, the Changing, and the Indeterminate (1965)." In *The New Media Reader*, ed. Noah Wardrip-Fruin and Nick Montfort, 133–46. Cambridge, MA: MIT Press, 2003.

Nesbit, Molly. "What Was an Author?" *Yale French Studies* 73 (1987): 229–57.

Neuhold, E. J. "The Formal Description of Programming Languages." *IBM Systems Journal* 10, no. 2 (1971): 86–112.

Nkiko, Christopher. "Book Piracy in Nigeria: Issues and Strategies." *Journal of Academic Librarianship* 40, nos. 3–4 (May 2014): 394–98.

Noll, A. Michael. *The Evolution of Media*. Lanham, MD: Rowman & Littlefield, 2007.

Norman, Donald A. "Cognitive Artifacts." In *Designing Interaction*, ed. John M. Carroll, 17–38. New York: Cambridge University Press, 1991.

Norman, Donald A., and Stephen W. Draper. *User Centered System Design: New Perspectives on Human-Computer Interaction*. Hillsdale, NJ: Erlbaum Associates, 1986.

Nuttall, Anthony David. *A New Mimesis: Shakespeare and the Representation of Reality*. New Haven, CT: Yale University Press, 2007.

Nygaard, Kristen, and Ole-Johan Dahl. "The Development of the SIMULA Languages." In *History of Programming Languages I*, ed. Richard L. Wexelblat, 439–80. New York: ACM, 1981.

Obama, Barack. "The 2016 State of the Union Address," January 12, 2016. Washington DC: White House, 2016. web.archive.org/web/20160328052623/ https://www.whitehouse.gov/the-press-office/2016/01/12/remarks-president -barack-obama-%E2%80%93-prepared-delivery-state-union-address (accessed March 28, 2016).

O'Gorman, L. "The Document Spectrum for Page Layout Analysis." *IEEE Transactions on Pattern Analysis and Machine Intelligence* 15, no. 11 (November 1993): 1162–73.

O'Gorman, Lawrence, and Rangachar Kasturi. *Document Image Analysis*. Edition reconstructed from book source files. Los Alamitos, CA: IEEE Computer Society Press, 1995.

Ohmori, Hiroyuki, Masanori Hosomi, Kazuhiro Bessho, Yutaka Higo, Kazutaka Yamane, and Hiroyuki Uchida. "Memory Element, Method of Manufacturing the Same, and Memory Device." U.S. Patent Application 20150097254 A1, filed September 4, 2014, issued April 9, 2015. www.freepatentsonline.com/y2015/ 0097254.html (accessed April 15, 2015).

Okiy, Rose B. "Photocopying and the Awareness of Copyright in Tertiary Institutions in Nigeria." *Interlending and Document Supply* 33, no. 1 (March 2005): 49–52.

Orr, William D. *Conversational Computers*. New York: Wiley, 1968.

Pajak, Henry G. "Electronic Library." Patent EP0472070 A2, filed August 9, 1991, issued February 26, 1992.

Pan, Hao, Xiao-Fan Feng, and S. Daly. "LCD Motion Blur Modeling and Analysis." In *ICIP 2005: IEEE International Conference on Image Processing, 2005*, 2: 21–24. New York: IEEE, 2005.

Parnas, D. L. "Software Engineering Programs Are not Computer Science Programs." *IEEE Software* 16, no. 6 (November 1999): 19–30.

Pasquale, Frank. *The Black Box Society: The Secret Algorithms That Control Money and Information*. Cambridge, MA: Harvard University Press, 2015.

Patel, Reena. *Working the Night Shift: Women in India's Call Center Industry*. Stanford, CA: Stanford University Press, 2010.

Pavan, P., R. Bez, P. Olivo, and E. Zanoni. "Flash Memory Cells: An Overview." *Proceedings of the IEEE* 85, no. 8 (August 1997): 1248–71.

Peirce, Charles Sanders. "Excerpts from Letters to Lady Welby." In Charles Sanders Peirce, *The Essential Peirce: Selected Philosophical Writings, Volume 2, 1893–1913*, ed. Peirce Edition Project, Nathan Houser, Jonathan R. Eller, Albert C. Lewis, André de Tienne, Cathy L. Clark, and D. Bront Davis, 477–91. Bloomington: Indiana University Press, 1998.

——. "On the Algebra of Logic: A Contribution to the Philosophy of Notation." In Charles Sanders Peirce, *The Essential Peirce: Selected Philosophical Writings, Volume 1, 1867–1893*, ed. Nathan Houser and Christian Kloesel, 225–28. Bloomington: Indiana University Press, 1992.

——. "Pragmatism in Retrospect: A Last Formulation." In Charles S. Peirce, *Philosophical Writings of Peirce*, ed. Justus Buchler, 269–289. New York: Dover, 1955.

Perzanowski, Aaron. "Rethinking Anticircumvention's Interoperability Policy." *UC Davis Law Review* 42 (2009): 1549–1620.

Petit, Annie. "Claude Bernard and the History of Science." *Isis* 78, no. 2 (1987): 201–19.

Petroski, Henry. *Invention by Design: How Engineers Get from Thought to Thing*. Cambridge, MA: Harvard University Press, 1996.

Petzold, Charles. *The Annotated Turing: A Guided Tour Through Alan Turing's Historic Paper on Computability and the Turing Machine*. Indianapolis: Wiley, 2008.

——. *Code: The Hidden Language of Computer Hardware and Software*. Redmond, WA: Microsoft Press, 2000.

Phelps, C. Deirdre. "The Edition as Art Form in Textual and Interpretive Criticism." *Text* 7 (1994): 61–75.

Piatkowski, Thomas F. "The ISO-ANSI Open Systems Reference Model: A Proposal for a Systems Approach." *Computer Networks* 4, no. 3 (June 1980): 111–24.

Piccinini, Gualtiero. "Computational Modelling vs. Computational Explanation: Is

Everything a Turing Machine, and Does It Matter to the Philosophy of Mind?" *Australasian Journal of Philosophy* 85, no. 1 (2007): 93–115.

Pihlström, Sami. *Structuring the World: The Issue of Realism and the Nature of Ontological Problems in Classical and Contemporary Pragmatism.* Helsinki: Philosophical Society of Finland, 1996.

Pike & Fischer Inc. *Digital Millennium Copyright Act: Text, History, and Caselaw.* Silver Spring, MD: Pike & Fischer Inc., 2003.

Piper, Andrew. "Of Note." In Andrew Piper, *Book Was There: Reading in Electronic Times,* 63–82. Chicago: University of Chicago Press, 2012.

Plato. *The Dialogues of Plato,* ed. Benjamin Jowett. New York: Random House, 1937.

——. *Euthyphro. Apology. Crito. Phaedo. Phaedrus,* trans. Harold North Fowler. Cambridge, MA: Harvard University Press, 1999.

——. "Phaedrus." In Plato, *Euthyphro. Apology. Crito. Phaedo. Phaedrus,* trans. Harold North Fowler, 405–580. Cambridge, MA: Harvard University Press, 1999.

——. "Timaeus." In Plato, *Timaeus; Critias; Cleitophon; Menexenus; Epistles,* trans. Robert Gregg Bury, 1–254. Cambridge, MA: Harvard University Press, 1999.

——. "Timaeus." In Plato, *The Dialogues of Plato,* trans. Benjamin Jowett, 339–516. London: Macmillan, 1892.

Pollak, Anton, and Josef Virag. "Writing-Telegraph." Patent US675495 A, filed June 28, 1900, issued June 4, 1901.

Postigo, Hector. "Information Communication Technologies and Framing for Backfire in the Digital Rights Movement: The Case of Dmitry Sklyarov's Advanced E-Book Processor." *Social Science Computer Review* 28, no. 2 (May 2010): 232–50.

Postman, Neil. *Technopoly: The Surrender of Culture to Technology.* New York: Knopf, 1992.

Poulsen, Valdemar. "Method of Recording and Reproducing Sounds or Signals." Patent US661619 A, filed July 8, 1899, issued November 13, 1900.

Prabhakar, Arati. "How Will Technology Shape the Future of War?" March 3, 2015. web.archive.org/web/20160729194906/http://www.newamerica.org/interna tional-security/future-war/events/future-of-war/ (accessed July 29, 2016).

Propp, Vladimir. *Morphology of the Folktale,* 2nd ed. Austin: University of Texas Press, 1971.

Purves, Dale, George J. Augustine, David Fitzpatrick, Lawrence C. Katz, Anthony-Samuel LaMantia, James O. McNamara, and S. Mark Williams. "Types of Eye Movements and Their Functions." In *Neuroscience,* ed. Dale Purves, George J. Augustine, David Fitzpatrick, Lawrence C. Katz, Anthony-Samuel LaMantia, James O. McNamara, and S. Mark Williams, 2nd ed. Sunderland, MA: Sinauer Associates, 2001. www.ncbi.nlm.nih.gov/books/NBK10991/ (accessed December 26, 2016).

Putnam, Hilary. "James's Theory of Truth." In *The Cambridge Companion to*

William James, ed. Ruth Anna Putnam, 166–85. Cambridge, UK: Cambridge University Press, 1997.

———. *Representation and Reality*. Cambridge, MA: Harvard University Press, 1988.

Ramsey, Frank Plumpton. *The Foundations of Mathematics and Other Logical Essays*, ed. R. B. Braithwaite. Eastford, CT: Martino Fine Books, 2013.

Randell, Brian, Maurice V. Wilkes, and Paul E. Ceruzzi. "History of Digital Computers." In *Encyclopedia of Computer Science*, 4th ed., ed. Anthony Ralston, Edwin D. Reilly, and David Hemmendinger, 545–70. Chichester, UK: Wiley, 2003.

Ransom, John Crowe. "The Concrete Universal: Observations on the Understanding of Poetry. II." *Kenyon Review* 17, no. 3 (July 1955): 383–407.

Raymond, Eric S. *The Art of UNIX Programming*. Indianapolis: Addison-Wesley Professional, 2003.

Reinitzer, Friedrich. "Beiträge zur Kenntniss des Cholesterins." *Monatshefte für Chemie und Verwandte Teile Anderer Wissenschaften* 9, no. 1 (May 1888): 421–41.

Rheinberger, Hans-Jörg. *Toward a History of Epistemic Things: Synthesizing Proteins in the Test Tube*. Stanford, CA: Stanford University Press, 1997.

Richards, I. A. *The Philosophy of Rhetoric*. London: Oxford University Press, 1965.

Ricoeur, Paul. *Interpretation Theory: Discourse and the Surplus of Meaning*. Fort Worth: Texas Christian University Press, 1976.

Riskin, Jessica. "The Defecating Duck, or the Ambiguous Origins of Artificial Life." *Critical Inquiry* 29, no. 4 (June 1, 2003): 599–633.

Rist, J. M. "Plato's 'Earlier Theory of Forms.'" *Phoenix* 29, no. 4 (December 1975): 336–57.

Ritchie, D. M, and K. L. Thompson. *QED Text Editor*. Murray Hill, NJ: Bell Telephone Laboratories, June 1970.

Roberts, M. J. D. "Morals, Art, and the Law: The Passing of the Obscene Publications Act, 1857." *Victorian Studies* 28, no. 4 (1985): 609–29.

Robshaw, Matthew J. B. "Abuse-Resistant Object Distribution System and Method." Patent US5400403 A, filed August 16, 1993, issued March 21, 1995.

Rogers, Rosemary. "The Demo." *MouseSite*, 2005. web.archive.org/web/201504152 03743/http://web.stanford.edu/dept/SUL/library/extra4/sloan/MouseSite /1968Demo.html (accessed April 14, 2015).

Rottach, K. G., A. Z. Zivotofsky, V. E. Das, L. Averbuch-Heller, A. O. Discenna, A. Poonyathalang, and R. J. Leigh. "Comparison of Horizontal, Vertical, and Diagonal Smooth Pursuit Eye Movements in Normal Human Subjects." *Vision Research* 36, no. 14 (July 1996): 2189–95.

Rowland, Henry A. "Multiplex Printing-Telegraph." Patent US689753 A, filed July 26, 1897, issued December 24, 1901.

Ruiz de Mendoza Ibáñez, Francisco José. "On the Nature of Blending as a Cognitive Phenomenon." *Journal of Pragmatics* 30, no. 3 (September 1998): 259–74.

Russell, Bertrand. *The Philosophy of Bergson*. Cambridge, UK: Bowes & Bowes, 1978 [1914].

Sartre, Jean-Paul. *Being and Nothingness*, trans. Hazel E. Barnes, reprint ed. New York: Washington Square Press, 1993.

Sattar, Atia. "The Aesthetics of Laboratory Inscription: Claude Bernard's Cahier Rouge." *Isis* 104, no. 1 (2013): 63–85.

Scholz, Trebor. *Digital Labor: The Internet as Playground and Factory*. New York: Routledge, 2013.

Schopenhauer, Arthur. *The World as Will and Idea*, trans. R. B. Haldane and J. Kemp. London: Paul, Trench, Trübner, 1906.

Searle, John R. "Metaphor." In *Metaphor and Thought*, ed. Andrew Ortony, 83–112. Cambridge, UK: Cambridge University Press, 1998.

———. "Minds, Brains, and Programs." *Behavioral and Brain Sciences* 3, no. 3 (September 1980): 417–24.

Seigfried, Charlene Haddock. *William James's Radical Reconstruction of Philosophy*. Albany: State University of New York Press, 1990.

Sellars, Andrew. "Petition of a Coalition of Medical Device Researchers for Exemption to Prohibition on Circumvention of Copyright Protection Systems for Access Control Technologies." Petition before the U.S. Copyright Office, Library of Congress, Docket No. 2014-07. Cyberlaw Clinic, Berkman Center for Internet and Society, Harvard Law School, Cambridge, MA, July 2014. clinic.cyber.harvard.edu/files/2014/11/Medical-Device-Research-Coalition-Petition.pdf (accessed July 14, 2016).

Seringhaus, Michael. "E-Book Transactions: Amazon 'Kindles' the Copy Ownership Debate." *Yale Journal of Law and Technology* 12, no. 1 (January 2010): article 4.

Shaked, Shaul. *Dualism in Transformation*. London: Routledge, 2005.

Shaw, A. C. "A Model for Document Preparation Systems." Technical Report 80-04-02. Seattle, WA: Department of Computer Science, University of Washington, April 1980.

Shaw, J. C. "JOSS: A Designer's View of an Experimental On-Line Computing System." In *AFIPS '64: Proceedings of the October 27–29, 1964, Fall Joint Computer Conference, Part I*, 455–64. New York: ACM, 1964.

Shelley, Percy Bysshe. *Essays, Letters from Abroad, Translations, and Fragments*, ed. Mary Wollstonecraft Shelley. London: Edward Moxon, 1840.

Shillingsburg, Peter. "On Being Textually Aware." *Studies in American Naturalism* 1, no. 1/2 (2006): 170–95.

Shklovsky, Viktor. "Art as Technique." In *Russian Formalist Criticism: Four Essays*, ed. Lee T. Lemon, 3–24. Lincoln: University of Nebraska Press, 2012.

———. "Isskustvo, kak priem." In Viktor Shklovsky, Osip Brik, Yevgeny Polovanov, Boris Eichenbaum, and Lev Yakubinsky, *Poetika*, 101–14. Petrograd: State Typography #18, 1919.

———. *Voskreshenie Slova* [Resurrection of the Word]. Petrograd: Tip. Zh. Sokolingaskago, 1914.

Shklovsky, Viktor, Osip Brik, Yevgeny Polovanov, Boris Eichenbaum, and Lev Yakubinsky. *Poetika.* Petrograd: State Typography #18, 1919.

Shklovsky, Viktor, Lev Yakubinsky, Osip Brik, and Boris Kushner. *Sborniki (Po Teorii
Poeticheskogo Iazyka)*, vol. 1. Petrograd: Typographer #3, 1917.

Shneiderman, Ben. "Direct Manipulation: A Step Beyond Programming Languages."
Computer 16, no. 8 (August 1983): 57–69.

———. "The Future of Interactive Systems and the Emergence of Direct Manipulation." *Behaviour and Information Technology* 1, no. 3 (July 1982): 237–56.

Shore, Andy. "Acrobat 2.0." In *Compcon '95: Technologies for the Information
Superhighway, Digest of Papers*, 379–82. Los Alamitos, CA: IEEE Computer
Society Press, 1995.

Siegert, Bernhard. "Cacography or Communication? Cultural Techniques in German
Media Studies." *Grey Room* 29 (fall 2007): 26–47.

———. *Cultural Techniques: Grids, Filters, Doors, and Other Articulations of the Real*,
trans. Geoffrey Winthrop-Young. New York: Fordham University Press, 2015.

Smith, Oberllin. "Some Possible Forms of the Phonograph." *Electrical World* (September 1888): 116–17.

Smith, Pamela H., Amy R. W. Meyers, and Harold J. Cook, eds. *Ways of Making
and Knowing: The Material Culture of Empirical Knowledge.* Ann Arbor: University of Michigan Press, 2014.

Sontag, Susan. *Against Interpretation, and Other Essays.* New York: Farrar, Straus
& Giroux, 1966.

Soyata, Tolga, Rajani Muraleedharan, Jonathan Langdon, Colin Funai, Scott Ames,
Minseok Kwon, and Wendi Heinzelman. "COMBAT: Mobile-Cloud-Based Compute/
Communications Infrastructure for Battlefield Applications." *SPIE Proceedings*
8403 (May 7, 2012). dx.doi.org/10.1117/12.919146 (accessed May 12, 2016).

Spencer, Herbert. *The Philosophy of Style: Together with an Essay on Style.* Boston: Allyn & Bacon, 1892.

Spolsky, Joel. *User Interface Design for Programmers.* Berkeley, CA: Apress, 2001.

Starosielski, Nicole. *The Undersea Network.* Durham, NC: Duke University Press,
2015.

Stefanita, Carmen-Gabriela. *Magnetism: Basics and Applications.* New York:
Springer Science and Business Media, 2012.

Steinhart, Eric. "Digital Metaphysics." In *The Digital Phoenix: How Computers Are
Changing Philosophy*, ed. Terrell Ward Bynum and James Moor, 117–34. Oxford: Blackwell, 1998.

Stensola, Hanne, Tor Stensola, Trygve Solstad, Kristian Frøland, May-Britt Moser,
and Edvard I. Moser. "The Entorhinal Grid Map Is Discretized." *Nature* 492, no.
7427 (December 2012): 72–78.

Sterne, Jonathan. *MP3: The Meaning of a Format.* Durham, NC: Duke University
Press, 2012.

Stoltz, Mitch. "Is It Illegal to Unlock a Phone? The Situation Is Better—and
Worse—Than You Think." Electronic Frontier Foundation, January 28, 2013.

web.archive.org/web/20150414213427/https://www.eff.org/is-it-illegal-to-un lock-a-phone (accessed April 14, 2015).

Susina, Jan. "'Why Is a Raven Like a Writing-Desk?': The Play of Letters in Lewis Carroll's Alice Books." *Children's Literature Association Quarterly* 26, no. 1 (2001): 15–21.

Swedenborg, Emanuel. *The Apocalypse; or, Book of Revelations, Explained According to the Spiritual Sense, Wherein Are Disclosed the Arcana Therein Foretold Which Have Been Hitherto Hidden.* London: J. & E. Hodson, 1901 [1812].

———. *A Treatise Concerning Heaven and Hell, Containing a Relation of Many Wonderful Things Therein, as Heard and Seen by the Author,* trans. William Cookworthy and Thomas Hartley. London: James Phillips, 1778.

Szabo, Nick. "Formalizing and Securing Relationships on Public Networks." *First Monday* 2, no. 9 (September 1, 1997). web.archive.org/web/20150414075111/ http://firstmonday.org/ojs/index.php/fm/article/view/548 (accessed April 14, 2015).

Takayuki c/o Fujitsu Limited Hasebe, and Naoya c/o Fujitsu Limited Torii. "Licensee Notification System." Patent EP0766165 B1, filed July 10, 1996, issued November 19, 2003.

Tanselle, G. Thomas. "The Concept of Format." *Studies in Bibliography* 53 (2000): 67–115.

———. "Textual Instability and Editorial Idealism." *Studies in Bibliography* 49 (1996): 1–60.

Taussig, Michael T. *Mimesis and Alterity: A Particular History of the Senses.* New York: Routledge, 1993.

Taylor, Frederick Winslow. *The Principles of Scientific Management.* New York: Harper, 1919.

Tenen, Dennis, and Maxwell Foxman. "Book Piracy as Peer Preservation: Computational Culture." *Computational Culture* 4 (November 9, 2014). web.archive.org/ web/20150825131658/http://computationalculture.net/article/book-piracy-as -peer-preservation (accessed August 25, 2015).

Terranova, Tiziana. *Network Culture: Politics for the Information Age.* Ann Arbor, MI: Pluto Press, 2004.

Thiele, Heinz H. K. "Magnetic Sound Recording in Europe up to 1945." *Journal of the Audio Engineering Society* 36, no. 5 (May 1988): 396–408.

Thurston, H. A. "Leibniz's Notation." *Mathematical Gazette* 57, no. 401 (1973): 189–91.

Turing, A. M. "Computing Machinery and Intelligence." *Mind* 59, no. 236 (October 1950): 433–60.

———. "On Computable Numbers, with an Application to the Entscheidungsproblem." *Proceedings of the London Mathematical Society,* ser. 2, 42, no. 1 (January 1937): 230–65.

Turner, Mark. *Death Is the Mother of Beauty: Mind, Metaphor, Criticism.* Chicago: University of Chicago Press, 1987.

Turner, Mark, and Gilles Fauconnier. "Conceptual Integration and Formal Expression." *Metaphor and Symbolic Activity* 10, no. 3 (September 1995): 183–204.

Turner, Raymond. "Programming Languages as Technical Artifacts." *Philosophy and Technology* 27, no. 3 (February 2013): 377–97.

Tweney, Dylan. "Dec. 9, 1968: The Mother of All Demos." *Wired* (December 8, 2008). web.archive.org/web/20150430043803/http://www.wired.com/2010/12/1209 computer-mouse-mother-of-all-demos (accessed April 30, 2015).

Uexküll, Jakob von. *A Foray into the Worlds of Animals and Humans: With A Theory of Meaning*, trans. Joseph D. O'Neil. Minneapolis: University of Minnesota Press, 2010.

Unicode Consortium. *The Unicode Standard: Worldwide Character Encoding, Version 1.* Boston: Addison-Wesley, 1990.

U.S. Bureau of Labor Statistics. "Displacement of Morse Operators in Commercial Telegraph Offices." *Monthly Labor Review* 34, no. 3 (March 1932): 501–15.

U.S. Copyright Office, Library of Congress. "Exemption to Prohibition on Circumvention of Copyright Protection Systems for Access Control Technologies." *Federal Register*, October 28, 2015. web.archive.org/web/20161227024042/ https://www.federalregister.gov/documents/2015/10/28/2015-27212/exemp tion-to-prohibition-on-circumvention-of-copyright-protection-systems-for-access -control (accessed December 26, 2016).

Vansize, William B. "A New Page-Printing Telegraph." *Transactions of the American Institute of Electrical Engineers* 28 (January 1901): 5–43.

Varela, F. G., H. R. Maturana, and R. Uribe. "Autopoiesis: The Organization of Living Systems, Its Characterization, and a Model." *Biosystems* 5, no. 4 (May 1974): 187–96.

Vasic, Bane, and Erozan M. Kurtas. *Coding and Signal Processing for Magnetic Recording Systems.* London: CRC Press, 2004.

Veselovsky, Alexander. "O metode i zadachah istorii literatury kak nauki" [Aims and Methods of Literary History as a Science]. In Alexander Veselovsky, *Sobranie sochinenii* [Collected Works], 1–17. St. Petersburg: Imperial Academy of Sciences, 1913.

———. "Psihologicheskii paralelism i ego formy v otrazheniah poeticheskogo stila" [Psychological Parallelism and Its Forms in Reflections of Poetic Style]. In Alexander Veselovsky, *Sobranie sochinenii* [Collected Works], 130–225. St. Petersburg: Imperial Academy of Sciences, 1913.

———. "Tri glavy is istoricheskoi poetiki" [Three Chapters from *Historical Poetics*]. In Alexander Veselovsky, *Sobranie sochinenii* [Collected Works], 226–484. St. Petersburg: Imperial Academy of Sciences, 1913.

Vessey, Iris, V. Ramesh, and Robert L. Glass. "A Unified Classification System for Research in the Computing Disciplines." *Information and Software Technology* 47, no. 4 (March 2005): 245–55.

Von Lohmann, Fred. *Unintended Consequences: Twelve Years Under the DMCA.* Electronic Frontier Foundation, March 3, 2010. web.archive.org/web/201504

28051638/https://www.eff.org/wp/unintended-consequences-under-dmca (accessed April 28, 2015).

Vriendt, Charles de. "Program Distribution System." Patent US1974062 A, filed July 8, 1933, issued September 18, 1934.

Wagner, Pierre. "Wittgenstein et les machines de Turing." *Revue de Métaphysique et de Morale 2* (April 2005): 181–96.

Walther, George H., and Harold F. O'Neil Jr. "On-Line User-Computer Interface: The Effects of Interface Flexibility, Terminal Type, and Experience on Performance." In *AFIPS '74: Proceedings of the May 6–10, 1974, National Computer Conference and Exposition*, 379–84. New York: ACM, 1974.

Weber, Jutta. "Keep Adding: On Kill Lists, Drone Warfare, and the Politics of Databases." *Environment and Planning D: Society and Space* 34, no. 1 (February 2016): 107–25.

Weik, Martin. "Neutral Direct-Current Telegraph System." In *Computer Science and Communications Dictionary*, by Martin Weik, 1096. New York: Springer, 2000.

Weller, Charles Edward. *The Early History of the Typewriter*. La Porte, IN: Chase & Shepard, 1918.

Wendt, Larry. "Sound Poetry. I. History of Electro-Acoustic Approaches; II. Connections to Advanced Electronic Technologies." *Leonardo* 18, no. 1 (1985): 11–23.

Wheatstone, Charles. "Improvement in Receiving-Instruments for Electric Telegraphs." Patent US158156 A, filed November 13, 1874, issued December 22, 1874.

Wigdor, Daniel, Joe Fletcher, and Gerald Morrison. "Designing User Interfaces for Multi-Touch and Gesture Devices." In *CHI '09: Extended Abstracts on Human Factors in Computing Systems*, 2755–58. New York: ACM, 2009.

Wimsatt, W. K., Jr. "The Structure of the 'Concrete Universal' in Literature." *PMLA* 62, no. 1 (March 1947): 262–80.

Winner, Langdon. *Autonomous Technology: Technics-Out-of-Control as a Theme in Political Thought*. Cambridge, MA: MIT Press, 1978.

———. "Do Artifacts Have Politics?" *Daedalus* 109, no. 1 (January 1980): 121–36.

Wittgenstein, Ludwig. *The Blue and Brown Books*. New York: Harper Torchbooks, 1965.

———. *Lectures and Conversations on Aesthetics, Psychology, and Religious Belief*, ed. Cyril Barrett. Berkeley: University of California Press, 1966.

———. *Philosophical Grammar*, ed. Rush Rhees. Berkeley: University of California Press, 1974.

———. *Philosophical Investigations: The German Text, with a Revised English Translation*, trans. G. E. M. Anscombe. Malden, Mass.: Blackwell, 2001.

———. *Wittgenstein's Lectures on the Foundations of Mathematics, Cambridge, 1939: From the Notes of R. G. Bosanquet, Norman Malcolm, Rush Rhees, and Yorick Smythies*, ed. R. G. Bosanquet and Cora Diamond. Ithaca, NY: Cornell University Press, 1976.

Wolpaw, J. R., N. Birbaumer, W. J. Heetderks, D. J. McFarland, P. H. Peckham, G.

Schalk, E. Donchin, L. A. Quatrano, C. J. Robinson, and T. M. Vaughan. "Brain-Computer Interface Technology: A Review of the First International Meeting." *IEEE Transactions on Rehabilitation Engineering* 8, no. 2 (June 2000): 164–73.

Woods, Michael. "Form, Species, and Predication in Aristotle." *Synthese* 96, no. 3 (September 1993): 399–415.

Wright, Walter. "Computing Attachment for Type-Writers." Patent US1162730 A, filed January 17, 1908, issued November 30, 1915.

———. "Computing Mechanism." Patent US1105170 A, filed September 28, 1908, issued July 28, 1914.

Wu-Tang Clan. *Once Upon a Time in Shaolin.* 2014. Cilvaringz and RZA, producers.

Youngquist, Robert, and Robert Hanes. "Magnetic Reader." Patent US3013206 A, filed August 28, 1958, issued December 12, 1961.

Zimmermann, H. "OSI Reference Model: The ISO Model of Architecture for Open Systems Interconnection." *IEEE Transactions on Communications* 28, no. 4 (April 1980): 425–32.

INDEX

abstraction, 16, 40–46, 60–68, 81, 84, 97–102, 157. *See also* form; perception; symbolism

access, 2–3, 17–18, 27, 42, 94, 113, 124, 127–30, 190, 199. *See also* affordance, legibility, interpretation,

Adobe Systems, 112, 128; Acrobat Reader, 16, 112; Adobe Acrobat, 193–94

aesthetics, 21, 50, 62–64, 98, 102, 108, 186

affect, 19, 74, 98, 105–108

affordance, 25–40, 47, 111–14, 123–35, 156–72, 179, 190–93, 206n11. *See also* media; metaphor

algorithm, 93, 141, 193, 198

Alice in Wonderland (Carroll), 35

alienation, 10, 203

alphabets, 134, 136, 140–42, 145, 150, 172–78

alternating current (AC), 172, 176

Amazon, 113

Amazon Kindle, 112

analog systems, 166, 176–77, 182–83, 185–90

analogy, 77, 79, 186. *See also* metaphor; symbolism

appearance, 101. See also *phantazpmenōn*

Apple Inc., 31, 42, 49

apprehension, 33, 61–63, 111, 166–71, 192–94, 227n51

Arca Musurgicae, 69

archive, 6–14, 18–26, 40, 63, 93–95, 132–34, 193, 205

art, 63, 65–66, 98–100, 103, 105, 108, 110

Art as Technique (Shklovsky), 62, 106

artifacts, 2–21, 56, 65, 98–99, 107–17, 155–56, 170, 192–93

ASCII, 176

asemiosis, 2, 23, 205n1. *See also* illiteracy

atomism, 79, 186, 205n10

augmentation, 162, 202

Austin, J. L., 94

authorship, 13–14, 55–56, 64, 107, 110

automation, 55–60, 93

Autonomous Technology (Winner), 60

autopoiesis, 14, 207n40

avalanche injection, 41